METTLE & HONOR

WISCONSIN STORIES
FROM THE BATTLEFIELD

Bob,
Enjoy these incredible
stories.

Mark Concannon

D1291931

OTHER PRODUCTIONS BY MARK CONCANNON

- Veterans Story Project, Milwaukee County War Memorial Center

- Mettle & Honor TV Documentary, Milwaukee PBS 2015

- Mettle & Honor, The Greatest Generation, TV Documentary, Milwaukee PBS 2016

- Mettle & Honor, Vietnam, TV Documentary, Milwaukee PBS 2017

- Concannon Communications, Branding Videos:
  - Brunswick Billiards
  - GE Healthcare
  - Marquette University
  - Concordia University
  - Milwaukee Public Schools Foundation

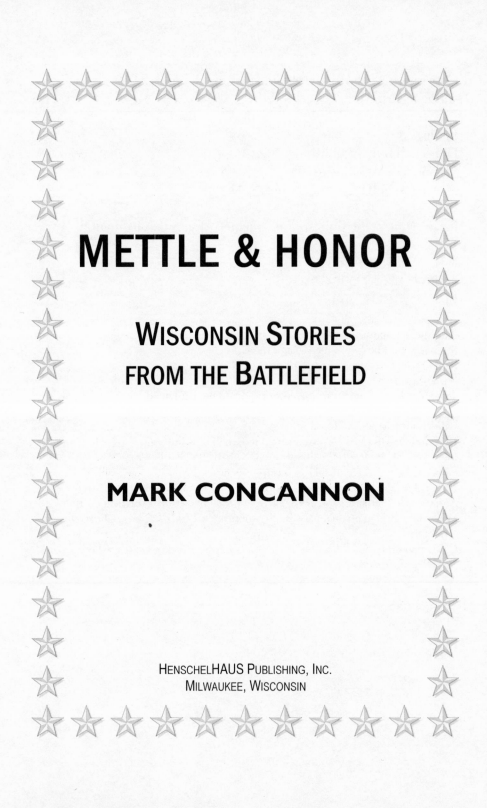

METTLE & HONOR

WISCONSIN STORIES
FROM THE BATTLEFIELD

MARK CONCANNON

HENSCHELHAUS PUBLISHING, INC.
MILWAUKEE, WISCONSIN

Published by
HenschelHAUS Publishing, Inc.
Milwaukee, Wisconsin
www.henschelHAUSbooks.com

Please contact the publisher for quantity discount information.

ISBN: 978159598-630-6
E-ISBN: 978159598-679-5
LCCN: 2018947753

Publisher's Cataloging-In-Publication Data
(Prepared by The Donohue Group, Inc.)

Names: Concannon, Mark, author.
Title: Mettle & honor : Wisconsin stories from the battlefield /
        Mark Concannon.
Other Titles: Mettle and honor
Description: Milwaukee, Wisconsin : HenschelHaus Publishing, Inc., [2018]
Identifiers: ISBN 9781595986306 | ISBN 9781595986795 (ebook)
Subjects: LCSH: Veterans--Wisconsin--Interviews. | World War, 1939-1945--
Personal narratives, American. | Korean War, 1950-1953--Personal narratives,
American. | Vietnam War, 1961-1975--Personal narratives, American. | Iraq
War, 2003-2011--Personal narratives, American. | LCGFT: Personal narratives.
| Interviews.
Classification: LCC E745 .C66 2018 (print) | LCC E745 (ebook) | DDC
355.00922775--dc23

Printed in Milwaukee, Wisconsin

This book is dedicated to all of the Wisconsin veterans
featured in the following pages,
the countless others who have served in all wars and
to two vets not from Wisconsin:
my father, Frank Concannon from Philadelphia, PA
U.S. Navy, World War II,
and my father-in-law, John "Red" Helling, Sr.,
from Joliet, IL, U.S. Army, World War II.

TABLE OF CONTENTS

PREFACE

I'VE ALWAYS BEEN A FAN OF MILITARY HISTORY. But it is one thing to read books or watch documentaries and movies about war. It is quite another to sit a couple of feet away from those who risked their lives on the front lines and hear them tell their stories, what it was like in the heat of the battle, how these soldiers who were mostly just scared kids when they joined the service performed selflessly and heroically.

World War II veterans talking about Normandy, Bastogne, Iwo Jima, and Guadalcanal. Astonishing. Sometimes almost unbelievable, and in the end, magnificent.

Those who served in Korea. The forgotten war.

Vietnam vets recounting tales of Tet and Khe Sanh and further hostilities faced when returning to the states. Heartbreaking.

Young Americans who enlisted after 9/11 to serve in Afghanistan and Iraq. Edifying for those who may believe millennials think only of themselves.

The interviews I conducted are all part of the Wisconsin War Memorial Center's Veterans Story Project, an oral history archive of Wisconsin veterans from all wars.

2017 marked the 60th anniversary of the War Memorial Center. In the early 1950s, several community groups saw the need for a fitting memorial to honor the soldiers killed in World War II. The community pooled its resources in a truly remarkable fundraising campaign that resulted in construction starting in 1955 and the War Memorial being dedicated on Veteran's Day 1957.

"A group of people got together and thought let's not do a statue, let's not have a flagpole, let's do a living, breathing memorial," said Dave Drent, the War Memorial Center's Executive Director.

"It was painstaking, they had to find a place to do it, they had to raise a lot of money. It took a couple of years but they raised the money, they raised $2.7 million. Those $2.7 million came from 70,000 individuals and businesses in the Milwaukee area.

"It was on marquees at theaters, it was on sides of busses. So the community got behind this. This is the community's War Memorial Center."

The Veterans Story Project is another effort to serve that community by preserving these important stories of individual veterans so that future generations can have a fuller understanding of the service and sacrifice of Wisconsin's military heroes.

By putting this book together, my goal was for readers to enjoy the same privileged experiences I had in interviewing these veterans. I will set up each interview with a short introduction and then respectfully give our veterans the floor.

What you'll read will not be PG or PC in the descriptions of combat, its sometimes devastating after-effects and personal opinions about a wide range of topics. These vets have more than earned the right to speak freely about their service.

—Mark Concannon

ACKNOWLEDGMENTS

MANY THANKS TO EVERYONE AT THE Wisconsin War Memorial Center, most notably Executive Director Dave Drent, Development Director Vicki Chappell, and Renee Riddle, who handles public relations—they have all been instrumental in coordinating and championing the Veterans Story Project. Our project is ongoing. If you're a Wisconsin veteran or know someone who has served in the military, we'd love to record your, his or her story. For more information on how to become part of our project, visit WarMemorialCenter.org.

Massive thanks to my wife Janet, who transcribed all of the interviews, organized them for the specific chapters, and offered invaluable advice on the writing, tone and feel of the final product. This book or any of my personal or professional efforts wouldn't have amounted to much without her.

And last but certainly not least, a major tip of the hat to Kira Henschel, president and CEO of HenschelHAUS Publishing, who took this idea and ran with it, providing wisdom and insight that only someone with her years of experience and exemplary track record could offer to guide this writer into what was for him uncharted territory to bring the project home.

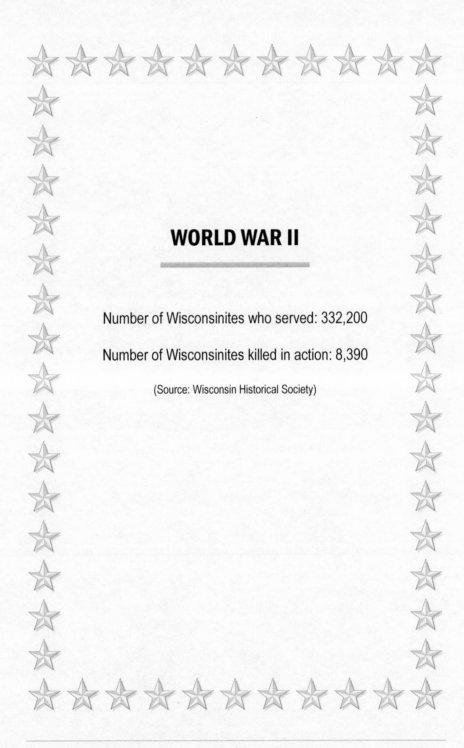

WORLD WAR II

Number of Wisconsinites who served: 332,200

Number of Wisconsinites killed in action: 8,390

(Source: Wisconsin Historical Society)

CHRIS ABELE

PEOPLE IN SOUTHEASTERN WISCONSIN are familiar with the name Chris Abele, the Milwaukee County Executive. But most do not know he is the grandson of a World War II naval hero.

Mannert Lincoln Abele was posthumously awarded the Navy Cross, the Navy's distinguished decoration for valor in combat, for his heroic actions in the Pacific Theater. Mannert Lincoln Abele's submarine remained lost at sea until the Abele family championed efforts to locate the craft some 60 years after it was damaged in battle and driven to the bottom of the ocean.

"I grew up in and around Boston, and I remember the house I grew up in," Chris Abele said. "On a wall, there was a picture of a submarine, a picture of a destroyer and there was a medal. And as a young boy, I wasn't clear on why we had those pictures there. And later I learned that the submarine was the *USS Grunion* that my grandfather, Mannert Lincoln Abele, or Jim, actually even his sons called him 'Jim' as kids, was commander of and his last command in World War II. The destroyer next to it was the *USS Mannert Lincoln Abele,* which was named after him in 1944.

"And the medal was the Navy Cross, which was posthumously awarded for his actions in World War II. The last time my father saw his father was a Sunday in 1942 at the Officers' Club at the submarine base at Mystic or New London, Connecticut. They used to go there periodically and it was a pretty fancy thing.

"My dad remembers feeling it sort of had this feeling of exclusivity. But the next day he shipped out, headed out for Pearl Harbor, which had been attacked about six months earlier. And on the way, the *USS Grunion* actually ended up saving 16 survivors from another American boat, the *USS Jack*, which had been sunk by a German U-boat somewhere in the Caribbean.

"We actually have a letter written by one of those survivors to my grandmother years later in the tone of 'for what it's worth, you should know that the reason I'm here able to write this letter and survive is because our ship went down in heavy weather and was sunk by a U-boat in the Caribbean. We all thought we were gone, then a submarine pops out of the water. And submarines, and I know enough about submarines to know it's difficult to do this in this kind of weather. But these guys took all of us aboard and I, the guy writing the letter, was dropped off in the Panama Canal. The sub then went to Pearl and then headed out to Dutch Harbor, which is in the Aleutian Islands in Alaska.'

"The long and short of it is, in the defense of some other American boats, the *Grunion* encountered a number of Japanese boats. It sank two Japanese sub-chasers, got hit—they're not sure what happened—eventually it was sunk. We know this now. We didn't know it for about 60 years after it happened until about 10 years ago. It turns out, I think there were only two submarines in World War II that were missing and that were MIA and not KIA because there just wasn't confirmation. It was unusual because the Japanese kept very detailed records.

"And decades later, my father and his brothers had all worked hard and had been able to do well and my father approached his brothers and said, 'Hey, you know, we've never known what happened with our father beyond the fact that he was in a conflict and was awarded the Navy Cross,' you know, the highest award the Navy gives.

"But technology's better now and so, through the Internet, we were able to do some digging. And so they spent a lot of time and a lot of digging and long story short, 60 years later, I remember being with my father and his brothers on a boat with a side- sweeping sonar that was being tugged along behind it. And this was along the Aleutian Islands—it was essentially the Bering Sea in Alaska. About as remote as you can get in the United States when they first saw a sonar image of the sub that their father was in.

"And I remember thinking in the sort of silence of all of us just looking at this image, the sub at the bottom of the sea, and the 70 men who had been on that submarine probably knew that when they engaged a larger Japanese force that there was a pretty considerable possibility that they might not make it back. But they engaged anyway. And you know, the importance of seeing the reality of people who make decisions about things that are bigger than themselves is something that's easy to forget.

"And we value that and we're worthy of continuing to live in it when we never forget the sacrifices that are made and decisions like my grandfather and so many others made to put country above themselves. You know, lay down their life so that we get to live."

Your family has an extensive military history...

"My grandfather on my mother's side, Henry Seton, drove ambulances in France during World War I. And actually, interestingly, my grandfather, when he was posthumously awarded the Navy Cross, wasn't the first relative to get the Navy Cross. His uncle, Arthur Abele, had also received the Navy Cross. And my grandfather Jim actually taught for at least a class his Uncle Arthur at the Naval Academy. He graduated from the Navy Academy in 1936. My grandfather did. But had at least one class with Arthur Abele, who also had set the bar with a Navy Cross."

Chris Abele has served as Milwaukee County Executive since 2011.

MARGE "PINKY" BEHLEN

SHE STARTED OUT IN LIFE AS Marge Behlen, but spent most of her days known as "Pinky."

"That name was given to me when I was in Illinois. Because there was a lady, I didn't really know her, but her father was administrator at the hospital where I trained as a nurse. I also went to high school with her sisters. So and I had red hair and I think—I don't like to say this but—a red face, too. And she said that every unit had to have a Pinky. And it was going to be me."

Pinky completed her nurse's training at Milwaukee County General Hospital in 1944 and shortly after her graduation, headed overseas to serve in Europe.

"It was almost like it couldn't not happen," Behlen recalled. "Nearly every nurse I knew was going because they were recruiting nurses for the services, and so, I just went along with them."

"I went for basic training at Ft. McCoy in Wisconsin. Well, I finished that and then I was in a post in Illinois. and we went from there to Providence, Rhode Island, and there we were barely there and we were...got on board a ship and went over to England.

"And in England, I was in a town called Chester and we lived in barracks there. There were about 15 nurses who were living in barracks there and we had to take turns starting the fire in the morning. So everybody had their turn.

"We had to wait there because they wanted us across the Channel into France. But we were unable to go there because the Battle of the Bulge was right there and that was the bloodiest, worst battle of the war almost. And they didn't want to take us there while that was going on because it was too close. So we did get on a boat and on the boat there was a place for the nurses to sleep. There were about 60 cots there.

"I had a friend who didn't worry about anything. We had our duffel bags and she said to me 'Pinky, don't worry about it. We'll get there.' And everybody was shuffling around trying to get a cot. So it ended up, my friend and I, did not get a cot. So we had to cross the Channel in a stateroom with the two chief nurses. So then we were, when we got there, it was...we left on I think it was Christmas Eve and we got to France and we had on our fatigues and we got on a train. And then we were supposed to go on a train from there to Rons, France. And we got on the train, it was Christmas Day and they stopped the train—I don't know, for a rest or something else—and we had turkey sandwiches for Christmas dinner."

Did you take care of many wounded soldiers in France?

"Yes, we did. But we were not like a field hospital. You would not see something like M.A.S.H. *(Mobile Army Surgical Hospital)* We were a more behind-the-lines hospital. And patients came there who had already been through a field hospital and they were being further evaluated as to whether they should go home or they were well enough to go back to the front lines. And those are the people we took care of. And our duties were to like regular simple nursing duties, like giving out medicines and making sure patients were available for their treatments and kind of cheering them up if they needed that. And just kind of being there."

What was the hardest part of your job?

"It wasn't hard at all. No, I liked it. I even liked going to work."

Did you have any memorable patients?

"I just remember a couple of patients and I believe I was the youngest nurse in that unit. That was the 199th General Hospital. And there was a young patient there who...I was assigned to work with four patients and he was one of them. He always wanted me to take care of him first. And he wanted me to take care of him best. And I don't think he wanted me to take are of anybody else. He was so loyal.

"And there was another patient there who was a very, very funny. And he would make rounds and pretend he was the doctor and he was on crutches and he stopped at one bed and he said to this patient, 'You know what? My grandpa died when he was 105 and five years after he died, he looked better than you do right

JOSEPH BIERSTEKER

ONE OF THE MOST HISTORI-CALLY underappreciated efforts of the war was flying "the Hump" a treacherous journey over the Himalayas to re-supply Chinese troops and the U.S. Army Air Force based in China as they battled to hold off the advances of the Japanese.

Hall-of-Fame baseball star Hank Greenberg was part of that mission, as was Wisconsin native Joseph Biersteker, who faced the constant danger of flying over uncharted terrain with unreliable maps, weather forecasts, and radio navigation.

"Flying over the Himalayas was a difficult job because of shifty winds and deteriorating weather usually going over," Biersteker said. "It made it, navigation, a bit difficult."

How did you get that duty?

"Well, when I went into the service, I went into the Aviation Cadet Classification Center and I qualified for pilot navigator or a bombardier. But because of my mathematics ability, they decided I should become a navigator."

"Everything had to be flown into China. All of our supplies. So usually we were carrying bombs or fuel. We'd put fuel tanks in our bomb bays and bring the fuel into our base in China."

"Flying over the Himalayas, we had an engine catch fire. And we didn't have enough fuel to get to our base in China and we were carrying 4,500-pound bombs. And we dropped them. They were non-fused, of course. So they didn't explode when they hit the ground. And we turned around to go back to our base in India but then didn't have enough fuel to reach our base in India. So we landed in Dacca, which is now in the country known as Bangladesh. And had to change an engine. And they flew an engine from our base in India to Dacca and we all were involved in changing the engine."

Was it a tough landing?

"No. No. We were on a mission to Japan and we were attacking the Navy, a big navy base on the main island, Honshu, and we were attacked by a fighter plane. We were in a 6-plane formation and we were one the far right side. And so we became his best target, I guess. And he hit us with two explosive shells. One hit our No. 2 engine and put it out of commission. And the other one entered our fuselage right behind my head and exploded at the top of the fuselage, rupturing a band of wires that were going to the instrument panels. And so we were crippled. And so we had to make an emergency landing in Iwo Jima. And they didn't want us landing on their main runways so they put us on a shorter runway. And then when we hit the runway, we found out that our fluid for the brakes had leaked and we ended up in a semi-log at the end of the runway. The plane never flew again."

"We did not have that many fighter attacks. We'd get anti-air craft fire. Over Singapore, that was a target that was well defended. And Tokyo, of course, was well defended. But we never got hit. Outside of that one fighter. The time we got hit, I was a little bit anxious, but most of the time, not...I was young. 20 or 21.

"I had credit for 36 missions. And most of them were to Japan. From India, we hit Rangoon, Bangkok, Saigon, Kuala Lumpur, and Singapore.

"The longest mission we flew was to Singapore and we were in the air for over 17 hours. The B-29 had two bomb bays, one forward and one rear. And in the forward bomb bay, we carried extra fuel tanks. And in the rear bomb bay, we carried four 1,000-pound bombs. And we hit a floating dry dock that the British had built before the war and anchored off Singapore to service their Navy in that part of the world. But the Japanese, of course, took over and they were repairing their ships fighting our navy. So we were sent down to destroy the dry dock. And we did sink it."

Were most of your missions successful?

"Yes, we were a very good crew and we worked well together. That brought about success. Our original crew was a very friendly group of people. We all got along very well. There were two of us who were qualified both as navigators and bombardiers. The idea being that B-29s fly such long missions, you may have to replace a navigator. But then...before we went overseas, the decision came down that one individual be declared the navigator and the other the bombardier. And the crew decided that I should be the navigator."

You and your brothers all served in World War II?

"Yeah, five of us...three of us went overseas, two that were left in the States."

Where did the two brothers serve overseas?

"My older brother was a commander in a tank unit. He was in the invasion of North Africa, Sicily, and into Italy. And my younger brother was a gunner on B-24 bombers flying out of Italy and the plane was shot up over Yugoslavia and he bailed out along with his crewmembers. And they spent three months behind German lines with partisans, who helped them walk out."

Both came back alive?

"Yep, everybody made it home."

Did the war change you?

"I think I had a more positive attitude. And so when I came home...before I went into service, I worked in a paper mill. Kimberly-Clark in the testing department. When I came back to the mill, the supervisor who knew me well from Little Chute, also. Told me, 'Don't stay here. Go to college. You've got an opportunity to get a college education. Take it.' And so I followed his suggestion."

Joe taught high school and college math, chemistry, and physics after the war, including teaching stints in Kenya, Nigeria, and Turkey.

BERNARD J. BYTHELL

THE BIG-SCREEN MOTION pictures saluting war heroes feature gallant troops storming beaches, engaging in fierce firefights, and jumping on live grenades to save their buddies. But for every two soldiers who see action, there is another soldier behind the scenes in a critical support role. Bernard Bythell was a company quartermaster who landed in France on D-Day plus 30.

"I went overseas in December of '43 and I went over on the *Queen Mary* and well, it was kind of interesting about the *Queen Mary*. I'll never forget, the first thing we heard when we got on board was, come over the loud speaker, 'This is a British ship, manned by British officers and manned by British seaman.' And I thought to myself, 'Yeah, but who the hell is paying for it?'

"We took six days to go over. It was not...because of the speed, the *Queen Mary*, it didn't have a convoy. *(Troop ships were often accompanied by warship convoys to fend off U-boat attacks.)* It went down the East Coast and then across to North Africa and then up to Glasgow, Scotland. And then from Glasgow, we went down to Cardiff in Wales and we were down there for a week and from there I went to Cheltenham, England and we were in Cheltenham from December of '43 to June of '44.

"And being there 6 months, the evenings, you go to town, the pubs and the French cafes and that. There was nothing wrong with that. Many of the GIs, I should say, a certain number of GIs, did get familiar with the British ladies. And they got very familiar with them, these ladies.

"Well, anyway, they would stay overnight with the British ladies. There was no curfew. As long as they were there for *Reveille* the next morning, well, that was perfectly all right. But the British 8th Army that was fighting in North Africa, well, they brought them home one night on leave and they landed them and they put them on a troop train and went up the coast, dropping them men off where in the towns where they lived. Well, they got in to Cheltenham that night at 1 o'clock in the morning. So when they got home, some of GIs were with their wives or girlfriends.

"When we got to France, those first few weeks, we were stationed out near St. Lo and it basically was in the woods, camped in the tents and all that. And from there, we moved into Paris. And my first experience with Paris—we got in there late at night and we were assigned our billets and the way that the billets were assigned, the officers were assigned the fancier hotels. The grander the hotel, the higher the rank the officer was. And the enlisted personnel, they were like smaller hotels and things like that.

"It was kind of interesting because I was a ranking non-com in our unit. I was a master sergeant. And so we get into this room after being out in the woods for a couple of months and here I am, a big double bed with a canopy with a balcony looking out onto the street. And a full bath. And it had a toilet and another facility in there that I didn't know quite what it was in those days. I learned it was a bidet. So I thought that was kind of interesting.

"Well, we were sleeping in beds for the first time in a couple of months. The next thing I know, my commanding officer is knocking on the door. 'Sergeant, are you going to get your men out?' I said, 'Yeah, I might as well. And so, they marched us over to a restaurant and this restaurant was a typical French restaurant. It had waiters with the black suits, white shirts, black ties. Linen table covers. Plates and knives and forks. And they served our first meal there, a breakfast. Well, that only lasted a couple of weeks before the Army took over and we had a regular mess hall with Army food.

"My weapon during the war was a typewriter. And I did not see any action. In Paris, our office was located on the Champs-Élysées just kitty-corner from the Arc de Triomphe. And that was where our office was. Now that building had previously been occupied by the German Luftwaffe. That's were they had their headquarters when they were in France. And of course, they went through and sapped the offices, make sure there weren't any mines or anything. But that was our office and our primary function there was to get parts, these spare parts to keep the laundry equipment in working order. And that was my primary job.

"Then I was in Paris from August of '45, was it to...well, I was there and then I was transferred out of there and I went to Reims. And I was in Reims for the balance of the war. And in Reims, it was kind of a quartermaster depot, a reclamation depot where they had all materiel, coats, and uniforms and things like that, would come back from reclamation. And it was kind of an interesting town because we in the United States Army maintained the depot. We had German POW labor. The actual compound was guarded by the free French and there was too much going on between the free French and the German prisoners that they actually took the free French off and brought in a Russian guard company. And the Russians were brutal to the prisoners of war.

"The unit that I had, I had a dozen enlisted men working under me in an office and I had a German major who was in charge and he spoke fluent English. He was formerly a pen manufacturer in Germany, prior to the war. But of course, he was a Nazi. He'd been drafted in the Army. We didn't have any problems with the German POWs at all. In fact, most of the German POWs were polite. They kind of took over the mess and so we had great meals and they were great bakers. So we ate very well with the German POW cooks and bakers and things like that. We also had a German barber. And that was fine. I had...I was a little apprehensive the first time I went in to get a haircut. But it was perfectly fine. So we got along fine.

"We didn't have a lot to do with the French people other than we'd go into the bars at night and things like that. I don't say that they were overly happy to see us. We were there and we were there for a reason. But...I was actually at Reims when the war ended on VE Day. And on VE Day, we actually had a parade in our pressed uniforms and things like that."

How did serving in the war change you?

"I went into the Army when I was just 22 years old. I had led a very sheltered life. My mother was a very prim and proper person. I don't think I ever heard the word 'damn' in our household at any time in my life. This was my mother and father. They were both very strict people. Well, I got back from basic training after two months of basic training and I was home on furlough for a Sunday dinner with my mother and father and my sister and my girlfriend, who was later my wife, and the first thing I remember saying as we got to dinner was, 'Pass me the fucking sugar.'

"Didn't go over very well with Mom at all. There was a little boy who'd gone off to war and came home with this kind of language. You learn that in basic training.

"In the Army, you did what you were told. You even went where you were assigned. And this is what I was assigned to and I was very happy with it. And, as I say, my weapon was a typewriter."

Bernard was a successful salesman after the war, working for RCA and Hearst Allied.

CLAYTON "CHIP" CHIPMAN

LIKE MANY OF HIS HIGH school classmates, Clayton "Chip" Chipman, felt a powerful patriotic sense of duty to serve his country during World War II, so at the age of 17, he dropped out of West Allis Central High School (he received his degree 70 years later at a special presentation ceremony) and joined the Marines, where he served in the Pacific from 1944 to 1946. Clayton told me he was "only in one major battle, Iwo Jima" dismissing other live combat encounters on the Marianas Islands as mere "firefights."

Can you tell me about your experience at Iwo Jima?

"On Feb. 19th, of 1945, I was in K323, a 4th Marine Division unit and we were on a APA troop ship and they woke us about 2:00 or 2:30 in the morning. They gave us a fantastic breakfast. We went to a church service, had Communion and we went down to our bunk area and they said, saddle up and put on your equipment. And then we went back up to our station where we went over the side and down the cargo net into the landing craft. And at that point, the veterans set the pace, the ones that had been in three previous battles. And nobody said a word. The first word I heard was, that morning, was 'Don't attach the pins in the grenade to anything on your uniform.'

"Nobody said a word. We all knew what to do. We practiced it so many times. And even on the landing craft when we got in it, there's so much I could add to it, but the next word I heard was from the lieutenant and he said, 'We need 2 volunteers, one of each 50-caliber machine guns to watch for Japanese planes.' And Cpl. Culp volunteered for one and I volunteered for the other. And everybody was below the sides of the landing craft except the two of us and the coxswain.

"And it was one of the better things I did. I saw the shelling on the beach and the exploding and black and gray and white smoke and debris going up from the naval shelling. And then came in the Corsairs *(American fighter planes used in World War II)* and they were given close ground support and they made their run. And the last one through was not coming out of his dive. And I was watching him, and they got so close that I yelled out, 'Pull up! Pull up!'

"Screamed it out. But you know he couldn't hear. We were over three miles out. And the plane crashed and there was a great, big ball of smoke.

"We rendezvoused in a circle with our company and we were pretty close to a battleship. And when the 16-inch salvos went up, the concussion was so great, it pushed our landing craft just about down into the water. I mean, guys were taking their helmets off, ready to start bailing. But as we went in, of course, the two of us were seeing all this stuff, and the Corsair went down. Then we saw a Piper Cub—we call it a grasshopper and it was a plane that was calling in the shots to the battleships—just a little one like you'd see around here. And it just all of a sudden, it didn't collide, it just nosed down.

"And then the next thing I saw was a white plane and I didn't recognize it and I thought it may have been Japanese so I watched it very closely and all of a sudden the whole tail dropped out. It didn't collide, it just went right down. And I started to think, you know, no parachutes. And my thought was, what the hell am I doing here? People are getting killed. Well, we got in and the ramp put down and the first thing I saw was about 10 to 15 yards of dead Marines, just in every position you could imagine. And the peripheral vision caught 3 lines of dead Marines, just lined up like they were ready to charge in.

"So that was the first impression. And the second impression was the noise. The noise. There was so much...so many shells exploding on our beach where we were going in, that you couldn't distinguish one shell from another exploding. It was just a roar. And the other thing that hit me was that it was the first time in my life that I didn't have control over what would happen. And I just psychologically realized that I have absolutely no control. And I turned to the Lord and started to pray.

"Can't run into anybody that would say they weren't scared. They were all scared beyond the English language. There's no word that covered how scared we were. And I talked to a lot of people, including a pastor, about that and everybody—there are no exceptions—they all turn to their god and I recognized something within me that, you know an athlete will go to a certain degree and all of a sudden, he hits a barrier and then his body takes over and it produced endorphins which is a natural stimulant that the body produces. But this was past that. It was way beyond that. And the pastor gave me a clue and he said that he feels that at that time, adrenaline took over and whatever the drugs are in adrenaline. And that's...We could carry more, we could move faster. We could think faster.

"And the next words I heard...Up until that time, no body said anything, except that lieutenant. And he said, 'Let's get the blazes out of here. This is no place for us.' So I took it as an order and started to move up to the airfield, which was about 250 yards away. And as I looked, I could see shell holes that were larger than the normal. And I'm sure they came from the planes and the bombs. And it dawned on me that they warned us about landmines and stepping on landmines and so forth. And I thought if that explosion in that hole, it had to explode the landmines. So I decided to go from shell hole to shell hole, crawling mainly. If you stood up, they'd cut you in half with the shrapnel. You couldn't hear the machine guns, it was so noisy.

"But going up the beach, it took...well, numbers, you got to watch number and writers and movies because numbers are different. On that day, Gen. Crulack, one of the Marine generals, said a Marine, on D-Day, a Marine fell every 50 seconds. One author figured that out differently. He said one Marine fell every 30 seconds. On that day, 30,000 Marines landed—on the total battle, it was about 73,000 Marines and naval corpsmen. The numbers I have memorized pretty much but on that day, out of the

30,000 Marines, 501 were killed, 197 were wounded. 99 had mental problems, you know a situation like that, your cognitive situation doesn't do you justice.

"But just to let you know, some of the carnage there and there's a picture of a fellow where his one ankle is shot off and just by looking at him, you know he died, bleeding to death. An another one that stood out in my mind was a guy that was laying on his back and he didn't have a stitch of clothing on and the only thing I could figure out was he was close to a blast of a shell and it just tore everything off of him.

"And then another one that stood out, of course there were a lot of them that stood out over the course of nine days, but a fellow Marine was laying on his face. He had his right arm out, his rifle was in his right hand, and I thought, 'Well, he's resting. And I thought, 'Well, I'll go up and ask if I can help him.' And I started to think, 'If he is having mental problems, how is he going to react if I go up to him?' So I passed him up. I thought well, if he's resting, fine, let him rest.

"So while I was there, there were other things, people jumping in the hole with you and so forth. As long as you went up. Actually, the plan I used was not a bad plan, because it took all day to go the 250 yards, mainly crawling, a few steps, but mainly crawling. But I was going from one shell hole to another and it wasn't always straight ahead. It was going to the side. And finally I did see somebody I recognized at about 4:30 or so, the shelling let up a little bit where you could talk some. And I saw somebody walking. And I didn't see anybody walk all day. They were crawling, if anything. And I called out to him because I kind of recognized him. I said, 'Where's K Company?' And he pointed and I looked up there and I could see our sergeant. He wore his helmet a little different than some people. I think he did it on purpose so people would recognize him.

"So the fellow that was in the hole was a Seabee and we buddied up together and we went up to the sergeant and reported in and took some ammunition to the machine gun and then the sergeant said, the Seabee will stay with us. We need every guy we can get. And he said, 'Dig in.' And so we dug in for the evening. And we were so tired, we didn't eat. We had battle rations, which was a special package for that day. And we had two canteens. We were just so tired, we didn't drink. The only thing we did was exchange information on who got killed and who got wounded. And that was it. And then...that's all day. You don't hear anybody talk. As I said, the whole thing...just a few words. And everybody knew what to do. They were in squads and fire teams and so forth."

You were wounded at Iwo Jima?

"I lasted nine days and we were coming up to an area they called the meat grinder, because so many guys were killed and wounded in that particular area. And on the right, to the right there was the amphitheater, and there was Turkey Knob, and there was Hill 382. We were coming up 382 along the second airfield. And the area was fairly flat, it was rough but it was so flat compared to the hills. And we got up to an open area that went in to this five or six area football fields, pillbox on the bottom of the hill and five caves on the end of a, end of the airport. And they were the height of the peak of a Milwaukee duplex. And we came up there and they just got tired of sending guys in there and getting them killed and wounded.

"So they ordered up a tank and when that tank came to that open, it refused to go in there because they had the pillbox firing at it and they were afraid of what might be in the caves. So there were five or six guys there and three of us came up who were with our outfit and one marine came up to me and filled my pockets with hand grenades and he says, 'Go close that...those caves.' So I took it as an order. I didn't know who he was. He was a stranger. So when the tank went in to work on the pillbox, I went close to those caves and throw the hand grenades up over my head and into the opening of the caves.

"If you're familiar with a hand grenade, it takes a little effort to throw it. And I threw it in four of the five caves and the last cave was full of Japanese and I emptied a magazine from an automatic rifle in there in case someone was hiding behind it. Well, when that was done, I looked for the guys that sent me in and they were gone. And I thought, well, I want to be with Marines. And the only Marines I could think of were in that tank, so I ran past the open area and I found a roll of Japanese money and I ran past a tank and hid up against a pillbox because I knew the Japs were going to send someone else to fire out. But my emotions took over and I wasn't thinking. I knew and everybody else knew that the Japs were going to shell the tank. Well, when some of the shells hit the tank, a piece went through my shoulder.

"That was about how I got wounded. And I made a foolish mistake but the alternative was hunting around to find some more Marines. So I knew the tank would eventually pull out and go back to the, lines and I could either follow it or ride on it to get back to the Marines in the line."

How long were you out of action?

"I was sent back to what they called a beach hospital, which was nothing but a big shell hole. And there was a corpsmen and a doctor. And the doctor commandeered a landing craft and he said take these dozen guys out to your ship. And it was the *Indianapolis*. And if you know history, the *Indianapolis* was sunk.

The sinking of the USS Indianapolis in 1945 resulted in the greatest loss of life from a single ship in U.S. Naval History. Of the nearly 1,200 crew members, only 317 survived.

"Well, they put us in bunks, the officer's bunks. We were bloody and dirty. They sprayed us with DDT before we went in. And here we were with mattresses, white sheets and next day they transferred us to a hospital ship. And of course, they made us take a shower even though you were a wounded man. So I spent a couple days on a hospital ship and that was one of the scariest situations I was in, because, at night, the hospital ship lights up like a Christmas tree and out there with submarines and everything, it was just very unpleasant.

"Well, we spent about a week on Guam in a jungle hospital. And then they took us to Hawaii and each place they would triage you and decide how long the wound's going to take and then they made the judgments whether you go back to the States or whether you stay in Hawaii or you stay on Saipan or Guam or through a hospital. And after being in a hospital, Schofield Barracks Hospital, the Navy hospitals were all full, there were so many patients, wounded guys. And they decided to close my wound so they operated on it, one day, they sewed it shut and they left it in and instead of a week, they left it in ten days because it was in a stretchy area. Well, they took it out, they took the stitches out in the morning and in the afternoon, I was walking with a friend and I bent down to pick up something and he said, "Hey, you're bleeding." So the wound broke open. Well, when I went to the doctor, they made the decision to let it heal from the inside out. So I spent about two and a half to close to three months in the army hospital.

"And then when I was discharged, I still wore a bandage for three, four weeks, a month. And we were put into regular units that they were developing and they sent us out to Saipan to do duty on Saipan in the Marianas.

"To this day, I feel that the war gave me a Guardian Angel and he's kept me out of trouble."

Clayton spent his post-war years as an elementary school teacher and principal in Milwaukee. He gave lectures about the psychological toll of war.

NEILAND COHEN

NEILAND COHEN ENLISTED IN the U.S. Navy in 1944. "I just went down to the recruiting office in Milwaukee and signed up. That was it," Cohen said.

He would eventually see action in many exotic ports of call in the Pacific Theater but just after completing basic training at Great Lakes, mistakenly thought he was immediately being dispatched to a faraway land.

"We picked the ship up in Evansville, Indiana and we sailed down the Mississippi. Three Coast Guard officers sailed the ship. We didn't do anything but exercise. And we took the ship down to New Orleans. And I'll tell you a funny thing. We asked the Coast Guard officers, 'Where are we going?' They said, 'You're going to Algiers.' Well, we thought that was kind of strange. How could they send raw recruits with nothing aboard the ship. There was nothing aboard the ship. It just was raw steel. So then the next day we asked the guy how can we go overseas when we don't have anything on the ship? He said, 'Don't go away. I'll be right back.'

"How can we go overseas when we aren't prepared? You said we're going to Algiers. Not overseas. Algiers, Louisiana. We didn't know that.

"While we sailed, the Coast Guard put the ship on the beach three times. They were stuck in the mud. And we sailed the—uneventful—down to New Orleans. And then they outfitted the ship in Todd Johnson's dry dock and then we took it out on a cruise in the Gulf of Mexico. And then after that, we sailed down to the Panama Canal, went through the Panama Canal and then to San Diego.

"And in San Diego, we...the Marine Corps trucks pulled up and they unloaded cases of Pabst Blue Ribbon beer. And so we took a tactic load of beer to Hawaii and we unloaded it. While in Hawaii, we had a berth between two battleships. There was enough space for an LST *(Landing Ship, Tank)* to dock. So we broke a steam pipe because he couldn't see. You couldn't turn any lights on. So he was relieved of command. So the executive officer took the ship to West Locks. That's where the amphibious craft was. In West Locks."

What was your job in the Navy?

"I was a ship's yeoman. A yeoman does paper work. Paper shuffling. Well, you know, like the Navy is famous for paper shuffling, as you may know. And I prepared sailing reports. Every ship has to submit a sailing report. On the sailing report, you list all the personnel aboard the ship. So they have a record. Then the regular stuff. Personnel files.

"We sailed to many, many ports. The Marshall Islands. Eventually, we wound up in New Guinea where the fleet assembled. I never saw so many ships in all my life. From looking out over the Bay, that's all you saw was ships. That was for the invasion of Leyte. And we made the invasion of Leyte. And then we went to Mindanao, and then Subic Bay. And then we were in Okinawa.

"I saw action five times."

Were you hit?

"The ship wasn't hit, no. But I tell you, we were tied up to a water tank on one side and another ship was on the other side. And a Betty bomber went over and I saw the bomb drop and it just missed our ship. The other ship got it. We had a one fellow who took shrapnel. He lived for three days."

I understand you witnessed an historic moment?

"I saw McArthur walk ashore *(at the iconic culmination of Douglas MacArthur's famous "I shall return" pledge when first evacuating the Philippines.)* Our ship was on the beach at Leyte and a fellow from the other ship yelled over to no one in particular. I was standing bow watch. The ensign and I were standing the bow watch and this guy yelled over, 'Hey, McArthur's walking ashore.' So like fools, we ran over there. None of us saluted. And we saw McArthur walking ashore. We were so in awe of what we saw, we didn't think of saluting. No one said anything either.

"I missed the Navy when I first came home. And then I joined the service, the Internal Revenue Service, where I was a revenue agent. So briefly, I missed the Navy.

Which was harder, the Navy or the IRS?

"Being in the IRS. You were supervised closely. You couldn't make a move without somebody criticizing you."

Neiland spent 35 years as an IRS agent in Milwaukee and Washington.

JOE DEMLER

OF THE TENS OF THOU-SANDS of Wisconsinites who served in World War II, only one appeared on the cover of *LIFE* magazine. His picture, with the caption "The Human Skeleton," was one of the war's most memorable images. But Joe Demler had to endure unimaginable suffering to achieve his fame. He first saw action at the Battle of the Bulge in 1944.

"I joined the 35th Infantry Division up at the... Luxembourg—Belgium border."

"And I was a scout...scout in Company K in the 137th Infantry division. And I was in a lookout...out in this farmhouse...one of these old stone, stone farmhouses, houses and I was on the second floor. And the weather was...the weather was snowing, cold and rain, freezing rain, rain. And the Germans broke through. We were on the right flank, flank of the 35th Division. And the Germans broke through and captured two companies of men. 360 some men.

"And this big German tank, tank shot, shot a bullet underneath into the wall of this old stone house, farmhouse. And I flew from the sec-...I was on the second floor. I flew from the floor up to the ceiling from the impact. We had no choice and we all fell out and we were captured. And the Germans took all our rations and all our whatever personal things we had. And then we were captured. And so then they had us all fall out and then they marched us back, farther in from the front line. And then we went to the interrogator.

"And the interrogator said to me, he said, 'The name Demler. That's German. German. What are you doing here?' And I told him it was my name, rank and serial number. So that's all I had to, according to international law."

You were taken to a prison camp?

Well, I tell you what. I worked at night. We had to work on repairing the railroads. So in Europe, in the United States when you have repaired the tracks, you had the ties...ties separate and the rails separate. In Europe, they were all welded together. So we'd place sections. If we could find the good piece, we would take it out. And while we were there working on that nights, the German guards would smoke, and when they lit up their cigarettes, our night fighters would pick them up and that's when we would get bombed and strafed.

"Like one night, it was like on the 4th of July. They had tracers, tracers and we were down, down on the ground. I was in this cemetery and the bullets just ricocheted off the tombstones. And lucky never to got hit because the...kissed the ground that I was laying on.

"So we worked...Our diet was made up of...a pound of cheese for ten guys. And so we had this German bread. This bread was made from rye flour, flour, sawdust, leaves, and straw. And that was our diet. Some days we didn't even get fed. And that's where I lost the weight and I got...contracted pneumonia and had no doctor care. And then we...water, we didn't have any water. The only water we had is when we ate the snow. We had no bathroom facilities. But the clothes I had on, I didn't have off in three months. The socks were rotted on my feet. My feet.

"But I'm one of the fortunate ones. I survived. The majority of the ones that were with me perished, perished. And you couldn't escape. If you would have tried, the first place you didn't have the strength from the diet that we had to be able to...to be able to...get through. When you had snow up over your hips and the cold weather would...We stayed in this one place, it was the top floor of a hospital. The next place, we were in a warehouse. We slept on the floor. We had no blankets. The only thing I had was my rain ...my big wool overcoat and the clothes I had on. So that's how that went. And then when we finally got the railroad repaired, they were going to take us to Limburg. So they piled us in railroad cars, we were in there four days, five days, I had no way of knowing.

"They didn't feed us those four or five days at all. We were locked in. I stood on the top of one of the dead soldiers because there was no room to move. And when I got to Limburg, we finally got some rations from the Red Cross, Red Cross, but most of us by that time died and passed on. And I was one of the fortunate ones. I survived."

You were down to 70 pounds?

"That's right, yeah. Right. I remember when I was liberated, the little hundred-pounders lifted me off the gurney and put me in bed. I would have lived...they figured I would have lived about three days. I had pneumonia. Part of my lung, I had over four liters of pus, pus in my lung. And part of my lung had grown tight on the bottom and I've never got the full lung back of capacity again.

"So when I was liberated...when I was liberated, the first day they said, anybody that has a tag on the bed tonight, tomorrow morning you're going to be operated. And I had a tag on my door so they took me to a field...I was in a field hospital. The first thing that they did when we got there—DDT is illegal now but DDT. They powdered up from top to bottom. Killed the lice. Those lice were wicked. They just ate away at you all the time. These were these big lice, so...they took a part of my rib out and inserted a tube in there. But they couldn't put me out because they didn't know how strong my heart was going to be.

"So when the pain got too bad, they would just give me more oxygen. But they got it open and...So whenever that would block up, the tube would block up, after that I had it in there for a couple of months, they would take a forceps and put a forceps in the...into the wound, open the forceps up and turn it so that it...get it to bleed and to drain again. And I'd be good for a couple of days.

"So then they moved me to Paris. And I was in Paris in the 48th General Hospital in Paris and there I hooked up with Col. Shaw who was the chief...the chief chest surgeon in there and one of the top ones in the world. And I was with him for a while. And he's the fellow that took care of President Kennedy when he was shot at Dallas. They moved me over the Evac Hospital in Paris where they were going to get me ready to fly back to the States. But my blood count was too low so they had to keep me there for a while.

"So I stayed there and finally I was flown form Paris to the Azores. The second day from the Azores to Newfoundland. The third day to New York. And the fourth day I came to Memphis. I was supposed to be sent someplace close to home. But they sent me to this hospital in Memphis. There was only 6,000 patients there. So while I was there, there I spent about two months and then I...they sent me home for two months to fatten me up and get my strength back. So they went to work and sent me home and when I came back, when I came back I was in Memphis until the 29th of November. And then I was discharged and sent home. Sent home.

"And one of the doctors...they had six doctors examine me before I went home and one of the doctors said to me, he said, "Son, you've been reborn. Go home and live a natural life and you'll be all right." So that's what I did."

What happened when you were liberated?

"When they liberated the camp, they took it over. We had...the fellow that ran the camp, his name was Stame. Now I don't know if this was his real name or not but they called him Sgt. Eisenhower. And I don't know, I don't know if he was...if that was his correct name or if he was what the guys named him. But I think they took care of him when the thing was over with. You know, before when we were talking out here about aircraft and that, when we was prisoner and we would work at night, all of sudden we'd hear these loud roars and that's when the Germans were testing the rocket they were sending. And every one of them guards would say, 'Oh, there's another one for that Prime Minister Churchill. There's another one, another rocket for Churchill.'"

How did you wind up on the cover of LIFE magazine?

"When I was liberated, John Florea, he was a photographer. He was for *LIFE*. And I think he was for United Press. He was a... he took pictures of us and all of them. It didn't only appear in *LIFE*, it appeared in *Stars & Stripes* paper. I've been in every paper I believe in the world. And I only met him that one time. And I feel bad that I never had an opportunity to meet him because he died here a couple of years ago. And I've had so many interviews and stuff, I'm probably the most publicized. In fact, when I was in Memphis in the hospital, I was the most publicized veteran there."

Did you ever think you weren't going to make it?

"You can't have a defeated attitude. You got to think positively. And that's how my life had always been. I always think of what... the good things and...that's why I take very good care of myself. You can't live a defeated attitude. You wouldn't last very long.

"You know another thing I haven't told you. You know once in a while...one day...they brought a horse in. And they went to work, shot the horse, and they had a big kettle and they made soup. And that was the soup. It was mostly water, water and the meat, but we at least got...we got the meat from the horse. One of the guys got an eyeball in his soup.

"But I thank the Lord every day. I always pray for all the guys that perished and had to suffer. Like one night, this fellow was sick and he couldn't fall out to follow work detail, and the guard shot him. He shot him in front of us to show us an example of try to break our morale down. And so I've seen a lot in my life. And you get to the point where you appreciate things that happen. And the little things a lot of time mean more to you than the big things."

Joe worked for 37 years at the U.S. Postal Service after the war.

GREG GABRIEL

THE DAY AFTER HE GRADU-ATED from high school, Greg Gabriel and a car full of his friends signed up for military service.

"If you were 18, you had to sign up," Gabriel said. "I was the only one in the car that was 17 and I was the only one who signed up for the Navy. No special reason except it looked better to me."

Gabriel served in some of the Pacific Theater's hotspots and although he "never fired a shot," Greg was on the receiving end of some friendly fire, a story he told with a smile.

"I had never been on a ship or anything. But the boys that signed up for the Army, they were gone in a few weeks. For me, it was kind of an unusual deal. There was a delay because the Navy had only three training stations in the nation: Norfolk, San Diego, and Great Lakes. You had to wait until the contingency. And they told me I'd be waiting for a few months. Turned out to be quite a wait. The war was on. And I signed up in the Navy and I had to wait to get in. And it was a little bit unusual. But I went to Great Lakes and from there to the West Coast and from there they assigned me a ship and I went to the Pacific. But I joined the Navy because it just looked good."

What did you do in the Pacific?

"My role basically was one of the coxswains on one of the boats on the ship. Battleships have many, many long boats—whale boats and workboats—and I was on a smaller ship. We only had two. And coxswain is like a seagoing taxi driver. Wherever we were anchored out, if anybody had to go to shore, it was the coxswain that had to take them there.

"We had to take the mail to shore. Supplies once in a while. Officers that had to go to shore had to be taken ashore and we had to wait for them. The little boat had a three-man crew: A coxswain to run the boat, a motorman to run the engine and a bow hook to tie up the front, or the bow. And we were together most of the time in the Pacific and I got it ashore all over."

What parts of the Pacific?

"Well, we were in Guam, Iwo Jima, Okinawa..."

Did you have some close calls?

"Yes and no. We got battle stars in Iwo and in Okinawa; we got there before they were declared secure. And when we got to Iwo, we were under air attacks a couple of times. And when we got to Okinawa, the kamikazes were in action there. And I think I spent the summer of 1945 with my clothes on because we were up on general quarters two, three, four times a night. The Japs happened to know exactly the range of our radar. And they would send in a couple of planes for aggravation. And you'd sleep with your clothes on, have your shoes half tied so you could jump into them and get up to general quarters. Sometimes you had three, four times a night. And so we were under attack.

"Our ship was not a prime target. The prime target of the kamikazes were the cargo ships carrying something and the destroyers because the firepower from the stern wasn't very great. So they could get in on the destroyer. These were the two primary targets but they sunk a lot of ships at Okinawa. So I did see some action.

"But if you ask me if I ever killed anybody or shot....I was a ... my assignment on the ship and in general quarters was one of the main battery men, was one of the quad 40-millimeters and we had to stand there until the all-clear came. But never got to fire a shot. I don't think...the only...the only time a shot was fired at me was when an airman from B-29 fired his pistol at me to get my attention. That's unusual."

You were on the receiving end of friendly fire?

"We went up at Iwo a couple of different times. Our job there, if something was damaged, we had to pull it back to Saipan, pulling something. And our way back and I think it was our second trip, we were pulling a damaged LST and a B-29 came over and we had recognition signals but they didn't bother with them. They were tapping an SOS right from the beginning. When I first saw them, they had bailed out because the plane was I think—I'm not positive of this—both engines were out on the same side. And that was almost very difficult to keep it in the air. And I know a B-29 can fly with two engines, one on each side, but when they're both out...

"So they bailed out and we were involved in the rescue. Pick them up at sea. In one of my whale boats, I picked up three of the airmen almost immediately. We got them back to the ship. It was April and the water was cold. And one of them we didn't find until after dark, and it was about ten o'clock in the morning when the plane went down. We saw the plane go down, too. We stayed after dark because he may have had a light. And we had eight of them and we were missing two.

"About 9 o'clock at night, the ship just happened to by chance, run across...he had no light. We just found him by accident. The next morning, we were talking about the airmen. They were still aboard ship. We took them back to Saipan and one of them asked who was the guy in the whale boat? And I raised my hand and thought it was something I accomplished.

"He said, 'You made a long run at me, late in the afternoon and you turned away and I thought you were just pulling a stupid joke. I took off my pistol and fired in your direction. Fortunately, I couldn't hit a barn with a .45. You were pretty safe.' Then he said, 'I was angry, upset.' He spent the next, you know, another six hours in the water. He was in the water from ten in the morning 'til almost nine at night. But we never found the tenth one. So the only shots fired at me were from an American airman lifting his pistol at me to get my attention."

Do you feel fortunate to have served in the Pacific and been able to survive unscathed?

"Oh, yes. Oh, yes. We didn't have casualties aboard our ship and I seen some in other places. No, I'm very fortunate. Looking back on it, as soon as I was out, I was proud of it. I was anxious to get out. I left home in '43 and got home in '45 so I was gone for two years."

Greg was a teacher, football coach, and athletic director at Wauwatosa East High School after the war.

JESSE HARO

FOR THE HARO FAMILY, MILITARY service is an integral part of their heritage. Jesse Haro was born in Mexico. He came to America when he was nine years old. He was drafted into the U.S. Army and experienced some of Europe's most intense action—at Normandy and the Battle of the Bulge.

Jesse's son David served in Vietnam at great personal sacrifice. But David prefers to talk about his father's military service, from the Greatest Generation.

"He was part of the 3rd Armored Division," David Haro said of his father. "Landed in Normandy. And went all through Europe, France. He was at the Battle of the Bulge. So there's a lot of history with my dad. And I'm very proud of him because as we were growing up, as Mexicans, we didn't understand that. My dad never talked about it. Most World War II vets do not talk about the activities that they had. And even if you probed him...'Hey, Dad. What did you do in World War II?'" he would just shrug, 'Ah, you know, I was a tank commander.' "

"I asked, "What do you mean, a tank commander?"

Jesse Haro told me about being shipped overseas to Europe.

"I remember it was a long trip," Jesse Haro said. "I thought it would be you get on a ship and in about two, three hours, you get off of the ship. No, it was a long journey."

"They trained in England," David Haro said. "Waiting for, I think he said, waiting for a year and a half there. Trained. Just waiting for the day."

"We were anxious to get into any activity that they might have because sitting in the camp doing nothing all day long," Jesse Haro said. "Sometimes it gets boring so we were ready for anything that came in front of us."

"He remembers when he got the call," David Haro said. "They just said, 'We're loading you guys onto the ships and the tank' and all that. And they were not told...because they were going through so many exercises.

"They just thought it was part of the exercise. When they were at sea, in the Channel, they were informed, within a couple of hours, they were going to land in Normandy. And Normandy didn't mean anything to them other than there's the beach out there and we're going to go over it. What was very emotional for him, because it was the second or third day for the heavy equipment, which of course, his tank was allowed to get on the beach until they cleared the mines and all that. He recalls very vividly and actually got very emotional and started crying, that when they were debarking from the ship, the bodies, just floating around.

"He said that was very emotional. Because they didn't have time to grab the bodies, get the bodies off the beach because they had to move forward. They were just...they were going so fast. And he teared up. My dad doesn't tear up. And he did. And I had to slow him down because I know it was very hard for him. And he just said he saw red and bodies floating on the beach. They're all laying, you know. It's sad because we don't...war is war. I'm glad he became a tank division because he was only 19.

"Because what I found out through history, Eisenhower knew that from Day One, there were going to be a lot of casualties. And he didn't want to send his veterans in from Africa because they knew what war was about. They knew that when they hit the beach, they were most likely going to be killed. So what he did, right or wrong, he got the younger guys, 18-, 19-year-olds, the young men that thought they were invincible. He needed men that were not going to be afraid, didn't know what was going to happen but were gung ho. And he needed that first front to go in. And right or wrong, he kept the veterans a day behind. So those young men took the brunt of it, not knowing what the older guys...and the older guys were only 21, 22, or 23. It's kind of comical because you think of in your 20s or 30s, all these men were in their 18, 19, 20 or 21.

"So when he landed in Normandy, they couldn't stop. They said, 'You don't stop. You keep forward. Keep forward. For about two or three days, that's all they did. They went forward until they established the beach."

"And then his story starts from the Ardennes, that there was fierce fighting in the Battle of the Bulge, of course. And that they just had to swing it. They were there. They were surrounded. And they just had to...Patton came through and opened a corridor for them to get out, or at least put the offensive on to the Germans because that was their last stand. So that was great. Had a lot of pictures of when he was in Paris."

In November 2015, at the War Memorial Center, Jesse Haro was presented with France's highest military medal—the Legion of Honor—for his distinguished service during World War II. David read the letter sent to his father by the French Embassy Consulate in Chicago.

DEAR MR. HARO,
IT IS A GREAT HONOR AND PRIVILEGE TO PRESENT YOU WITH THE KNIGHTS OF THE LEGION OF HONOR MEDAL. THROUGH THIS AWARD, THE FRENCH GOVERNMENT PAYS TRIBUTE TO THE SOLDIERS WHO DID SO MUCH FOR FRANCE AND WESTERN EUROPE. SEVENTY YEARS AGO, YOU GAVE YOUR YOUTH TO FRANCE AND THE FRENCH PEOPLE. MANY OF YOUR FELLOW SOLDIERS DID NOT RETURN, BUT THEY REMAIN IN OUR HEARTS. THANKS TO YOUR COURAGE AND TO YOUR AMERICAN FRIENDS AND ALLIES, FRANCE HAS BEEN LIVING IN PEACE FOR THE PAST 6 DECADES. YOU SAVED US AND WE WILL NEVER FORGET. FOR US, THE FRENCH PEOPLE, YOU WERE OUR HEROES. GRATITUDE AND REMEMBRANCE ARE FOREVER IN OUR SOULS."

Jesse Haro worked at Milwaukee's Square D company as a machinist for 40 years.

David Haro served in intelligence with the U.S. Air Force during the Vietnam War.

PHILLIP HOJNACKI

PHILLIP HOJNACKI BEGAN HIS World War II service stateside in 1942, training army troops as a staff sergeant drill instructor. It was a sometimes daunting task.

"You teach them how to march to start with," Hojnacki remembered. "You know some of these guys don't know their left foot from their right."

Hojnacki prepared thousands of men for battle, then joined the fight on the frontlines in Europe himself in 1944 as a member of the 36th Division, H company, 142nd Regiment, immediately after D-Day. Like many veterans, Hojnacki was wounded and survived another close call that led to many years of pondering "what might have been."

Hojnacki and another soldier also enjoyed an unexpected break from the hostilities when they stumbled upon what turned out to be a "happy hour" near the German border.

"They were shelling the road we were on as we were walking up and me and my buddy and there was this big house. We didn't know what it was. It was just a house. But it was open to the basement. We ran down in. It had been shelled before. But we had access to the basement. We ran in there and boy, did I love it. I walked in about a foot of wine. It was a winery and these big barrels? They were in huge barrels like that. Maybe 10 feet high, I don't know. They were broke. And it spilled on the floor. So him and I, we took our canteen cup and half of the barrel was full of wine yet. I always tell that story. We would have stayed there all day. We would have got schnockered. But we had to move."

You spent your first years in the service training troops. What did you teach them?

"We had firing ranges. We fired bazookas, and like I say, you teach them how to take guns apart. I could take a machine gun apart in the middle of the night, when I was blind, I could tell you 108 parts on there because I did it so often. And later, when I got overseas, I was in charge of a section of machine guns, that was a Browning 30-caliber. But my job was mostly, I didn't even fire the machine gun.

"Because I had a section and I would tell them where to position them, you know the most advantageous area and maybe where there was maybe a gulley where they could sneak up with the mortar specialist. We had sound power wires, that you would take on the road and I could have a phone and take it to either one of my guns so that you could communicate.

"Yep, that was just a basic training. They were just going out. They didn't know where. And I didn't know where."

Drill sergeants usually don't have many fans among the troops they train, but one of your soldiers actually wrote you a "Thank You" note?

"Yes. (*Begins reading letter*) 'We've enjoyed our association with you and will always be grateful for the instructions that you have given us. We've drilled and sweated along with you and now it's over. That is, the basic training. This ain't goodbye. Not by a long shot. We've got a job to do and a big one at that. And some day, we'll meet again. Perhaps in Tokyo or still better, in Berlin. So you see, it ain't goodbye. We just say until we meet again, we wish you good luck and God speed. We're going to give them Hell. We're your boys.'

"That's the part that I feel so thankful, that they'd even say that. I don't doubt, you'd have to look all through the second war and all the wars, I don't think anybody ever thanked whoever gave them the training. You just accepted it. But this guy did that.

"These were guys who were leaving in 1942, I'd say. And when they left, I don't know where they went because at that time, we were in Africa. So they could have ended in Africa, or surely they were in the War because The Big Event didn't happen until 1944 with the invasion. But they could have went through Africa, they could have went through Sicily, and Italy. There were several invasions over there."

You were wounded in Germany. How did that happen?

"It was a big missile. We were in this little village, matter of fact, I just took a prisoner down before it, I see that son-of-a-gun coming in the air, a big ball of fire, and I'm kind of really laughing. "Hey, wait a minute." It's coming more and more toward me and all of sudden, it started to whistle, and we used to call them Screaming Mimis. That was the name that we gave them as soldiers, you know. Because you could hear them screaming.

"And I tell you it was coming more and getting louder and I hit the ground and I had my leg hanging over the side and the bomb exploded right off, right across the road from me. Incidentally, the whole town was burning. The Germans had that thing zeroed in. I didn't know if it was our artillery that did it, or theirs. But the, I don't know, I got hit and had to start hobbling later, and I can tell you about that one day especially."

Where were you hit?

"Right in the bottom of the leg here. Well, my leg got stiff later and I had to hobble. And we went up this hill anyway and we went up this hill between buildings. The buildings were all burning. Both sides of it. Just previously it must have bombed out. And there was a plantation, you know like up North, where you have these pines, and the Germans put these big logs in the road and it was about 10 feet across, filled it with dirt and had more of these pine trees.

"Because we laid there half the night. And there was an American tank that was burning over there, that the Germans had knocked out. Because when you hit that, you couldn't get any farther. And the Germans must have had it zeroed in, so when that thing was burning half the night, then we moved up the road and then we went in to some old farmhouse because there was a...I can remember there was some grape orchards down the hill. Maybe it was part of a winery, I don't know.

"I remember one time somewhere in Germany, there was a German tank over a hill. I'd say it was about a mile away. It was kind of an open field. And there was a red brick building. Me and him, my buddy, were walking down the road and the rest of our unit was around the corner and I had just passed an American soldier, a young guy, nice-looking kid, he was laying there with a bullet hole right through the helmet, out the other side. So I always thought our American helmets at that time, they sure as hell weren't Kevlar. Yeah, he was just laying as dead as a doornail. Well, anyway, we got up to that corner and all of a sudden, we stopped here. The red brick was about seven feet high. And that German tank on top and that 88 was a fast gun and when they fired them, you could hear them. And it knocked a hole in that wall.

"When I talk about it, even then, we were able to take out some insurance. I didn't think I was ever going to make it. I took out some insurance so my mother could maybe buy a house. Anyways, that thing was still smoking, he fired a second shot right through the same spot. That tank, it has just got through smoking. And I said to my buddy, 'Let's go.' And we ran through that damn hole where they just blew two holes through there. But he never blew another one. That tank took off again. I think we were getting near the Rhine River and he had to have his asshole back there somewhere. Pardon my language.

"Honest to God, I must have been a little goofy because I don't know why we did that. We could have went around the corner. I think I was trying to time the shells and I figured we'd make one in between.

"We were somewhere sometime, again you didn't know where the hell we are, they never tell you. You always moved. At least we were. And we was stalled. And there was a heavy woods. And we were on the dirt road, and as we were going, we got stalled. So naturally we're walking all the time, we're tired. And we went and sat on the right side of the road and it was kind of narrow, a dirt road. And the whole unit was stalled up ahead. And as we sat down, the grass. There was a ditch in the road, and my buddy sat down over there by me and as we sat down—oh, my God, and I said, 'Hey, don't move.'

"Right between us in that grass, there was a German shoe mine, they called it, shoe mine. I don't know how they spelled the word shoe but it was just a brown box, just stained, about this big. We knew about what you might call you know, personnel traps. You know, it could be a helmet that you pick up that could blow you up. But this thing was hidden in the grass. And I said, 'Tony, don't move.' We'd of sat on that.

"So a little while later, while we were sitting there, here come walking down the road from here to there and they had the litters you carried the wounded, two guys and the medics had the young kid on there and his leg had blown off completely on both legs. The flesh and the legs were just hanging there. And he was knocked out, of course. I don't know if he ever lived.

"But what happened is, farther up that road, he must have stepped on one of those or sat on one. And that's what could have happened to us. But what I did is I had some toilet paper and I didn't want anybody else to sit on it. But I didn't do it right, either. Anyway, I took some toilet paper and I made a circle around that so that anybody the rest coming back down that would obviously see, 'Oh, what the hell is that doing with that circle around it?'

"But what I should have done was is just walked across the road and told the other guys to get off the side. I should have taken my rifle and blown it up. I didn't do that. To this day, I'm still wondering, I didn't do the right thing."

But you saved your friend.

"Well, yeah, because I seen it. But what about somebody walking back, somebody who didn't know, except that I put that toilet paper and it might have caught their attention. Otherwise, I don't know how many of them they strung along. Obviously, the German soldiers figured, they're not coming back. So they're just going to threw these things along there. Hell with them. They could be laying there yet.

???WHAT DID PHIL DO AFTER THE WAR? OR WORK HISTORY LIKE OTHER CHAPTERS???

BILL HOLMES

Every veteran who survived World War II felt fortunate to return home safely. But Bill Holmes felt more fortunate than most. He escaped death first after a harrowing experience in battle and then after being badly mistreated in a POW camp. Holmes lived to tell the tale, which included a happy ending; rescue by an American legend.

"I was a flight engineer. I did practically everything but fly. I always referred to it as the third pilot. If something happens to those two guys, you're the next guy. That B-24 is like a flying boxcar. As a matter of fact, that's what they used to call it. A big plane. Very cold. In those days, you wore so many clothes you could hardly move. Long underwear. Regular underwear. Uniform you used in flying suit. And they're plugged in. After around 12 to 15 thousand, it's below zero. And there was no oxygen so you had to wear an oxygen mask all the time and that was very uncomfortable. That's always the wrong place, you had to be careful. So you had to squeeze it because it would freeze up from your breath. That's how much good it did.

"I got shot down, I think it was the third mission. We were flying...most of our targets were either oil wells or refineries. And that day we were going after a refinery which was near, well, near Istanbul. It's...those countries were all German in a sense. I mean they had...I guess it was really Istanbul. Because that's where one of the big refineries was. Actually, we could see these planes flying off to our right. They were Messerschmitts. One of things you learn is aircraft identification, you know. That's how we knew which one it was.

"So we could see these Messerschmitts. 'Oh, boy, here it comes. Make sure the guns are all set.' We finally figured out what they were doing. They were talking to aircraft people on the ground, telling them our air speed and altitude to make them more accurate. And they were. 'Cuz they got us. They hit us in the No. 2 engine. It was also right on the wing where you fill the pipe full of gas. It was right there. I looked up. I had a window so I could get the pilot gear, keep him from freezing, they can't see the gear.

"That was also one of my jobs. Secure down locked gear. Secure. So I look out there and see all this water. So I called back from the waist, I said, 'Do you see anything?'

"He said, 'Yeah, heat water.'

"I said, 'Don't light a match, that's 100 octane.' So of course, you don't go far without. So rather than take a chance on the thing blowing up, we jumped. And that's another experience.

"Well, you never figure you're going to use the thing (*parachute*). I wore what they called a chest pack. Most people wore a seat pack or a back pack. Well, chest pack's also a little bit smaller than the actual canopy. But I was standing out on the catwalk of the bomb bay watching the pilot go this way.

"Because I wore a chest pack, you had to be careful when you opened it, you don't want to be facing down. Because when you opened it, the back of that pack will knock you out as...I saw guys in prison camp obviously did that. They had big gashes across the top of their heads because the back of the pack is something solid anyway. So you're supposed to get over on your back so when you pull it out, you know, but is it going to work? Well, obviously it did.

"But when we finally get down, I thought, 'It's such a strange feeling. Am I falling? I'm just laying here.' Well, like I say, you're up 15,000. You got a long way to go. And then finally you get close and you realize, 'Yeah, whoo.' So I came down through trees. And the canopy got caught. I came down and bounced. Hanging in there. Well, how do you get out? Usually you have chest, but you have leg straps, too. Well, of course, all your weight and all your clothing. You're got it all bunched up. So you're trying to find it. But obviously, I did find it. But I tell you what, the troops were... the SS troops were there. And they knew exactly what we carried. They wanted to know, I threw the gun away as soon as I got on the ground because I thought I would get caught with it.

"But they knew we carried .45s. They knew we had a pistol belt with spare clips. First aid kit and all that. And they were very upset that I didn't have spare clips. And trying to convince them... well, I didn't speak German, they didn't speak English. But the message gets through, believe me. So they finally realized I didn't have...But they took my flying boots. My regular GI shoes were hooked on my parachute. Well, they came loose when I jumped when the chute opened. So all I had was the flight boots—huge boots not made for walking. So they gathered it up; they wanted that chute. They did get the chute. Some German bride probably had a great wedding dress. I think in those days there actually were silk. So it was, then they led me off to a...we moved around so much...partly because we were kind of in these transit camps at first. And then they moved us to a more permanent camp.

"But as the Allies were coming in, the Germans kept moving us back, deeper into Germany all the time. So finally, they kind of ran out of space. So we're in this barracks building, whatever it was. You slept on the floor, there were no...it was a great hotel. Like I say, they wanted everything and they did. They took anything that had value at all. But then you go to the interrogation center. These guys got...oh, boy...these interrogators speak better English than I can. They know. 'You were a flier?'

" 'I didn't say I was a flier.'

"So I keep doing that. Of course, they had all the information already. But they are so good. But finally, well a little time in solitary, you don't have to talk to us. And that's what they do. They march you out to solitary. And that is scary. The cells are not very big, needless to say. There are barred windows that frosted. Same with the door. There's no bathroom. It used to be above the door. There was a red handle and when you had to go, you pulled that red handle. If some guard happened to see, he'd come marching up with a latrine.

"You might go a day or two without any food. I weighed 90 pounds when I came out. You might go a day or two, the food was so bad. It would be old bread of something like that. But like I say, you might go a day or two without anything.

"I was a POW for I think it was nine months altogether. It was ...it was an experience I wouldn't want to do again. Boy, I couldn't do it. I couldn't handle it."

Were you part of a work detail?

"No, they had the Russians and so made them work. They moved us around so much. I can't remember which camp it was in but there were moving us to this camp and another. We were going through a tunnel and finally, I realized it was a gas chamber. You could see by the way it was built. You could see these...I thought, oh, this is it.

"We get into the tunnel, and outside to lead where they're taking us here, all these bodies are stacked up. And they had been through; they were Jews, as far as I could figure out. So if you were Jewish, forget it. But they board us on a train, 40 guys in a boxcar about that big. They kept moving us around. Well, they were using us as a buffer.

"But I'll never forget when they, Patton, came and liberated our camp. That was something. They came in on a tank. His ivory-handled pistols. And oh, you...was he a hero. And we broke into the German part of the camp where the workers...and we stole everything that wasn't nailed down and a few things that were. Anything that looked like food, we ate, whether it was good or bad. But, oh. So I had a few souvenirs. I had a helmet, stuff like that. I don't know what happened to it but...Well, it was something I wouldn't want to try again."

Did the prison camp experience change you?

"Probably, yeah. Probably a lot more serious than I was before and a lot more appreciative of things. God knows. I'd say I appreciate anything and everything. Whether food or clothes. And you're terribly lonely. And everybody else is too but like I say, they did move us around. They had...this one barracks we were in, was it the English? I think it was the English flew over at night and bombed.

"And like I say, this one camp was right near Nuremberg, right near the big stadium, which was a likely target. Most of the camps were located near military targets. And this last one was like I say near Nuremberg. And the British come over, one come over at night and the other come over in the day. But they'd drop a flare, which was to tell the pilots where to drop. Needless to say, you get a thrill a minute. It was an experience I'll never forget but II wouldn't want to repeat it. I wouldn't be able to handle it now.

"I couldn't do it again. But you should learn everything that happened. Learned to appreciate life a lot more. Food and a lot of things that...My dad was a World War I vet but he'd been gassed and had bad lungs. So I got home, he really didn't want to swap any stories. He thought mine was far worse than his."

Bill spent his postwar years working in the family business, which sold building materials.

ED IHLENFELD

IN A WAR THAT RAGED FOR SIX years claiming millions of lives over multiple continents, there are legions of stories about courage under fire, gallantry, and battlefield swagger. A Milwaukee man was directly involved with perhaps the most memorable story in Europe, a story that has been re-told countless times, most famously in the movie *Patton.*

"I was drafted on a Friday the 13th, 1942 and I was discharged on Nov. 19th, 1945. I don't know if the Friday the 13th was a bad omen," said Ihlenfeld, who was interviewed by his family in 2004. He passed away in March of 2016.

"I never mentioned this before but I've killed a guy. With a hand grenade. I don't know if it was me or if it was a guy who was with me but we were in a jeep going into Carrington and we saw somebody...snipers shoot from a store window, shot the fire out. I was sitting on the back of the jeep and he shot the tires out underneath and of course he had to come to a stop.

"We ran up to the store and I threw a hand grenade up and the other guy went up the steps and threw it in...the hand grenade... and it was no more. We went up and here's this young German guy was literally hamburger. Just tore him apart. And I often think about that. His mother's probably still waiting for him to come home."

When did you get shot?

"In an invasion. Oh, yeah, on the way down, I was shot. And I was laying there and I could hear German machine guns right nearby and this friend of mine from the medical company, Tom Doyle, saw me laying there and he came over and he helped me. He says just put your arm over my shoulder and I did and then we struggled and he took me into a first aid station...actually it was a base hospital...and there they said that the bullet had just gone in my leg and went right around the bone and out the rear. So they sewed it up and I laid there about three days and they said you can go back to your company.

"Well, later on, this Tom Doyle, the guy that helped me, we were on our way up to Bastogne, Belgium, in 10-ton trucks and they didn't take us into Bastogne. They took us on the outskirts and then they dumped us out. There was a big haystack there and this Tom Doyle, the medic that I was...he was from Chicago...I got to know him quite well.... He says, 'Ed, come on. Let's sack out in this haystack.'

"I said, 'No, they want us up in the town of Bastogne.' Which we knew was just ahead of us. And I said, 'I'm going to go on further.'

"And he said, 'Ah, I'm staying back here.' So he stayed and in ten minutes, that whole...the Germans came and surrounded that haystack and all those guys that stayed back were taken prisoner, including Tom Doyle. And I later found out that this Tom Doyle died from dysentery in the German prisoner camp. I felt bad about that.

"And then we were up in Bastogne, and then the Germans surrounded us up there. And we were surrounded for 10 days. And that's when they sent us this letter to surrender. I got all the wording...Christmas letter there. And that's when I...General Taylor in the meantime had gone back to Washington DC to prepare for us to go to Japan and fight in the Japanese War because they figured the German war wasn't going to last much longer.

"So while Taylor was gone, the assistant division commander, who was General Tony McAuliffe, was is command and, of course, I was assigned to the Chief of Staff and Commanding General's section or office.

"Anyway, when the Germans asked us to surrender, McAuliffe read it and he said 'Nuts.' And he said, 'What am I going to answer?'

"And then the general says, 'Oh, why don't you tell them *Nuts.*' He said OK. And then I was sergeant.

"Put this sheet of paper in the typewriter. Write this to the commanding general...to the commanding general of the army, of the German Army: 'Nuts in capital letters and sign it the commanding general.'"

"So I did. Never think anything further of it. And then this German emissary of whatever brought the message over, took it back and that's how things started."

(In the movie "Patton," George C. Scott, playing the title role, reacted to hearing the story of General McAuliffe's reply by delivering the brilliant line, "A man that eloquent needs to be saved.")

"Well, we waited and waited because they were going to annihilate us with I don't know how many German artillery and Panzer Divisions and so forth. So we sat kind of tight in Bastogne waiting for them to come. And then one day, we heard the German tanks starting up, so we had to go out on the line and see if they were going to attack.

"That company commander throws a bazooka at me and says, "Hey, you take a bazooka and knock on any tanks that come this way." Another guy had the ammunition. And boy, was I happy they didn't come because I didn't know how to shoot one of those things. Just had a general idea. They have three markers on them. One, one hundred yards, two hundred yards, and three hundred yards. So we had to estimate how far they tank would be and then use that particular sight to sight it in. And those bazookas were like a rain gutter, you know? Six or seven feet long. Round pipe. And you held it up and aimed and another guy put the ammunition into the back.

"But we didn't have the...we were all set, loaded, waiting for them to come. You could hear the rattling of it. And what do you know? That's when the weather broke. We were covered with clouds all the time. I think it was the day after Christmas the weather broke and the Air Corps P47s and P51s came in. They were given positions by the liaisons, who also had a new kind of colonel assigned to us to coordinate the air corps. Give them targets and you gave them targets where the tanks were and the P47 guys just came in and literally destroyed those tanks. Blew them up to pot.

"And that was the end of Bastogne. Oh, and after this had all subsided, we were in the basement of a Belgium army barracks and there's a knock on the door. And I opened up the door and there Patton was standing. Oh, my gosh. You know...I always feared him because they said he was old blood and guts and that he had literally treated guys bad. And then I saw these...he was a big guy. He had four stars on his helmet shining on. And his ivory-handled guns and he had a sheepskin jacket on.

"He said, 'Where's the commanding general?'

"And I said, 'I'll get him for you.' So I moved real fast and I went into the Chief of Staff's private room and it was Col. Higgins. By then, he was a brigadier general.

"And I said, 'General, Gen. Patton's here to see Gen. McAuliffe.' And he couldn't believe me.

"He said, 'Who?'

"I said, 'Patton.' Oh, my gosh.

"He quick put on his helmet. He went and got McAuliffe and the two of them went into the office there and talked to Patton."

What was it like when you finished your service and came back to the United States?

"We came through Patrick Henry, Virginia. And then from Virginia, I went to Ft. Sheridan, Illinois. And there they just discharged me and gave me an overcoat to wear on the way home and then I had that barracks bag. And I took the North Shore from Ft. Sheridan to the end of the line in Milwaukee, that was 6th and Michigan. And I got off at 6th & Michigan, that was in November. It was kind of cold. And I walked up to 6th & Wisconsin and I got a street car to take me home.

"When the streetcar stopped on 18th and Hopkins St., and I got off and I walked across the street, and my parents...I could see my mother looking out that front door...yelling, 'He's coming home!'

"My mother and dad met me at the door. It was around 9 or 10 o'clock at night. And then they called up my sister Norma Sue, and she and Eddie came over with Sherene and Carol, and Jimmy was just a baby then.

"I went over the Franks' Tavern. Well, we visited for about an hour or so and I wanted to get over to my favorite hangout. My mother got my car running, had the guys from the service station service my car. I had a '36 Plymouth convertible coupe. And she got them to get it running, so I went over to the neighbor's garage where it was stored and started up and I went up to 24th & Hopkins St., Frank's Tavern. There's where all the guys used to hang out and I thought that there'd be more guys there, you know, to celebrate homecoming. And lo and behold, there was nobody in the tavern. It was almost midnight. Frank was so happy to see me and that. We were sitting there talking and along come a guy by the name of Bud Melvin. He had just been discharged from the Army, too, and he came over there that night. During the succeeding days, guys were gradually filtering back but there was quite of few of them that were killed."

Ed enjoyed a distinguished career as a Milwaukee Police Detective after the war.

JOE KLUCARICH

LIKE MANY YOUNG PEOPLE across America, Joe Klucharich and his college buddies from the University of Wisconsin–River Falls were swept up in a wave of patriotism after the attack on Pearl Harbor.

"Pearl Harbor was on a Sunday afternoon. Monday morning we went from River Falls to Minneapolis/St. Paul to enlist in the service," Klucarich said. "All my friends from college, yeah, we jumped in three or four cars. Took off. Practically emptied out the River Falls university. Yeah, the guys just took off to volunteer for the service."

Klucarich enlisted in the Marines but not because it was a particular lifelong ambition.

"The lines were very long for the Army and the Navy and we found a short line and we went in there and that was the U.S. Marines. So that's how it happened that we joined the Marines. They had the shortest line waiting for them."

Klucarich reported to the savage boot camp on Parris Island in South Carolina.

"We always said, 'Let's go to war. War will be easier than boot camp.'"

After taking several tests during officers' training in Quantico, Virginia, Klucarich was part of an elite group sent to Harvard and M.I.T. for 10 months of schooling on electronics, radio, and radar. Klucarich became a communications officer for a fighter squadron in the Pacific, where he had critical responsibilities of making sure the planes could maintain radio contact.

"Every day, we went through the radio and the radar of every plane. We had 24 planes in the squadron. So my crew that I had, radio radar crew, and myself, we went through every plane to make sure that that pilot would have communications with all the other pilots in the squadron. And of course, most important, with the skipper of the squadron. And communications with all ground unit.

"We had a portable ground unit and I had an operator in that ground unit that was in communications then with the planes when they were in the air. And with the skipper. So that was my job with my crew that I had with keeping communications open. And we used to change frequencies every day. Otherwise the Japanese could tie in to what our frequencies we were telecasting at over the air. So we changed frequencies all the time. So every plane, we used to change the frequency so they couldn't home in on our frequencies."

Was that a bit of a chess match?

"Oh, yeah. I'd sit in a plane and then my other crew members would sit in other planes and we'd make sure we could communicate with one another. And I usually sat in the lead plane, the skipper's plane. His was the most important. We had to make sure that communications was 100 percent with the skipper. And then he could communicate with the ground unit and he could communicate with all of the pilots.

"You had to be in total communications all of the time. And of course, when they flew, when we were stationed on the Marshall Islands, then the squadron would fly to other islands and they bombed those islands to neutralize the Japanese planes and their airstrips there. So we neutralized the Japanese planes pretty good.

"We lost a couple of pilots but not bad. I got to tell you a story about one pilot. He was up in the air and he got on the tail of a Zero (*Japan's top fighter plane*), homing in on a Zero. So he called back to the base, our base communication center, and he said, "I got a Zero cornered up here." Well now, he's up there 10,000 feet. He's got a plane cornered.

"We told him, 'Tell us what corner you're at. We'll come and get you some help.' But he was a great pilot. He was a great pilot. He got on the tail of the Zero with his prop. He chewed off his tail rudder. Lost control. The Zero went down.

"We were supposed to go into Iwo Jima. And the invasion of Iwo Jima was Feb. 19th, 1945. We were supposed to go into Iwo Jima, we sailed up there but we couldn't get into the airstrip. The fighting was that fierce. It was terrible. We couldn't get in so we sat out on the ocean aboard ship for a while but nothing doing so we had to go back to our base.

"And then shortly after that, then we went into the invasion of Okinawa. And that was Sunday morning, April 1st, 1945. But we couldn't get into Okinawa either. So we had to go to a small island adjacent to Okinawa. And that wasn't too far from the southern island of Japan.

"So the planes, the bombers from Japan, they has an airstrip in Kyushu—Sasebo was the big airbase in Japan—so they would bomb us on the island of Hashima. And then once the airstrip was secured on Okinawa, we left Hashima and went to Okinawa. And that's where our squadron was. We stayed there 'til the end of the war. And then when they dropped the atomic bombs, after the surrender, then we went into the occupational forces in Japan, in the island of Kyushu. And the city of Sasebo.

"We took over one of the big Japanese air bases in Sasebo and made it our air base. We brought all of our planes there. So we stayed there until war ended, the peace treaty was signed and everything. And from there, we, on our way home, sailed to Tokyo. Spent a few weeks in Tokyo. And from there then on our way home, we went through the Aleutian Islands back to California, San Pedro, California. Yeah, that was the tour of duty."

How did the Japanese react when you got there?

"They were very, very good. We met a lot of families when we were...Sasebo was a big city. And probably not too many people knew it but they were very, very poor. They sacrificed everything for the military. And the civilians in Japan had to sacrifice food, clothes, everything. So the people there were poor. They were destitute. So we tried to help them out but they were very nice. We had absolutely no problem.

"We were very careful, though, where we went. We never worked alone. We always went two, three or four of us. Always went together. And we went to their theater presentations. They had some beautiful theater presentations in the city of Sasebo. So we used to go to their presentations but we always sat in the very back row. So just in case. There was caution. We were very cautious. We never took any chances but the people were very friendly. They invited us over to their homes for a little luncheon.

"And as you entered the home of the Japanese, you took off your shoes at one level, went into the next level, squatted on the floor at a little table. You didn't sit in a regular chair. You squatted on the floor, had a little lunch with some hot sake. And sake was their rice wine. Now I don't know if you had any hot sake or not, but just the fumes would get to you. All you had to do was inhale the fumes of that hot sake and that was enough. But they were very good. They people were very good.

"But I got to tell you a story, talk about the customs of the Japanese. In the city of Sasebo, the farmers didn't have land in the city, so they would go out in to the countryside where they had plots of land where they would raise rice and other food. Well, their custom was the man would be riding in the two-wheel rickshaw and the woman would be pulling the rickshaw with the baby strapped on her back and the man would be sitting in the rickshaw. So we, as Marines and young and foolish at the time, we used to stop them and make the guy get out and pull the rickshaw and we'd put the woman on the back, let her ride, with the baby strapped on her back. We changed the custom of the Japanese.

"I always say I was very proud that I served and I'd do it again. If I had to, if they called me tomorrow, I'd be right there. But I know they wouldn't want a 94-year-old guy back in the Marines. No way. But yes, I was very proud and I'm proud today. I'm very proud today my service with the Marines been very good."

Joe spent his post-war years teaching math and physics.

ALFRED KORTH

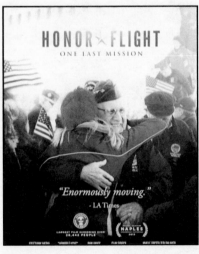

ALFRED KORTH ANSWERED the call for duty and reported to enlist in the U.S. Navy, but eventually wound up getting drafted by the Army. He served under a military legend and was wounded in combat, an injury that he still felt the physical effects of for 20 years after the war ended. Korth also witnessed some of the war's most horrific scenes that resulted from years of Nazi brutality.

"I went to Europe, yeah, and we landed in I think it was Scotland, and we landed there. It was a...because all the other places were crowded. And then from there on we marched to England and there's where we... we stayed there for long time then. And waited for...to get our equipment and stuff. I was on the anti-aircraft artillery. So then you went to work and they put the...besides Germans were sending these flying bombs to London.

"So they put us right in the path there, where the bombs were coming over. So that was with practice for us, until the invasion come. They was following it back down, you know. We had to duck. We were right in the path of their range. That bomb was coming down. It went down like that and they kept following it down. All the while I was there, that's the only one that we ever got because that...the planes that the English had, they didn't have any of them that go fast enough except one. By the time that one got turned around, that bombs already exploded in England there.

"Then the invasion come. They started that...It was a long procession that we was...we was the last ones to go there. We went there 40 days afterwards. We landed in France because we had to protect all the people, all the equipment and stuff that was in England, because we had over 4,000 ships there, they were sending to England, I mean sending them to France. Then when they got them troops all in down there, then they has to use the ships to start bringing the ammunition and the gas down there. So that's why we had to stay back until that was all, everything was set up. Then they finally had us go to France there.

"My unit was the 6th Armored Division Half-Tracks. General Patton was our general. He was a go-getter, you know. General Patton. Nothing stopped Old Blood-and-Guts."

Did you ever talk to Patton?

"Never. He just went by us once. That's all I saw of him. We were in France, just entering it. The German fighters start coming from way behind there and start strafing our column there, you know. And then old Patton, he comes right there by us. 'Let's get 'em going,' he says. He kept going there and we went around to the other side there.

"And we got ahead further and after a while, we found out that sure enough that the Germans had come through there and they had strafed that place, the parking area where we was. They strafed that all up and bombed it and stuff. So then from there on, we went to...oh, what's the name of that town? ...Brest, I think that it was.

"We stayed there for quite a few months. Because the rest of the first part of the Army already had all the other places cleaned up, you know. And then Brest was the only one left. And they had us over there to protect the infantry and stuff that was attacking Brest because the Germans was flying over back and forth, you know, and strafing all that stuff.

"And then after a while, we had this...it was a long ways across the canal. And we had the 250 calibers and one 37 millimeter. So the only thing that would reach the other shore on the other side was the 37 millimeter. So they had us strafing, knocking those cars and whatever was driving around down there. So then we'd start shooting at them. So, of course, in the meantime, our tanks, they was way in back of us. There was kind of a hill-like and then once in a while, they'd come over and shoot a few shells up there and the first thing, the Germans, they found out.

"They found out that where it was coming from. And then we was behind a bunch of trees and bushes and stuff. There was cracks of stuff. And then all at once, one of them must have found out where we was sitting there. And then they start shooting at us, there strafing. They didn't get close enough there to knock us out."

Were you ever wounded?

"Yeah, I was in a...I had a big shell landed...We got stopped...oh, I don't even remember what town it was...we got back up by some Germans behind old trees and stuff. And we start shooting...What you call them...the mortars. They start shooting the mortars. One guy got killed in our crowd there. I got wounded there. That's where I was wounded. Then I landed in a hospital for two weeks. they had a big Stuka (*German fighter plane*) head there. And besides, I had pieces inside of my head. And my hands and stuff. Lucky I had a raincoat on. An overcoat. The shrapnel didn't go through the rest of my body.

"I been picking shrapnel out...this stuff start working out and the last piece I got out, I was...June, 20 years later. I'll picking on it. Got it all out, yeah. All the little pieces. Them mortars, you know, they break up in thousands of pieces and stuff like that."

You were there when some of the concentration camps were liberated?

"Yeah. Buchenwald Prison Camp, you heard about that? The guys in that book (*LIFE magazine*) we liberated...The Germans, they had all these people, you heard about that? The Germans, they had these people lined up, clothes off, laying on the side there. Waiting to go into the gas chamber. And when the Germans found out that we was getting close, then they quit hauling them all out. Drove them all out. I don't know where they took them. But there was this guy who was alive yet. He was...skin and bones...legs all skinny.

"Bodies piled up like cordwood. Big trench there were they had all these dead people. They went and dumped them in the trench. Those that they gassed, you know."

Are you proud of your service?

"Yeah, you betcha. Hitler, he wanted to keep going. We finally got rid of him."

Alfred received a Purple Heart Metal for being wounded in action. His picture is the cover image for the award-winning documentary film, "Honor Flight: One Last Mission."

JULIA LANNIN

JULIA LANNIN (NEE McCALL) was a U.S. Army nurse stationed in Africa with the 33rd General Hospital unit in 1942. She also served in Rome for 20 months. For Lannin, the call of duty was a family affair.

"I had three brothers I knew would go in," Lannin recalled. "And I felt like I had to go, too. To help take care of the boys." And she would take care of many boys with expert medical care, infinite empathy, and a sympathetic ear that never tired of listening to young men dealing with physical and emotional trauma thousands of miles from home.

While she was in Africa, Lannin met her husband Gordon, an army drummer.

Lannin reported to Ft. Jackson, South Carolina, was sent to Ft. Patrick Henry, Virginia, and shipped out to Africa, landing in Casablanca. She quickly discovered that in addition to being a trained healthcare professional, it was valuable to be a good businesswoman.

"On the troop train ride from Casablanca to Bizerte, on this troop train, they almost ate us up with bed bugs. We all just scratched. It was terrible. But we had C-rations all the way except we ran into a British outfit and we sold them...we gave them our C-rations for kidney pie."

So it was a good trade?

"Yeah, it was a good trade. For us, it was a very good trade. We'd buy fruit from the Arabs, grapes, a lot of the stuff we couldn't eat because they said it would make us sick. Anyway, I got tired of the C-rations. Our ship was sunk with our supplies. So we landed in Bizerte and they put us in a wheat field. So we slept on the ground between the furrows, you know? That's where our bedrooms... and we had them pup tents over us. And old Germany came up every night at 9:00.

The Germans would attack then?

"Well, see, the Mediterranean was loaded...The ships were all loaded with mustard gas. And then there was a German...There was a British outfit on one side and ammunition on some other side. And we were right in the middle of all of this, you know and...

Oh, my God. Remember when the war started in Iraq? This bought back so many memories because we were right in the middle and our colonel yelled to us, 'Crawl down on your bellies to the bottom of the hill.' This ack-ack was going up all around us."

You were in the middle of live fire?

"Oh, yes. But you know what? None of us got hit. Oh, some women went over to see German planes that were shot down at night. I never wanted to see that again."

Did you treat many soldiers who were in bad shape?

"Those shrapnel wounds, they were so bad. They were so bad. And it took weeks to get well. Some of them never got well. They had to be shipped back home. All we had to treat them with was sulfa powder in those days. You know, you'd dress them every day, clean them up and sprinkle sulfa powder on the wounds. And some of them were paralyzed. You know, it hits their spine and they were paralyzed all the way down. And then they got bedsores, you know. Oh, God. It was bad."

Was it tough to be in that environment all the time?

"Well, you know, I wouldn't have missed that for the world. You know, the patients, a lot of them came back if they were severely, in severe, severely injured, they didn't stop at the evac hospitals or the station hospital, they came straight back to us because we had a lot of neurosurgeons in our group. And one guy came in and we got five bad ones in one day. And I was in charge of the ward. Oh, my God, but I went back to check one, I checked every one of them over. But this one boy and I don't even remember his name and I touched his lips with the thermometer and he screamed at me.

"And I touched him up here and he screamed again. Very gently. So I called my surgeon, I called the surgeon and told him what was going on. He said, 'Julia, call the operating room. Set it up right now. I'll be there.' And it was a bullet in the pituitary gland. And I saw him get well and go home."

How did that make you feel?

"Oh, I was proud. You know, you had to be on your toes. To know what was going on. You felt so bad for these, you know, you see these little boys. They were babies. I was 22 years old and I was older than they were."

Did you have to work fast?

"One time when we got to Rome—we were sent up into Rome for about 6 or 7 months—and we were working 16 hours a day. And sleeping on an army cot on the porch, open porch, and one night I was so exhausted, you see they couldn't serve us food because the kitchen was in such bad shape and the Germans had left this building a bad, bad mess and we had to get our patients taken care of first.

"And for days, we had peanut butter and jelly sandwiches for lunch every day, every day. But it was nice. Best jelly you ever had. And they got a...well, anyway, I want to tell you....I went off the ward. I went back to my bed and I cried. I was so exhausted. And one girl came up to me and she said, she knew what it was all about, and she said, 'Julia, you need a cigarette.' And so I smoked a cigarette."

The war in Europe ended and you were almost sent to Asia?

"We were on our way to Naples. And they woke us up at 3 o'clock in the morning to go down to breakfast because we were going to board the ship for India or someplace.

"They gave us blood sausage and bread for our breakfast. That was not a good breakfast. But anyway, when we got back to our quarters, they said that the war had ended. We got word that the war had ended and we would not be going. And a lot of the other people were allowed to come home. We had to stay until December."

Your three brothers served and your sister Olivia also served as a nurse. Did everyone make it back home safely?

"All made it back. And my one brother, he was sent home to die because he had rheumatoid arthritis so bad and they had him in a hospital in Phoenix and they raised his temperature. They had given him fever therapy. I never heard of that before but I guess it is true. And it didn't work for him. So they sent him home. And they said he couldn't live too much longer. But guess what? When we came home, he was sitting there in a chair and the only way you'd know he was in pain, he'd be very white. And he went to Furman University. He graduated with honors. And became a multimillionaire.

Are you proud that you served?

"Oh, I wouldn't have missed that for the world. You know, I have a lot of notes. I wrote about this one boy. I had this one patient. He got shot in the neck and was paralyzed from the neck down. His name was Holding and he was from Texas. And I had to have an emergency surgery over there after our hospital closed. When the hospital ship came in to get all those patients, a boyfriend of mine came to see me. He was captain of a minesweeper and he came back to see me and he said what can he, he wanted to do something for my patients since he could do nothing for me.

"And I told him to bring ice cream. And I'll never forget the day he came to the hospital ship; it was loading all these patients. This guy Holding was the last one to board and one of my foremen came over and got me and took me over there to see him. He said to me, 'Thanks for the ice cream.' Anyway, one of the nurses on the hospital ship came back and told me that he was so bad, they radioed his family to come and meet him at the dock. And he died on the dock. So you see, at least we kept him alive to see his family."

Julia continued her nursing career in a civilian role after the war. Her mother was presented with an award for having five children in the service at the same time.

WILLIE McCLAIN

WILLIE McCLAIN WAS drafted by the military right after his 18th birthday and served in the Pacific in the U.S. Marine Corps.

"I served in the South Pacific. I was at the battle that captured Iwo Jima."

"We didn't get going on the first waves. The 5th Marine Division, all them. They went in there first and we was at Hawaii. Not that Hilo, Hawaii, but at that Honolulu. That Marine base was right over there just opposite of the where them Japanese bombed all them things. And we stayed there. We did some training there. LST (*Landing Ship, Tank*) because that's what we went in on when we went down to the battle there at Iwo. We stayed there a few weeks and took training. We took swimming training, you know, combat swimming and all of that stuff there. And then when we got ready to go, we loaded up on that LST and went on down to Iwo.

"Well, Iwo was quite an ordeal, you know. The first time that I had been into anything like that, although I must say, you know, when I went in, I wanted to go into the Navy because all of my friends was in the Navy. And then the recruiter there, I was in Jackson, Mississippi and he looked at me and I told him what I wanted to do, and he said OK and so he went in the room, another room, and come back out and he told me and the other guy with me there, 'You going into the Marine Corps.' And so I never argued the point, you know, because I never knowed anything about the Marines, you know. When he said that, I said, 'Well, I wanted to go into the Navy.'

"He said, 'Well, you're going into the Marine Corps.'

"So that's that and I went and they shipped me up there and we got into it and I was thankful after I got there because I enjoyed that service that I got there. They really was up to date with everything. They could teach you everything and they could do it right, you know. And we had a captain was our company commander and he was awesome. In training and talking to the people that were the personnel there. And I just enjoyed that and it made a difference, you know, because I wasn't used to that, you know. And he was a white man and he was talking to me like that and it made a difference. Because usually it was all the other way where I come from in Mississippi, see?

"And I just enjoyed the way they...the training went. It was hard but it sure was fair. And I enjoyed it. And it made me realize how good it is to come together with strength. And that's the thing about it. When you're pulling and pushing, you ain't getting nowhere. But when everybody' s pulling the same, then you going to make a difference in what you do, you know, really. And I just enjoyed it. Best thing that ever could have happened to me.

"Iwo Jima was the toughest battle, I think, ever was. I really believe that. Because the time, you know, when they bombed that place, we thought ... everybody thought it was going to be just a few days, two or three days, you know. But it wasn't. *(The battle lasted from February 19th to March 26th, 1945)* They had it well fortified. And we saw that after we got there. They had those pillboxes from one side of the thing to the other, you know like. It was something.

"And we got out there and we was going, you know, my group and the Japanese threw a hand grenade at us, you know. It come... one guy was over on that right side of me and I was over here. We saw it when he threw it and this guy, when he threw that, he just ready for it. When that bomb, that grenade got there, he didn't try to take it and throw it, he just scooped it right back at that Japanese and killed him and tore him up. Hit him right in the stomach, just tore it up, really.

"So that was awful, I tell you. That battle was, it was awful. And you see so many people coming back from there all hurt up, you know, and it was just...It took your nerves. You just wanted to do something in it. Whatever you could to try to help. And we did. And I was happy about that.

"That was the closest call we had with that things, that one was, really. It was really action, you know. The only thing, if this guy hadn't of been as swift as he was, got that thing back on it, we all probably would have got killed because we was right at an ammunition dump. I was never wounded.

After the war, you had to fight some different battles back home?

"Well, I tell you how it was for me. I went...when I got out, I got married and I bought some land and I build a house. And when I build the house, I bought some land and everything, I had to go down and pay my taxes. And I went down to pay my taxes, and when I went to pay, I went over to register to vote. And the register there told me, said, 'Well, I can't help you boys. We going to have to wait to see what they doing in Little Rock, what they going to do in Little Rock, Arkansas,' he said. 'And then, we'll know what to do.'

"I said, 'How long do we have to wait?'"

"He said, 'I don't know. Your guess is as good as mine.'"

"And then we left...we left from him and went back got in line to pay our taxes and he went over the sheriff's and got him and pointed us out to him, you know, and he come over there and he got us, you know and he said, he looked and come over there and looked at us, me and another guy, he was my brother-in-law. The sheriff said, 'What's the matter with you niggers? Y'all want to be white?'

"I told him, 'That's out of the question. I said we wants to vote. Register to vote. We done fought for this country and we come back and can't vote?'"

" 'Well, I can't help you boys,' he said. And then he took us over by his office and he gave us a shellacking and pulled, he had a gun hanging up one side. I got in between one of them and my brother-in-law got in between the other one and then he looked and kind of calmed down. He stopped calling us niggers. He called us 'you boys' instead. But anyhow, that's how it happened there. And I never got to vote until I come to Wisconsin. And I enjoyed that. I been here ever since."

After moving to Wisconsin, Willie worked in the railroad business at J.I. Case for 25 years and later worked at St. Luke's Hospital for eight years.

JAMES McKEE

JAMES McKEE WAS DRAFTED by the U.S. Army in December 1942 and soon discovered that he and his fellow African-Americans who served in the military would be fighting a war on several fronts: against Axis oppression in Europe and Asia and a battle with racism in his home country.

After he was drafted, McKee had to travel to another state to report for duty.

"They did not take blacks in Milwaukee back in during the war when the war started," McKee said. "They didn't mix the races in McCoy, Ft. Sherman. You had to wait, you had to go to the Ft. Custer, Michigan, which is Battle Creek. Michigan, that's where we had to go. We didn't like it but we had to do it."

"We stayed in Michigan a while. We was inducted there. Then we had to get a train, they put us on a train and then I end up in Mississippi. Mississippi. I don't believe...I saw some things down there I don't believe and I still don't believe it."

What kinds of things did you see in Mississippi?

"When we got there and I got down there, if you're a white man coming down the street, you had to get off by him and let him pass. I didn't believe that. And I saw it. But we had to do that. We was soldiers and they was saying "Get off the streets, son." We'd knock him down. And we didn't have a whole police guard. We had... There was several uprisings, if you know what I mean. Because they didn't want you downtown. We got the place then. We had an officer named Bondhill, his name was. He was a beautiful commanding officer. And he tell everybody, 'When you come on this base, you're under my rules. There's no discrimination on this base. This is in Mississippi.'

"And he said, 'Now, you're going to work here. Everybody going to treat you the same. If you don't like it, don't come in here." So that's one of the experiences. We had another experience that I can say something about down there. A girl come in there. She's...she said she had been raped. And they was going to come in and take a....get the people. It was about...I say it must have been about 10,000 of us. So they going to come in and get the guy that did it. So the commander say, "No, ain't anybody coming into my jeep." Now see—pulled a jeep with guns on them. He says the first man that come through that gate ain't going to be followed. He said, 'OK, you bring her in here.' So they lined up all the guys in squadrons, you know. Which was about 300 to a squad.

"She picked out eight different men. She picked eight different peoples. And every one she picked out wasn't in town that night. And you know what she said? 'He didn't rape me but he looked at me all right.'

"And another thing I didn't like about Mississippi, the governor was Bilbo. That's what the governor's name was—Bilbo. Cuz they made a record out of that when he died. "I'm going back to Mississippi cuz Bilbo dead." So that guy told Roosevelt no blacks were going to carry guns in Mississippi. We trained with wooden guns. So we went to the rifle range then, the rifle range, they had to carry them out there. We couldn't take no rifle. They carry out there and then you go out there and practice. You come back with your wooden gun."

What were you training for?

"Well, I trained to be...an expediter man. I tell you what expediter...you know what expediter mean? I know you do. If you see it on television now, it's that jeep that says, 'Follow me.' You know what I mean? When planes that are landing, you tell them where to park. That's what expediter is. Then I was a refueling operator. You know, you wait around for two hours to fill them big planes. And after that, then I got to be a 345, which is a ...that's a big truck driver. Truck driver. I learned to do that. I went to MP school. So I have been through a lot."

What was your rank?

"Well, I ended up as a sergeant. Yes, I ended up as sergeant."

What happened after Mississippi?

"They threw us on a train. We went to a place in Washington state called Moses Lake. I don't know whether you guys have ever heard of it or not. It's still there. It's a big, pretty-good-sized city now, but it was an air base then. So that's where we went for the extended training. And we trained out there and we trained out there.

"That is where I got hurt. I got hurt there in Moses Lake. So we was on maneuvers. We was out on maneuvers and I was telling them how to jump out of the trucks when the airplane come over, I jumped out and the guy behind jumped out of his truck and the truck rolled over me."

What injuries did you suffer in that accident?

"I got everything. I got my arm...When I got to San Francisco, Camp Stone in California, that's San Francisco. They let everybody over overseas but me. Because I wearing the brace, you know. And they send me back to a hospital. I had to go back to the hospital and then they send me to Sioux City, Iowa, and I joined another outfit. They said we'd get back to California. The last time I told them, 'I ain't going back this time. I'm going to stay.' And that's what I did."

What else was hurt?

"My back. My back. My back. That's why I was wearing a brace. See, I'm still wearing one. They fused it together, you know. So that's why I went through a lot. Still going through a lot with that back. That's why I been in this wheelchair because of my back. I can't do nothing. And they treat you pretty rough when you was in service. You can take my word for that.

"I fell, you know when they was teaching you how to fall, and if you guys allow me the moment, you fall with your rifle and stuff, the weight. I slipped and fell and my hand went under me when I fell on that. And they say it was just...they just taped it up. And told me is wasn't nothing wrong with it. My hand swole up this big."

That was another accident?

"Yeah...You asking me and I'm telling you. If you was black, you didn't get the best training. I mean you got it but you was treated like a horse. And you know when you got to go anywhere, you went on this side and I went on this side. Even when I left Michigan for Mississippi, when we got to Evansville, Indiana, you had to get...we had to get...you had blacks had to get on the front, you had to get in the back. They wouldn't let us mix. We all in the Army. We all going to the same camp. It makes me mad to talk about it. We didn't understand this."

In California, there was an incident where the military was serving German prisoners at a train station restaurant, but they weren't serving you?

"When I came back into California, I was shipped out there. So they come in and ask all the guys that was in the Air Force, who was in the Air Force? And I happened to be in the Air Force. And they sent us to Victorville, California air base. That's where Roy Rogers got his home. And we had to park. They were flying all these carriers, they was flying all the planes and parking them in Victorville city and we had to be there to park the planes. So we did that and helped.

"I left Victorville the 31st of December 1945. I get to Houston, Texas the next morning. That's where we had that trouble. Them guys *(German POWs)* were in there set up in big, nice chairs. Waitress...crazy girl getting around there. They wouldn't let us in the door. Now that's in Houston, Texas, I think it was, in this train station there's a restaurant. That hurt. I never been so hurt. But it did and them guys teased us bad. That's when we got back on that train, they teased us a good way up. And they had been joking with us, you know. But they had this guy, I think he was the captain of I think 105 *(German prisoners)* that they captured, you know, in Germany.

"And I asked him, 'How do you speak so much...how do you speak English so good?'"

"He said, 'Hell, I graduated from Harvard.'"

"I said, 'You did?'"

"He said, 'Yeah, I went to Harvard and graduated from Harvard.' And then he said, 'I went back to Germany and the war started. I got to be a submarine captain.' He did, he speak better English that I did. But hey, he was a very...you know, he escaped several times so...he said one time from California and almost got to Mexico and all that stuff. And he...that's the guy. That's the submarine captain. He was a smart dude. and he escaped several times from the San Bernardino and he almost got into Mexico...a couple times."

Were you proud to have served?

"Well, I'm glad we changed some things. I'm glad. A lot of things changed after the war. Everything changed. Now you know you had 24 million mens in uniform. And when the war was over, they just dump you out on the street. They didn't care what happened to you. You didn't get no money, no nothing. You just out there. In fact, when the war ended, they didn't even tell you that. You didn't get nothing. They didn't even give you nothing. They just dump you on it. We got discharged. You just out there. If you starve, and a lot of them did freeze to death, right here in Milwaukee."

James served in the U.S. Army from 1943 to 1946. After the war, he began a long career with the Milwaukee County Sheriff's department.

DAVID MELTZER

WHILE EVERY WAR AMERICANS have fought has involved great courage and personal sacrifice, World War II was the conflict where our national way of life was most at stake, defeating the Axis goal of world domination.

"At the time, yeah, we thought we were saving the world," recalled David Meltzer, who served in Europe with the U.S. Army's 95th Field Division, Artillery. "Because there was a guy who took over all of Europe and he was going to eliminate Great Britain. But our attitude was, you know, we have the opportunity to make the world free and people can be people."

Meltzer enlisted in the Army Reserve in late 1942 and after being stationed in Virginia and Pennsylvania for officer and engineering training, shipped out to England in the summer of 1944.

"We went down to the Navy pier in Boston and the bands were playing and our hair was standing up and we marched up that gangplank. We were going to save the world. And we landed in England, Liverpool, and that was in late August and as were going through London on the train to our Miles Standish, there was a buzz bomb attack in London, and we had to wait on the outskirts of London while they were being attacked. And that was our first exposure to what was to be, you know, war.

"And then we waited until September and then we were sent over to Normandy, Omaha, and then we camped there, waiting for our assignment. And that's when we go into the Red Ball and then after three or four weeks, we were finally called to combat and we started out with Patton's 3rd Army."

Did you ever see Patton?

"No. Our captain, Hendricks, would go out whenever, whenever there was a...every morning, he'd go for the staff meetings and never with our outfit, no. We weren't up where he was mostly with the tanks and the infantry up front. "

Patton moved quickly?

"Well, at the beginning, that was the problem. He was moving so fast. And then we had Montgomery *(British General Bernard Law Montgomery, commander of Allied forces in Europe)* who was also competing and so Eisenhower gave him more of the supplies and Patton was told to back off. But he's one of those fighters who he figured as much ground as he could take, he'd take. And when we'd go on...when we'd get some stuff at the Quartermaster at Omaha, we'd come back and only go so far and we'd have to look for his marks, which direction he went to find where there were camps, and we'd dump off gas or ammunition or food, or whatever it was that they needed.

"We spent 151 days in combat, starting Oct. 20, 1944, to defend points along the Siegfried Line. One thing I remember in one town, the infantry was having trouble getting house to house in the city and there's a road going into the town and we were stationed just outside at the top of the road and, of course, we used to be on duty, privates and PFCs, not officers, and we'd be on two hours and off four. So one night we were on duty and it must have been midnight or two o'clock. And, of course, we have a machine gun in our front farm field and we were standing guard and my buddy, he was from Green Bay, he had unloaded wheat and coal up in Green Bay when he was a civilian. Chevoir was his name.

"We were guarding and all of a sudden, we hear noises and he says...and you know this is a guy when you're in a tavern you think he'd protect you , and he said, 'Dave, what do we do?'

"And I said, 'We have to challenge them.'

"So we said, 'Who goes there?'

"And you hear, 'Brooklyn.'

"And you say, 'Dodgers.'

"That was the password, so you knew that they were friendly, not the Germans. Stuff like that. And then were also, one morning, we were getting ready to go out on our assignment and we hear machine guns going off in front of us and all of a sudden we a Messerschmitt coming up. So we all run out with our...we had carbines. We didn't have rifles; we were in the Artillery. And the machines guns were going off and the plane got hit, not by us but it came over us and circled around and ended up at the end of the field in front of us. And, of course, some of our guys went down and captured it and, of course, the feeling was, the gun that they had was a trophy they liked. But I remember that incident.

"Everybody asked me if I was in the Battle of the Bulge. Of course, we were at the west end of the line so we were the last to go into the Bulge. But we were...we had to march from where we were in the line. It was November, December. We had driving in bad weather and we had to put tarps on our truck guns—they were reddish-blue—so that we wouldn't be hit by enemy, or friendly fire from our airplanes.

"One night we were...we would park and there was some bombs that were coming in and we lost one of our trucks and a few guys. But we were always within a few...then range of danger, but other than the infantry and a few in the artillery, we were on a firing line. None of us were threatened by them. My job...Buckley...Jim Buckley and I, who was from Boston, a tough Irishman, he was a little older. He wasn't in ASTP. He was a great, great guy and drove 40,000 miles in the service with our truck all over Germany and France, servicing the artillery and the infantry. When we were on the move, we emptied our artillery shells and the infantry someone would get in our truck. We'd have to keep moving, you know, to stay with them, even with the front line.

"Lifting a hundred pounds was nothing. When you're 20, we were there to get it over with and go home and go back to our normal life. When we went overseas, when you're 20, you have a long life and it's going to be the other guy that gets it, not you. And we just felt we had a job to do. No question, we just did it and when we came home, of course, we were given a gift. We got 36 hours in Paris on the way back. On the way back, to begin to get trained to go to the Pacific."

Did you go to the Pacific?

"Hell, no! We came home in June of '45 and we had a month's furlough. And when we were on furlough, of course, the bomb was dropped in Japan in August, two of them. And they were still going to send us over, so we did a slight protest. We petitioned, complaining that we were all veterans who had 65 to 100 points and we shouldn't have to go overseas. Well, finally they did cancel the move and we went down to Camp Shelby Mississippi to be discharged."

Did you feel fortunate to come home?

"Absolutely. But none of us had any control over what happened to us. But those of us who did should remember that there're a lot of us who didn't. And we should respect them because we were lucky. They gave their lives to make this world and this country better. The one thing I always say is we had one Normandy. The guys in the Pacific, they had it much worse. They has a...every island they landed in. The Marines and the Navy. It was a much tougher kind of war because every place that they landed was an Omaha or a Utah beach. They had to go out on a beach and the Japanese were much harder to fight that the Germans. Because once we got into Germany, it was a complete collapse.

After serving in World War II, Dave enjoyed a successful career as an advertising executive in the Milwaukee area.

ROBERT MISEY

ROBERT MISEY JOINED THE Marines in 1943, a decision based on a friend's recommendation.

"A friend of mine living in the same block joined the Marines about a two or three months before I did. And he sent me a letter from San Diego. And he told me about the wonderful trip he had from Milwaukee to Chicago and in Chicago, he got on a Pullman train and he had a Pullman berth and ate three meals in the dining car. And it took them three days on that train to get to LA and from LA, they went to San Diego. And he wrote me about this wonderful trip. And I had never left Wisconsin. So that appealed to me. And that letter was the reason I joined the Marine Corps."

"I had the same trip and I enjoyed it. I had never left Milwaukee. If you can imagine having a Pullman berth in a Pullman car. You eat three meals a day in a dining car, watching the gorgeous scenery. Was great. I really loved it."

Once his enjoyable cross country excursion ended, Misey reported to boot camp, a hellish experience for most that Misey handled with aplomb.

"It was not too difficult. I was quite athletic and I learned a lot of lessons in boot camp. I learned to be organized. I learned to be self-disciplined. I learned neatness and I learned order. And those are the characteristics that I still follow to this day.

"After boot camp, there were about 60 men in our platoon and most of them went to Camp Pendleton for fleet marine force for the Invasion. And only one or two of us did not go. They sent me to Chicago. I went to Wright Junior College in Chicago and I was in the...they wanted me to be an electronic engineer. Electronic technician. So the summer of '43, I was at Wright Junior College, which was very nice because I could come home every weekend for liberty.

"In September, we were transferred to the Naval Research Lab in Virginia and Washington DC. And we were there for a whole year. From September of '43 to May of '44. It was a very organized school. We went to classes in the morning. In the afternoon, we had lab work. After lab work, we cleaned the laboratories. And then we were free until that next morning at 8 o'clock.

"We learned all kinds of equipment. I learned...in fact, one of the things we had to do would be to make our own radio. We actually...it actually worked. Then we studied electronic equipment. At that time, radar was very new and it was very secretive. When we studied radar, when we completed our class, a Marine would come and pick up our notebooks. And when we would resume classes the next day, he would bring them to us and we would put our notes in the book and they would take them away. It was that secret.

"Well, anyway, when I gradated from that school, I was in Marine Aviation and they assigned me to a fighter squadron. My duty was to keep all the equipment, the communications equipment, running properly. And I was in the fighter squadron. We went to from Cherry Point to Columbia, South Carolina and then we began to work our way across the country because we were scheduled for the invasion.

"We went to Walnut Ridge, Arkansas, and from Walnut Ridge to San Diego. From San Diego to the Marshall Islands. When we were on the Marshall Islands, they dropped the atomic bomb. So we went on to Guam and we started going back. So I was in the Marine Corps for three years and I never saw any combat.

"It was very exciting to work with cutting-edge technology. Most of the people in that class went on to continue their electrical engineering work. But I was interested in liberal arts and literature and English. I wanted to be a lawyer and I didn't want to be an engineer.

"I am very grateful to the Marine Corps because everything, anything that has happened in my life that was good, that gets traced to the Marine Corps. I told you before, I learned those habits of discipline and organization. And it afforded me an opportunity to go to college and to go to law school.

"And when I finished law school, I came back, took the bar examination. I had some money left over and I decided to make the Grand Tour of Europe. Well, it was in August of 1952 when I gone on aboard a ship in New York City going for England. And on this ship, I met this lovely girl and she turned out to be my wife. And she was a New Yorker but she wanted to come back with me to Milwaukee.

"So she did come back and we got married and we came back to Milwaukee and I continued to practice law. And we've been married now for 56 years and we're living together in the Catholic Home. So anything that was good in my life, I can trace back to my tour of duty in the Marine Corps."

Robert became an attorney and, when this interview was recorded in 2015, was still practicing law.

LARRY MYLES

LARRY MYLES JOINED THE Marines in August of 1941, several months before the attack on Pearl Harbor.

"Hitler invaded Poland in 1939. And it was a case where you sort of got a gut feeling that something's happening. And instead of going on to college, which I wasn't very...I wasn't the brightest one in the class, my friend Bob Donnen and I decided we were going to try the Marines. And we didn't think they would take us because we thought they wanted the perfect specimen. Well, in 10 days they said, you'll be in San Diego and that sounded exciting.

"We went to San Diego. We thought we were in paradise. Palm trees and beautiful, beautiful sunshine."

Paradise would soon turn to a much starker reality for Myles, especially during his harrowing experience in battle on Guadalcanal.

You enlisted before America declared war and reported to basic training. Did you pretty much know that you would eventually see action?

"Well, with our bayonet practice and with some of the other training that we were going through, it was always the chance...the chance. And I'm wondering, I wondered once in a while what's everybody so mad at the Japs for? I couldn't understand why the Marines were so mad at the Japs. Somebody knew...expected something. They didn't know where it was going to happen but they knew it was going to happen some place. But we didn't know that. But anyways, we just did what we were told to do. Because we didn't have anything else on our minds for the most part, we were fast learners. We wanted to be Marines and so we did everything we were told to do and trained to do."

What happened to your unit after Pearl Harbor?

"At boot camp, I thought all Marines were riflemen, and they are. But I thought I'd be sent for advanced training for machine guns, for mortars, for whatever. Surprisingly, a handful of us were sent over to North Island, the naval air base in San Diego, which is out in the bay. And because I loved aviation, I was fascinated with it, my dad was involved in it World War I. He was with the Observation Squadron and photographs of him training, involved with those aircraft. I just marvel at the aerodynamics and so on.

"To this day, I don't know why they sent me over there. I learned that they needed radio and gunners. And those were the men they were training to fly, and primarily at that time, with the dive-bombers.

"Unbeknownst to us, we had...when Pearl Harbor hit, we were going to school. We were in school for a short time and they pulled some of us Marines out of school. It was primarily Navy. But they pulled some of us Marines out and they sent us over to another base about 20 miles outside of Honolulu. It was formerly a blimp base but apparently the Navy lost a couple of blimps in storms and so on and they discontinued that particular branch of the Navy and a Marine fighter squadron was originated there.

"And the next thing I know, instead of being radio, being trained in radio and gunnery, I'm working on an aircraft, on the Brewster Buffalo. It was a clumsy, awkward, I think one of the dumbest aircraft that the Navy ever allowed a pilot to get into. *(The Brewster Buffalo was criticized for being too heavy and difficult to handle, especially against Japanese Zero fighter planes.)*

"But we were removing the tanks, gasoline tanks, and installing bulletproof tanks. Self-sealing. And so that gave me a lot of insight to aircraft which I, again, you do what you're told. We still had guard duty. We were still doing Marine stuff. And had no idea where you're going from there. And, as it turned out, when the Brewster Buffalo squadron aircraft was sent up to Midway and was involved in the battle up there in June of '42, they lost all of the big, clumsy, dumb Brewster buffalos. It was a crime to put a pilot in one of those things.

"And then along came the Wildcat. And I loved the plane. And we were working on it and the next thing I know, I was, not having gone to school but being a fast learner apparently, they put me in charge of this plane. At this time, as far as I can seem to recall, there's 24 planes to a squadron and each squadron has a crew of people that would, you've got the pilot and then you've got the crew chief—at that time they were called plane captains—and that plane captain was in charge of that plane to make sure that it was combat-ready. It was fueled, gas and oil, and ammo. So then we went up to...went up to Midway and trained and the squadron was formed.

"The next thing you know, we're on a ship that's carrying us to —we had no idea where we were going—and we really didn't care. We were Marines and we're going someplace. We don't know what we're going to be doing. However, our particular assignment was taking care of those aircraft to make sure that they were flight- and combat-ready for the pilot. Some of the finest guys you ever want to meet in your life were those guys. We ended up on Guadalcanal.

"The Marines had landed on August the 7th on Guadalcanal in '42. And we came up, the squadron came up sort of piecemeal. Our group came up about two and a half to three weeks after the initial landing. The initial landing was unopposed. But in the time that the troops got in there and we started continuing to finish the airstrip that the Japanese had built, was starting to build, we...there had been fireworks. The Japs wanted that fuel back and they were doing everything possible to do that. We were sent up and put aboard a World War I destroyer. We had a World War I helmet. We had a World War I rifle. World War I practically everything. Mess kit. We were put aboard this World War I destroyer that had been brought up to date. And they put Higgins boats *(landing crafts designed for amphibious landings)* there. So we would get in the Higgins boats and they'd put us ashore.

"And then they'd run back. That's the way they brought— piecemeal—they brought men in there until they could get the...

some transports in there. The volume of the manpower that was needed. So there I was at Henderson Field with my...with my beautiful Wildcat. And it was an exposure that you just take for granted because that's what happens in life. Everyday is not going to be the same as the day before. So there was bombing and strafing and shelling. And the beautiful foresight some of our military, upper echelon, some of the gasoline that we were putting in the aircraft we were pumping, hand-pumping out of 50-gallon drums.

"And they could well be contaminated, in which case the pilot's life is at risk. And so somebody had the foresight to provide chamois cloths. So we were filtrating this fuel out of the 50-gallon drums into the aircraft through a chamois. And it's just remarkable to me the foresight that was given to all the necessary things to go into a place. And this was the first Allied offensive in the Pacific.

"And just prior to us going ashore, with the Marines landing on August 7th, the following day, I think it was the 8th or the 9th of August, four of our cruisers, allied cruisers, were sunk by the Japanese who had snuck in there.

"They, at night, snuck through a picket patrol ship out there and sunk three American cruisers and one Australian cruiser. Well, when we were just offshore waiting to go, there was a lot of debris floating around. And it wasn't until later that we realized what that ...where that debris was from.

"Guadalcanal was 80 miles long, 25 miles wide. And all you had, it was like a baked potato. And all we had was a little...a little perimeter of maybe about two, two and a half miles. On this whole giant...the biggest island in the Solomons, in that chain, southern island. And so it was, the Japs wanted...they were pouring troops and construction in there. You can imagine how badly they wanted that airstrip back because their whole intention was to complete the rim, including China and Burma and then Australia. And they needed that...they needed the base of the Solomon Islands, that airstrip, which would be in range for attacking our Navy. So if we had the Navy, we had Guadalcanal and the airstrip and so on. And that was the reason that that's as far as the Japanese went in conquering, in completing the rim.

"This was the first Allied offensive and they knew it and if they lost that, if they lost the Canal..."

Were you wounded?

"I got harpooned many times by mosquitos. And that's what, after I got home, I realized I had been harpooned by these female mosquitos, which causes the blood deficiency, and the spleen enlarges, and so on. And fortunately, I imagine it affected more of the Japanese than it did us, because many of them were starving because the power of our Air Force to sink, destroy many of their troop ships and ships to prevent a lot of landing that would have happened, reinforcements on their part. But as far as being hit, no. No, I wasn't touched.

"The Japanese wanted the airstrip; they wanted to destroy the airstrip because we were operating off of it. We were a very significant piece of real estate. And therefore they put everything, every force that they could possible put in there to take us. And by the grace of God, the grunt Marines, the most honorable of all the machine-gunners, and the Howitzer guys, they kept that perimeter from being broken which saved...which was very beneficial to us continuing to operate off the airfield.

"At one time, a short time, everyone's...you're so busy being involved, surviving, trying to find food to eat, among the few mess kitchens and so on, every once and a while you figure you're not going to get out of there alive. But that didn't bother you that much. Because you were so busy, involved in what you're doing. And you had a lot of confidence by virtue of the fact that in boot camp, I was a sharp-shooter with the rifle. And it was a case where you just had a tremendous amount of confidence. And you weren't by yourself. You were surrounded by a lot of your fellow Marines who were probably ten times more Marine than you were.

"By the grace of God, I'm happy that I was exposed to it. Because you don't know, at one moment, you're going to meet your Maker.

"I didn't feel any different. I didn't feel any different at all. I wasn't mad at anybody. I wasn't mad at the Japs. I may have been had they broke through and tried to do what they do to the Americans. Nah, I have no feeling whatsoever. When we came home from the Canal, that's when I got hit with the malaria. I was down at Great Lakes and they...you'd think they'd know all about it by virtue of the Panama Canal experience. Put in a glass enclosure in isolation in this ward. Doctors are coming in and they're checking the spleen. Watching either it's going up or it's going down. If it goes too far, it's the point of no return. But by the grace of God, it wasn't my time."

Larry became a successful executive at M&I Bank, where he worked for 40 years in mortgage and commercial lending.

EUGENE PALUBICKI

EUGENE PALUBICKI WAS drafted in 1942 and had a choice between joining the Army or Navy. He chose sea duty.

"My mother didn't want me to. She wanted me to stay home but I couldn't stay home."

Palubicki's mother fretted for years as Eugene and his two brothers served in World War II. All three Palubicki brothers returned home alive, but Eugene saw many men who did not.

Palubicki went from working at Milwaukee's shipyards to sailing the Pacific and witnessing some of the bloodiest battles of the war from a more agonizing perspective than most military men had to endure, including a distant view of the most dramatic event in the Pacific theater.

"I got mail from Uncle Sam. He said he'd like to see us at his party. He said either you volunteer or we'll draft you.

"I took my boot camp at the Great Lakes. And after I got off of boot camp, then I filled out the, well, I took an exam. And I was able to go to service schools. So then I went from there to Navy Pier and I spent about four months, or four or five months, at Navy Pier learning aircraft engine repair, aircraft engine maintenance.

"I thought I would report to an aircraft carrier. Instead, they sent me to San Diego, California and there I went to a diesel training school. And I thought then I'd be on a larger ship or something like that. But instead, they were just beginning to go from island to island at that time. I went to a small island there called Tulagi, just as close to Guadalcanal, which was one of the major battles in the early part of 1942. I was involved in...I got into the 3rd Fleet. And there was the amphibious fleet for the Pacific Fleet. And we started the war...that's where my war really started right there.

(The battle of Tulagi in August 1942 happened during the first Allied landings at Guadalcanal.)

"And I went to several islands and the last time was we had a big repair shop on a small island in the Russell Islands. And we were training then with the 1st Marine Division. We stayed there about three months and we were geared up, we loaded up. They didn't tell us where we were going. We picked up everything and went aboard ship. And we didn't know where we were going. But we did end up to in the island of Peleliu, on the Palau Islands. And they called that the "Bloodiest Victory." And the 1st Marine Division lost about the majority of the whole Division. They fought that one...they fought that war there on Peleliu.

(28,000 Marines and infantry fought on Peleliu. There were 9,800 casualties, 1,800 killed in action.)

"And there's where I spend most of my time—on Peleliu. And during that time, it was really the hardest and the most combat that I've ever received. We'd take in the soldiers, the live ones, and brought the dead ones back because there was no place to bury them. They were on the beach and they were on all floating in the water or laying on the beach. There was no place to bury them. So then we'd take them off to sea at night and bury them out to sea at night. I don't know now how many we buried there but it was quite a few. Go out about two or three miles, and then we'd go back.

"We'd take in supplies. We'd take in bombs, and gasoline and everything they needed to fight them. And eventually, they built out of Quonset huts, they built a repair unit. And it was our duty to repair all of the engines and that on an LCVP engines, those are the landing craft that they used to land these troops in the island of Peleliu. And I spent most of my time there. It took three months before they could really secure that island and I spent a lot of time there.

"You grew up fast. You grew up very fast. They tell you what to do and you did and they always said, 'There's the right way and the Navy Way and the Navy way was the right way.' It was a good experience for me. Knowing what I know now, I would do it again. It was something to see that many people get killed. You take some live people in and bring the dead ones back out. And sometimes they'd bury them right in the sand there, because they didn't have no place to do it.

"And I remember riding on a patrol boat and you could see a Japanese soldier on a beach and he'd pick up a rifle and fire a shot. And one time I heard the *zzzz* go right past me. And I was glad that he was a bum shot.

"I was aboard ship, aboard ship not too far from where they dropped the atomic bomb. It might have been, seemed like it was close but we were a hundred miles from there. But we could see the light. We could see the light when those bombs were dropped. From there then we went back, we went back to another island there. Because we didn't have to go ashore at Iwo Jima. I spent the rest of my time there.

"But I did have the opportunity to be in the area when they signed peace treaties on the *USS Missouri*. And I have in my possession a paper, whether it will ever be worth anything, memory-wise or that, it is a copy of the...copy of the surrender of the Japanese in 1945. And I spent the rest of my time waiting to go home. And I got home in February of 1946.

"Even to this day, I can get emotional. I guess I was very fortunate to get back."

Do you ever struggle with memories of your wartime experience?

"I had some small problems. It's something that happens to you that you don't know is really happening. It's your old inner feeling after you've gotten so far from anything that happened day after day. It hits on you. You think about it and you think you're afraid but you shouldn't be afraid. You don't sleep. You've got one thing on your mind all the time, 'What's happening? Is there something happening?' Your pulse rate and things rise up and at night you'll dream that it was worse.

"The last time I started was about a month before I got home. I didn't want to turn into the sick bay because I was afraid they would keep me back there. But I did have that problem until I got home. After I got home and was back with my family again, I did see a family doctor and he did treat me and took about a week or two and I was feeling fine. But it's something that crawls on you at a time and you don't know what's happening when most of it is around fear, your fear that this is going to happen and everything bothers you. You're a bundle of nerves."

Eugene and his two brothers served overseas in World War II. All three brothers returned home alive.

BOB PESCHMAN

AMONG THE WISCONSIN veterans who served in World War II, few experienced a wider variety of scenarios than Bob Peschman, a member of the U.S. Army's I Company, 353rd Infantry.

Peschman's ship arrived in England days before D-Day. His unit stayed on board awaiting the invasion.

"We lived on a ship for about two or three days," Peschman said. "And we played a lot of craps."

Did you win?

"Well, a little bit. Jesus. I was only seven.....18. They used to call me 'The Kid.' The rest of the fellows were around 27, 28. And there's this young punk, 18."

Then came the invasion.

"Omaha Beach got really hit. They lost a couple thousand guys. I would say we were nothing but bodies to fill the holes. We went in on Utah Beach and I don't know how it happened. We climbed down the rope ladders to get to our landing craft. And the landing craft took us in and it hit a rifle shot or a shell. But the initial invasion was over. And then we came in the next day, I guess it was. And we landed and three German soldiers were coming down, walking down the peninsula at Cherbourg. And I don't know if they surrendered or we captured them. But we took them. Took their guns from them. That's the first gun though, I never saw it again. And some other company took them over after that. And we were assigned to our different divi....I don't know how that works, though.

"I ended up in the 90th Division. And it lasted from June 6th or 7th to July 13th. That's when I got shot. I didn't get shot. A shell exploded in my hole. In my foxhole. And I had to wait....I had all sorts grenades and ammo. After the shell hit, I put my hand down...I looked at a couple of them. I think he was dead. Because then I felt my leg and I come up and I was all full of blood. And then I called the medics. And they came. And I remembered, they carried me down on a stretcher, right across the field where the Germans were shooting machine guns and they never shot a round while they were carrying me across. That was pretty nice of them. At that time.

"And then I went back to England again after that. That's was July 13th. I got on the boat, ship, and I laid there on a stretcher on some type of bed. And it was all nurses. 'Get me somebody here. Get this...*she said 'crap.'* Get this crap off of here.' I had grenades. I had the BAR *(Browning Automatic Rifle)* and ammunition. I had the M1. I wouldn't give up my M1. I had that ammunition and I had a little guy helping me carry it, especially the ammunition from the BAR.

"I could hear the bullets going right past my head. They go crack, a real loud crack. And then I'd fall down. The German probably said, 'I got that guy.' But I was just dropping down because I could hear bullets going past my head. I was a young kid and they walked me up in the middle of a field. But we had a lot of experiences. They counterattacked us one time and our lieutenant was hit—I don't know if he was killed or not. But he was gone. And another lieutenant come up and he didn't know beans. He said to me, 'Solider, take your BAR and go by that rock and if a tank comes over the hill, open up on it.' I says, 'Not with a BAR. I want a bazooka.'

"The tanks never came over. I could hear them. Running back and forth. Our tanks and their tanks having a battle but they never came. There was a road going into the hedgerows. They never came down that road. I never would have shot at them. I'd have dropped the gun down and blew me away.

"But I don't remember much about moving because we were crawling most of the time from hedgerow to hedgerow. But the Germans found us with them 88s. One day, we were advancing on St. Lo and the German, I'd say for sure, he opened up with a Burp gun and he hit the three guys. The guy in front of me and two right behind me. And missed me. And I had the BAR and I let out a whole magazine of shells go up the tree. And A company was coming up and they shot up in the tree and the German fell out. I don't know if I hit him or if they got him. But we got through there all right.

"Then we went on to St. Lo. On the way there, that's when the Germans got me. Then I went back to England. After a period... they put me in the Amputee Ward, that scared me. I wasn't afraid of nothing because I was a kid. And they put me in a amputee ward and I just laid there. At night, these guys were 'I could feel my hands.' Didn't have no hands. Or one guy had his foot, he could feel his foot. And he didn't have a foot. I said, 'Man, this is not for me.' The next day, the doctor came in and looked at me. He bawled the nurses out some for...because I had gangrene in my wounds. From them couple of days. I don't know how it formed that fast, but...Then they put me in a hos...took me out of the Amputee Ward. Put me in a regular ward for a number of days. For weeks, I should say.

"After they let me go back, let me go back, then I was a little afraid. I was scared. Because I could see what...I policed up bodies. We fought and fought and then they cleaned out them from fighting, you had to pick up the bodies. And a semi would back up and we'd treat them like cord wood. One guy on a hand and leg. And another guy on a hand and leg and throw them up on the truck. They were stiffer.

"I was there for...Nottingham was a good town. Lots to do for a bum, or you know soldiers. But then I got back and had a few experiences. They put me in the MPs for a while, for about two weeks, to get my legs back. And then while I was in the MPs, I had two experiences, really with the MPs.

"General Patton come up with his caravan and I wasn't on duty but I had my helmet, empty helmet, and my gloves and stuff and then I was just walking along down the street. And then three jeeps pulled up and I could see General Patton, but he didn't talk to me. The lieutenant talked to me and he says, 'Solider, where's your CP *(command post)* ?' You know, I didn't know. I didn't know really. But a lot of traffic was going that way. I says, 'Go straight ahead, take the first swerve to your right. And you're bound to run into it.' And then they took off. He saluted me. I had to salute back. And I took off, too. But that was quite an experience. He had his pearl pistols, too. He had them.

"I had another job that I probably shouldn't mention. I was MP in a cat house with 11 women working there and it was all soldiers. I mean I looked out the front window and I couldn't see the end of the line. But your medics was in there inspecting them, because the second day, they threw one out. And another girl was there immediately. And we had five on a...they put me on the second floor, had five women there. One on the third, three on the first. But we had 11 women, five, six, seven, eight, nine. We must have had five on the first. And all we had to do was take the soldiers' guns and knives so they wouldn't take them in the room.

"They averaged a guy, what, every ten or 15 minutes. I'm out. I'm out. And they asked for another one. One guy's getting dressed and some other guy in there. One girl called me in her room and she had a suitcase full of money. French money. Stuffed into the big paper. And all I was thinking, 'How am I going to get... to come up with the money and throw the suitcase out the window' but we never did it.

"And then I was back in the 90th Division again. And St. Lo... we went through St. Lo lickety-split. We had it and then the Germans counterattacked and pushed us out of town. And it took us two weeks to retake Metz. That was Metz. Because they had some tricky pillboxes. With pillbox sitting there and we were attacking that pillbox and all of a sudden that pillbox went down and another one came up. The only place I ever saw that. Was in

Metz, right outside of Metz. The manure, they always had manure piles. They had that built...pillboxes.

"I met interesting people. One girl gave me two beer mugs. I still got one. I broke one. She used to run a tavern. And we used to get in the houses and sleep in the potato beds. And we'd sleep in the potato beds and you'd watch the rats. Tried to shoot them.

"I was in Germany, too. Yeah, I seen the concentration camps. I can't remember the name of it but we were the first ones there. And they had...it as terrible. They had a big trench. I don't know how long but the width was...it was 20 feet. But it was 60 to 80 feet long and it was full of bodies. They were very...I'm not skinny but they were skinny. And they sure showed us the furnaces where they cremated them. They even had lampshades, they showed the lampshade was made from human skin. The shade fit on a lamp. I didn't care for that place at all. The fellows that finally get saved, they were happy. But they were very...they were dead.

"But then I had another experience. Besides the war. After the war was over, Hitler finally killed himself. He'd have waited six months, we'd have all been *Sieg Heil*-ing right now. But he rushed his...he had a B2 and a B1 rocket and the B2 had wings. And our planes could just hit their planes in the wing and knock it off course. But then they come out with the B1. That sucker was dynamite. And at the time, it rose straight in the air and you couldn't even see it. The B2 you could see. You could see them flying.

"And I was in Bristol when one hit. In the hospital. But a number, I can't give you a mile...there was a railroad track and it was built up about eight, ten feet off the ground. And each one pulled in on the other side. And the hospital didn't feel the explosion. But it was a good thing. Because they had that perfected pretty good. We were supposed to try and capture that near the end of the war, try and get von Braun, *(Wernher von Braun, a top scientist in Germany's rocket development program)* especially. Any German scientists we could get a hold of.

"But then I had the misfortune of raiding Hermann Goering's castle. After the war, they used to call us, our company out, I mean, 4 o'clock in the morning and we'd take a drive us through the town and then they'd get the foghorns going. Everybody'd get out of their houses and into the street. We're going to search their houses. And all we had to do was find anything pertaining to Nazis —flags, guns, pictures, anything.

"But we got assigned Hermann Goering's castle. And our squad went into there. There was only about eight of us. But two of the guys...we found Lucky Strikes in the Green pack. I don't know if you ever saw them. Lucky Strikes cigarettes in the green pack. They're little, short cigarettes. Case after case. I mean big boxes full of those things. And I also...GI wristwatches. They had those, 12 on a sheet. Where it was. And they had cases of that, too. But the two guys that went to search that room, found her jewelry and she could talk a perfect...she could talk English better than I could.

And after we left, she went and reported that her jewelry was taken. And of course they knew it was us. Well, we got back to our barracks, they guys came around and gave me three pieces. A broach. A bracelet. And a necklace. Had to be worth a few dollars in 1940. So they came and with a foghorn, 'Say, you soldiers that raided the castle and took the jewelry, if you put it outside the door, nothing will happen.' So I took my three pieces out the lockers and threw it out on the floor. But two guys that took it, they tried to get out a window. And they were waiting for them. They got court marshalled and I never saw them again.

This was Goering's wife's jewelry?

"Yeah, all the stuff they had stole. They had different stuff. Pictures and stuff on the walls. He was up in the mountains a little. Yeah, that was quite an experience.

"When the war ended, the German war ended and then they took our company and says, 'The next day or so, you're going to be shipped over to Japan.' And we were in a forty-and-eight boxcar and on our way to Marseilles, France. And then Harry Truman dropped the bomb. There's a story with that, too. He dropped the bomb and the war ended and we didn't...they cancelled our trip to Japan, thank goodness. If I had not have been to....

"We were there in that car and the German people come running up to the French people, this was in France. They come running up to tell us, 'The war's over. The war's over!' And they wanted us to sell our blankets and our jackets. I sold everything. A dollar. Two dollars. Because I didn't get paid for 13 months. They never caught up to me. I'd be on the move all the time. But had a lot of different experiences."

After serving in Europe, Bob returned home and worked at the A.O. Smith Company as a foreman and trouble-shooter.

JULIAN PLASTER

JULIAN PLASTER HAD A definite plan for how he would serve in World War II. But that plan took an unexpected turn, including an incident where he was nearly knocked out of action by the unlikeliest friendly fire before he engaged in formal combat.

"I was walking down Wisconsin Avenue and I saw the Navy there and I thought, 'Hey, I'll join the Navy, have a nice, clean sack, you know?' White sheets," Plaster recalled.

"And I got as far as Pearl Harbor and they connected me with a Marines outfit. And I ended up in a foxhole. We would follow the Marines into these different islands and I was a cook. But the maintenance guys would take care of aircraft. Quite a shock. The first island that I got on... I thought, 'My gosh, here I'm going to be ...I was supposed to be in the Navy.'

"When I first got there, the first time, I was with about five or six other Navy men, and we landed with about 15 Marines. And I was given a pair of gloves and a shovel and says start burying the dead. That was my first experience.

"My first body that I picked up, in his hand, in this Japanese soldier's hand, was a picture of an old woman. His thoughts were probably home just like mine would be.

"The stink was terrible. And bodies out there in the South Pacific, the humidity and the heat, you know, they would blow up. And it was like picking up dead pigs or animals, you know. Maybe they'd fall apart. And you're very nauseated. I think all of us that was in there, we lost a lot of weight because we couldn't eat. But that stink stayed with you. It was terrible.

"It wasn't so bad there because I didn't know these guys. But about two weeks later after we landed there and were loading our supplies, the Japanese come back and they hit our ammunition dump. And that island is flat. You and I could run across it in about four or five minutes. And we thought the island was going to sink. Because all our ammunition, and there was no place to hide. The bombs were just blowing off. And there was one tent that I was in, there were six of us and the next day there were only three. That was emotionally disturbing, when I had to go and pick up somebody you knew, somebody you had been with for a couple of months. And it stays with you."

You were almost killed before you saw action?

"Before I even got to my first battle, I was on board this troop transport. We were in one of those rooms there and we were playing a game at one of the tables and the guy was in a corner playing with a .45 and the sergeant says, 'Hey, just leave the gun alone. You don't play with guns like that. Not in a confined area.' And I was sitting there and all of a sudden, for some reason, I got up to grab the dice that I was playing, that gun went off, hit the stool in front of me, underneath where all the wood was, and hit the bulkhead. And the wood just scratched me. I didn't have my shirt on, but I had slivers in there and it cut me. And I reached and all I saw was blood, and I thought, 'Oh, my God. It's a .45.' And they took the .45 and they peeled it off of the...And there it is. *(Julian shows me the slug.)*

"That's the slug that they peeled off the steel bulkhead. It's a .45. A .45 would make a big hole in you...goes in small and comes out big."

You could have been killed.

"That's right. Before we even got into battle."

Did you have any close calls in combat?

"The night of the bombing, February 12th, we got to the foxholes, two of my buddies I was with, they forgot their helmets. Well, I had my helmet, so I went back to get their helmets. Well, I come out of the tent, and I was only about 10 or 15 feet, and with the bombs going off, the concussion blew me right back into the tent. Not a scratch. I was very fortunate.

"I had a lot of faith in God before the war and the war strengthened my faith. You had to have faith to endure what you had. Faith, in order to give you the strength to go through each day what you had to go through. Not to give up and not to let it consume you. That was the worst part, I think. We'd sit there and we'd talk, you know, about burying the dead and some of the guys, they become nervous wrecks. They're picking up dead bodies. But it also taught me one thing. And I've always believed this.

Appreciate the ones that you have, right? Your loved ones or your friends. Because you don't know how long you're going to have them. God never said that you could have them forever. And that has helped me...well, I lost my son when he was 15. So I accepted the fact that, hey, he's better off where he is. And then my wife died. And as your relatives and your friends die, you've got to accept the fact that, hey, you had a beautiful time with them. Enjoy it when you got up today. And don't say, well, tomorrow, 'I should have done this or I should have done that.' How many times are you at a funeral and you hear that, even at the hospital? Oh, I should have called. Or I should have done this.

"I was very fortunate. I figure God must have had a reason for me to be here. I mean, I'm 92 now and I feel very fortunate that I got my health and I'll do whatever the Holy Spirit inspires me to do."

Julian has written poems that have appeared in *Stars and Stripes*, an iconic American military newspaper. This poem is entitled "The Old Man Remembers."

The old man is no more
The Temple is crumbling
The old man looks back
At his walk through the battlefield of life
The old man never dodged the opportunity to serve his country
The old man remembers stepping into the battlefield of war
The old man remembers the bombs of anxiety, fear of losing a friend
The old man remembers coming home to face more challenges of taking a partner, being a parent, a neighbor

The old man dodges the bombs of deceit, hatefulness,
discrimination, unemployment.
Again, the bombs that lose the friend, the loved one
The old man can't dodge the bomb of his temple
The old man is no more in his temple
The temple is crumbling to dust from which it came
The old man's temple is no more
But wait. The spirit of the old man springs forth as a flower
from the dust
The spirit of the old man will flourish because it's being
cared for in his God's garden
The spirit of the old man will now find peace and content-
ment
The temple of the old man is gone
But the spirit of the old man lives on
Because of the living care in his God's garden.

Amen

Julian worked as a foreman and industrial engineer after the war.
He also taught Sunday School for 55 years.

VERN RADTKE

IT DOESN'T HAVE THE notoriety associated with Normandy, Iwo Jima, or Guadalcanal, but the battle of Hurtgen Forest in Germany was the single longest battle in U.S. military history. It began on September 19th, 1944 and raged for nearly three months, finally ending on December 16th.

The U.S. 1st Army suffered 33,000 casualties, killed and wounded. The Germans zealously defended that stretch of their home soil, as it would later serve as a launch point for their desperate counteroffensive, which resulted in the Battle of the Bulge. Vern Radtke saw action in both of those brutal conflicts, which was not what he originally signed up for.

"I was a student at the University of Wisconsin at the

time and I did enroll in an Army Air Corp Meteorology program," Radtke said.

"However, I passed everything except the physical. My eyes weren't good enough. So as a result, I didn't enlist right then. I thought, 'Well, I'll wait until I get drafted,' which I did in October of 1943. Once I got into the service, I was inducted at Ft. Sheridan in Illinois. And while I was there, they gave us a battery of tests. And that was to determine if we were eligible for a program called Army Specialized Training Program. ASTP as it was called. And I qualified for that.

"So a bunch of other guys were separated out and we were sent to Ft. Benning, Georgia for infantry basic with the thought that when we got out of infantry basic, we would be going on to college. Well, after about 10 to 12 weeks of infantry basic training, we were informed that the college program was being discontinued and that we wouldn't be going to college but we would be going on to another infantry outfit. Which we did.

"We wound up going to the 87th Division in Columbia, South Carolina. I trained there with them for, I don't know, about five or six months. And then many of us were pulled out of there as infantry replacements to be sent overseas. And we were. We got sent over in about October. And wound up in England. And then from there, we were transferred into France. And eventually fed up into the front lines into various divisions.

"I happened to wind up with the 1st Infantry Division. Got in there just about the time, that the 1st Infantry Division was locked up in what was known as the Hurtgen Forest. It's not a well-known battle. But it was a nasty one. We were in the trees all the time. And under heavy shellfire. And so our casualty rates were pretty high. Then we moved out of there and because we were in bad shape, they put us in reserves for about a week. And that's about the time that the Battle of the Bulge broke loose. So we were put back on the line again. And then spent some time in there until about mid-January we were mopping up the Battle of the Bulge about that time.

"And our first assignment was...this was at night...was to surround an artillery battery, a 155 artillery battery. There are long guns and they can fire a shell about eight or nine miles. So we surrounded that artillery battery and nobody bothered to tell us that they were going to fire because we thought everything was supposed to stay quiet so they wouldn't give away their position.

"Well, about the middle of the night—I couldn't tell you what the hour was—it was the middle of the night and they opened up. I thought the world came to an end because these guys were firing right over the tops of our heads. The sky lit up. The noise was horrendous. And it scared the hell out of us. But then after that, they took us on another assignment where they just fanned us out in a line and we just started working our way through the woods trying to pick up any stragglers...because the Germans were all over the place.

"We didn't know where they were. And they captured a lot of our equipment and they were using it. And of course, you've heard stories about them going in teams and passing themselves off as GIs and so on. Didn't run into any of them but we did have a couple of skirmishes in the woods with a couple of small patrols and what have you. After that, we were moved to another area and that was sort of a...I don't know, we were just put in kind of a holding position. We were on the flank of the total movement, the total Bulge. And so our job was to hold the flanks so that they wouldn't widen out and expand. And they were moving forward and they finally stopped them from moving forward and our job was to keep them from moving sideways which we did."

Did you have any close calls?

"Well, I don't know what close calls are. I had some shrapnel come into my foxhole one day. But fortunately, I had learned a little trick. In a service manual that I had seen the barracks, back in the States, in which if you're in soft ground, instead of taking it straight down, you also dig sideways. And I did that. And I think that probably saved me, because I did get some shrapnel in the hole. A lot of guys that didn't do that and unfortunately, they became casualties.

"That's one of the bad parts about being in the trees. You get a lot of tree bursts. And the shrapnel all come down on top of you. And so that's about the closest thing that I can remember. Oh, and we had one day when we got shot at pretty good because we had run off across an open road. But nothing too exciting. I didn't knock out any tanks or pillboxes or anything like that."

Were you scared?

"Oh yeah. All the time. All the time. Because you never knew when it was going to be your time. Any guy who says he wasn't scared is a liar. So yeah, I was scared all the time.

"I got a pretty good case of frostbite. So I was sent back to the hospital. And before I knew it, I was in England. In the hospital there and I spent about six weeks in a hospital there. When I came back, when I got out of the hospital, they designated me as limited duty which they did for a lot of guys, but especially the frostbite cases. Don't know really what that meant but I was physically capable.

"Anyway, I got sent back to France and got put in a camp down there and by that time, the war was winding down pretty well in Europe. The light was at the end of the tunnel burning brightly. And so I got assigned to a team of guys that were processing service records for guys that were...they had a point systems that they had established in Europe. And guys that had enough points to go home, could go home.

So I was put on a team to process those service records to determine who was eligible and who wasn't. So that lasted for about four or five months. After that, I was kind of a floater. I maintained my limited duty status. They kind of bounced me around. I was in...let's see...from there, I think I went back to a place outside of Paris. And I spend some time there as a teletypist. After that, I ended up getting sent to Germany because they were gradually consolidating. By that time, the war had ended in Europe.

"Whether I can say I wouldn't have missed it for the world, I'm not so sure about that. But I'm glad I served. I always kind of chuckle...I mentioned to you earlier about the fact that I didn't pass the physical for the...well, it was Army Air Corp at that time. I used to laugh about that because I wasn't good enough to be a meteorologist because of my eyes. But I was good enough to be an infantryman. I always thought that was a little ironic. My eyes were good enough shooting and that sort of thing but not for looking at the clouds. That always struck me as a little funny."

Vern became an industrial engineer after the war and worked in manufacturing for G.E. and other companies.

HENRY RATENSKI

HENRY RATENSKI DIDN'T WAIT to be drafted into the service.

"Once we graduated from high school we would be almost automatically drafted into the service," Ratenski said. "And that generally would be the Army. But we had alternatives in that we could pre-enlist in the service of our choice."

Ratenski pre-enlisted and chose the Army Air Corps, where he would become an Air Force Cadet. Little did he know then that he would wind up being part of one of World War II's most historic moments.

"I went to navigation school. And that's about a two-month

deal. Graduated from navigation school, and that is where I got my commission as 2nd lieutenant. And at that time, radar...radar was starting to enter, you now, the military life and the technology of warfare. And generally, navigators went to Boca Raton, Florida, where the radar courses were.

"The navigator would be qualified in both this little radar and also in the basic navigation of methodology.

"I was on the island of Guam. It was the 315th Bomb Wing. 315th Bomb Wing would have been the 5th wing of B29s that bombed Japan. We were the 5th and the youngest one in that sense. We were special. Our airplanes were special. Our airplanes were secret and we were pioneers at precision radar bombing.

"The planes were so brand-new that we didn't even train. The airplane that we picked up in Harrington, Kansas wasn't even calibrated yet. So our first missions that we were on, when we were on Guam, we got there on June 5th, 1945. June 5th, 1945. That's when we landed. We were like one of the very first airplanes. And so we practice a little on a little island just north of Guam. That was our practice mission. Then we had an official practice mission on another one of the Japanese islands which were still...they were still occupied by the Japanese. And then on June 24th, 1945, we had our first mission over Japan. About 30 of our airplanes were ready for it. And we had our very first mission.

"And tell you the truth, I was never scared on those missions because at that time, at that time, I was in control of that airplane. On a bomb run, since I was, since I was the navigation, since I was the bombardiering, radar-bombing, and navigation officer, I was controlling that airplane over the target at that time. And prior to that, the six or seven hours prior to that, I spent all my time trying to study the map. 'Will I be able to to determine or to identify that little blip, you know that little blip on my screen that that is part of the target?'

"So I would say I was so occupied, let's say tremendously occupied, with making sure that we hit that target that nothing else mattered in life. Because you can imagine if I got back to the base obviously and we missed the target obviously and think like that and sending up a big B-29, obviously endangering 10, you know, nine other crewmen, obviously I'd never live it down. So I had one fear on my missions. Hit that target!

"And so we had 15 very, very successful missions. When we concluded, when the war came to an end, we had our 15th mission. I don't know whether it...it turned out to be a rather historic thing, too. It happened to be the last mission of World War II. I was on that mission. It was the longest mission ever attempted in World War II. Roughly 3800 miles. Non-stop. We didn't even refuel. We had 132 airplanes fly over Japan that night. It probably would have been like from one o'clock in the morning to...I'll let you in a secret, the last bombs of World War II, I would say were bombed that fell at 3:39 in the morning. I don't think the history books have that.

"That was the final, final, I would say, mission of World War II. And the final bombs dropped on Japan and at that time, they were down there, the Japanese foreign diplomatic corps was at that time getting the final, final documents for surrender. At that time. In fact, at 3:39, that's like 20 minutes to 4, at 10 after 4, the Japanese diplomats in Tokyo, forwarded those documents to Switzerland. Those were the surrender documents. Switzerland, the diplomatic corps, the Japanese, and the Swiss, they transferred that over to Washington DC, then like U.S. time, like 6:30 in the evening, 7:30 in the evening, Truman got on and announced the end of the war.

"We're coming back from our last mission. We were over Iwo Jima. We traveled 800 miles from Iwo Jima, you know from Japan. We still had 800 more miles to go. Four more hours before our war was over. But Truman got on the Saipan radio and announced that the war is over. That would have been August...the morning of August the 15th, 1945. That's the surrender date.

"The atomic bombs were dropped on...first of all, it was August 6th at 8:15 in the morning. People think that when we dropped the bomb, the war was over. After that, we had another atomic bomb. We had 1,600 additional B-29 missions after Hiroshima."

Henry was a successful businessman at Applied Power after the war and, at this writing, is still a competitive ballroom dancer.

JOSEPH SOMMERS

JOSEPH SOMMERS GREW UP with two sisters. He was the only son in the family, which could have exempted him from serving in World War II.

"I could have stayed out of the military because I was the only male in the family," Sommers said. "But at that time, you just went for your country. It was automatic."

Sommers landed in Europe immediately after the Normandy invasion and saw the wreckage that remained from D-Day. He was wounded in a German artillery attack but quickly rejoined the action as a member of General George Patton's legendary 3rd Army and its historic mad dash across the continent.

"We went by rail to Massachusetts, Camp Miles Standish.

There we boarded a ship, the *West Point*. It was at one time a luxury liner and they turned it into a troop ship. And the first questions to the captain of the ship were. 'You know, we're out there, where's the convoy?' And he said, 'There's no convoy. This ship can outmaneuver any submarine or any enemy vessel. Don't worry about that.'

So we went across the ocean from Boston, Camp Miles Standish, to Liverpool, England. And across the whole ocean, we took a zigzag course in order to avoid meeting up with enemy submarines or ships. Took us 12 days from Boston to Liverpool.

"When we got to Liverpool, we were in a staging area and we stayed there for two nights and then we boarded the LCTs and crossed the English Channel. And we got across the English Channel and landed on Normandy. Omaha Beach was...we seen all of the D-Day destruction and the trucks that were still in the water. Tanks were in the water. They hadn't been brought ashore yet. Well, then we got on land and went into our first phase of fighting in the hedgerows in France.

"And it was very difficult because you had height, width, and length of the hedgerow, poor observation and you did mostly small-arms fire and hand grenades were used to get at the enemy. Well, we got through the hedgerows and we captured quite a few enemies and we sent them back to the rear lines as prisoners of war.

"We went across in 12-man boats loaded with ammunition and weapons. And the Germans on the other side had machine guns and artillery that were directed at us and they fired at our boats and some were lost. And we did lose...we had casualties from that experience.

"We went in and again, with small-arms fire and hand grenades and we got the commandants, who we called *Obersts*, colonels, that were in charge of the garrisons, that surrendered to us and this was strange. And they marched all of the troops out of the garrison and to our rear lines. Our troops took over and took them back to the rear lines. And they were then prisoners of war.

"Well, we were all out doing security work at the back of the fort, the side of the fort, at the front of the fort. And the forts were, I would say, 15-inch-thick concrete. When they built something, they built it to last forever. And that afternoon, at 3 o'clock, two tremendous explosions came about. They had everything wired with high explosives and the fort moved from the inside out towards us and we were out in the front of the fort. And it got all of those that were inside of the fort looking for enemy materials. And it got those people in the rear of the fort.

"And, let's see, eight of us were killed in action. And 47 were wounded. I was one of the wounded. I was in front. Chunks of concrete just blew. This had to be tons of explosives that were in these forts and there were six or seven forts.

"And that happened and we were laying on our spot because this concrete came out and flew in huge chunks. And clouds of concrete, of cement, or concrete, were formed and we couldn't breathe. And I was totally unconscious. And they set up a battalion medical aid station in Metz, that we had just taken and they set that up and we were taken there and I guess later that afternoon, I came to. And that was a terrible experience.

"But after that, we were in the 3rd Army and that was George S. Patton's Army. And he was the kind of guy, he's be there at a jump-off, when we left. Very excellent posture. Big, tall man and he would tell us, you know, 'Don't go into a field and dig a trench to lay in. Take that next big city. Take the next city. Take the next city.' That was his way of operating. And we did just that. Washington never knew where you were. They were always angry at him and always battling away at him.

"I was in the hospital for a few days and all of those with good arms and good legs and mobility, he had given an order that they should be taken out and sent back to their units and combat, which I went out and those that were ready to go went out and once again got back in combat. And took a lot more cities in France. Liberated them. And then when they got Germany, liberated those cities."

* * * * *

In November 2015, at War Memorial Center, an officer from the French Embassy in Chicago travelled to Milwaukee to present Sommers with France's highest military medal—the Legion of Honor for his distinguished service during World War II.

How did it feel to get the medal?

"Well, it felt very good. After so many years. I say it would have been nice to get it sooner. Got it sooner. However, so many individuals passed away and killed in action and never had a chance to get involved in medals or anything. And this was a rare thing that happened. A wonderful thing."

Joseph's grandson Jack, wrote a poem to honor his grandfather:

Veterans Day Poem
By Jack Summers

My Grandpa Joe
Is the best guy I know.

He fought in World War II
For me and for you

When I look at our flag
I think of Grandpa Joe

And the freedom he fought for
So long ago

I love being free.

I love being me.

I love Grandpa Joe.

After the war, Joseph worked for the Square D Company in the electrical equipment business.

JOHN WALLEN

JOHN WALLEN BECAME A member of the U.S. Army Corps of Engineers after he got a "special invitation from Uncle Sam" to join the American military. He was shipped to England just before the Normandy invasion, waited off shore for orders to attack, and was dispatched to France on D-Day plus seven. It was a journey that took him through much of Europe and resulted in a brush with royalty.

"It was not very traumatic, if you know what I mean. When I figure I came the day after D-Day 6, I came the next day and there was nothing on the beach. Nobody as there because they had cleaned everything up."

What was your job?

"Well, I drove...engineer stuff. Engineering, you have to lift stuff, heavy weights, and you know I learned that from when I worked for Froedtert Malt; I carried hundred-pound bags like this off the conveyor belt. Maybe a thousand bags went into that boxcar. And then I took off the boxcar and then I had to jump up on that thing to let it go out. So it only went about two blocks from my house on Lincoln Avenue. And then I had to tie it down and then release the brakes.

"I didn't see much action. Because everything seemed to be way out, you know. Because all these different countries you have to go through.

"I had different generals. We changed generals and everything else. It was well known: You have to go whoever says Uncle wants you here, you're going to be there."

You were involved in the Battle of the Bulge?

"Battle of the Bulge, yeah. Very cold. I had these combat boots, they was only the lifesaver I had. These big combat boots were the same thing the paratroopers wore. And I loved those because they kept my feet warm. Because when you went through them forests there, mighty cold."

Did you have any close calls there?

"We were shot at but we had no close calls. We built a bridge. Twelve of us had to go pick up this...we had a real long wooden thing. Six guys on that side, six guys on this side. We lifted this thing up and put it right on this pontoon. We had to get it up on top and do that. Raise that... all of them lift that up, put them on the pontoon boat and went across the Rhine.

"Before that, we knew that the Germans had blown up their Ruhr Dam. They destroyed that so we lost a lot of people there. When you get a combination of a dam, so much full of water, plus all the water—the Rhine is a very deep river too.

"We crossed that bridge and began heading for the next one because we were travelling all the time. We were on the move all the time. Then I had to get up to Holland because that was just a stopping point. We had to go to Holland and I went in there and a guy gave us some food. And I was always interested with the beautiful windmills and everything they had there. Beautiful country because they had these flowers. They're famous for everything, you know. Flowers and stuff like that.

"I got to Germany. I had to fly from the Alps. But I get in the plane, go down from the German Alps, go all the way down to Nice, where the two individuals everybody knows, Grace Kelly and Prince Rainier, lived. I was there, too. But the Prince told me, 'You don't go gambling here.' I said, 'No. We're not allowed to gamble.' Because that's a big casino there."

You talked to the Prince?

"Prince, yeah. Prince Rainier. He spoke very good English. I never saw Grace Kelly because this was way before they met." *(Kelly met the Prince in 1955).*

Was he a nice guy?

"Talked a little with him. But I said he...more or less using his language but I said I didn't *comprendre* too much French then at that time because I was just learning some of it.

"When we got into Germany, we got on the road, the Germans were befuddled—they wanted to know where's all the, the whiskey, the liquor, the cognac. They couldn't find any of it because the French were very smart. They buried all these big cognac bottles, 100-year-old Cognac, underneath the ground. And the Germans could not find it. So the French were not that dumb. The French were smart. They put everything underneath...under the ground. The Germans could not even find it.

"I'm proud of my service. Because I had to do a lot of learning. I was very happy to get home. Because I got the best country in the world."

John spent his post-war years working at the Froedtert Grain & Malting Company in Milwaukee. In November 2015, at Milwaukee's War Memorial Center, he was presented with France's highest military medal, the Legion of Honor for his distinguished service during World War II.

DON WHITAKER

DON WHITAKER NEARLY became part of a select group of soldiers to see action in both the European and Pacific theaters. Whitaker got his draft notice the day after his 18th birthday in July 1943. His military career took some unexpected turns and was forever altered by his musical talent.

"I was sent down with the infantry in Camp Alexandria, Louisiana for basic training. I shouldn't say that, after the basic training, and we had all kinds of maneuvers and extra training and that sort of thing. And then we were transferred to San Luis Obispo, California. And so we got additional training out there. I think they were thinking about South Pacific at the moment. And then with the Battle of the Bulge in Europe, plans got changed. We were sent to Boston and overseas. We landed at La Havre, France. We started in the battle at Cologne, Germany and finished near Mannheim, or Heidelberg.

"When I was first assigned in the infantry, they gave me some training in what they called the Scout," Whitaker recalled. "And then I found out The Scout is the first one out there looking for things. My eyes at that time were 20/600. I couldn't even see the enemy, let alone find out where they were. And so I volunteered for heavy weapons so I got training. In addition to the rifle, I got training in the .38- and .50-caliber machine guns and mortars and hand grenades. All that sort of thing.

"And then the company I was assigned to, they had a lousy bugler. I sent home for my cornet and practiced bugle calls when I knew the captain was in his office. And so after a certain length of time, the first sergeant came over and says 'Captain wants to see you.' I said, 'Okay.'

"And so the captain said, 'You know all these bugle calls?'

"I said, 'Which one do you want to hear?' Because I knew all 18 of them.

"And he said, 'You're the new company bugler. He takes your place on the machine gun squad.'

So I was happy. We had one other guy that was not very happy. But anyway, when you're not doing that (playing the bugle), you put pins in the map for orientation. You fill the Coke machine. You help sort the mail. You unroll the captain's bedroll when you go out on maneuvers. You get to ride in his Jeep. You didn't have to walk there.

"And so after a certain length of time, the first trumpet in the band was 36 years old and he was a farmer and if you were that age and had family home and what they considered a profession, due to the advantage of the United States, you could get discharged. So I tried out for that position—there were 51 of us that tried it—and I got the position. So I was in the band by the time we went overseas. My motto was, 'I'm willing to do my service but I wanted to see what I could do to come back.' So it was better than the Scout, I tell you.

"We took turns playing reveille. We had company buglers at that time. We took turns doing it, yes. When we...I don't remember the rotation now. When I got in the band, I was considered the division bugler, so I played for funerals and a number of ceremonies and had to be in a Class A uniform. That sort of thing."

Did you see action?

"I was never face to face with a German soldier. However, it was close enough they were doing artillery duels over us, yes. And two members of the band got Purple Hearts because when they were on top of busses—trucks I should say—snipers wounded some of our people. So we had close calls, let's call it. But I never was wounded. So I was happy about that.

"When we got to Cologne, they took away the instruments and then we were kind of a labor pool. We could stand on a corner and direct trucks in a convoy. We guarded prisoners until they could be transferred back to the corps. We were perimeter guards for the divisional headquarters at night. That sort of thing. So a lot of miscellaneous job but nothing to do with the music. Then when VE Day came, then we did a lot of decorations, you know, with the band, so we played a march, they handed out the medals and so that was the sort of thing we did every day.

"In Germany, if the town or city said that they were an open city, you know, flashing a white flag, we would not damage the town. We would just drive on through or around it and so on. In one of those situations, we had a convoy going through a town that had flown a white flag and it was an ambush. And we got partly into the city, they started firing, you know, from buildings from both sides. So the CO just did a U-turn and pulled outside and he lined up all his howitzers and he shelled that town until it was nothing left. Nobody living. Not one brick on top of another. And that's too bad. But that's war."

You saw a lot of bombed-out remains?

"That's true. Pieces of bodies. Pieces of animals. It was sad when we drove through them after that shelling. So, you know, that's another thing that changes you, you see something like that."

After VE Day, your band performed concerts for German citizens in local parks. What was the reaction from the German people?

"It was mixed. Some of them were amused. Some of them wondered what we were doing. There were some who were obviously very upset that we were there. It was mixed reaction. We had one little 12-year-old boy that threw a hand grenade at us. And luckily it only wounded a couple of guys. That was it. So where he got the hand grenade, I don't know.

Their grenades were what we called the potato mashers because it had a handle on it. Americans they figure everyone could throw a baseball, so that's why the American hand grenades were round like a baseball. And so, over there, they didn't have that kind of training so they used this charges on the end of a handle and threw it that way."

After Germany, you were transferred back to the U.S.?

"We got sent back to Camp Gruber, Oklahoma. And then we thought we were done. But then they sent us down South Pacific. I think we were probably intended for the final invasion of Japan. And I think I read on your program or somewhere that they were expecting 10 million Japanese casualties and something like 2.7 million American casualties. So when they dropped the atomic bomb, we were delighted because we knew that was the end and we didn't have to do that.

"When we were in the Philippines, one of our guys—this was after VJ Day so we were just sitting around doing things—and this one guy was out every day. We couldn't figure out where he was going. And he was sending money home. Hundreds and hundreds of dollars going home. And we knew he wasn't in a big poker game. We couldn't figure out what he was doing. But the Army couldn't open first-class letters to him and he was getting, you know, maybe a dozen a day from his wife.

"So what we finally found out when the bubble burst was that he found out that there were a lot of Singer sewing machines in the Philippines and nobody had any needles. His wife was buying the needles for $5... for 50 cents a pack, sending him many packs. He was selling them for $5 a piece. And sending all that money home. And he learned Tagalog, which was the language over there, so he could communicate with all these Filipinos. So he wasn't about to tell. Somebody else finally caught on.

"So then he went and they were selling surplus blankets at that time. The Army was trying to get rid of them. They were selling them for 50 cents apiece. He bought us, you know, hundreds, and was selling them for $5 apiece. So he made money on the war. We found out later that he had been employed by a department store in Tulsa, I think, and had been a man who ... went around and collected overdue bills from customers. But he also carried merchandise in his car. He not only collected what was due but he sold them new merchandise on time."

Don played the trumpet professionally in Chicago and became a music professor at the University of Wisconsin in Madison.

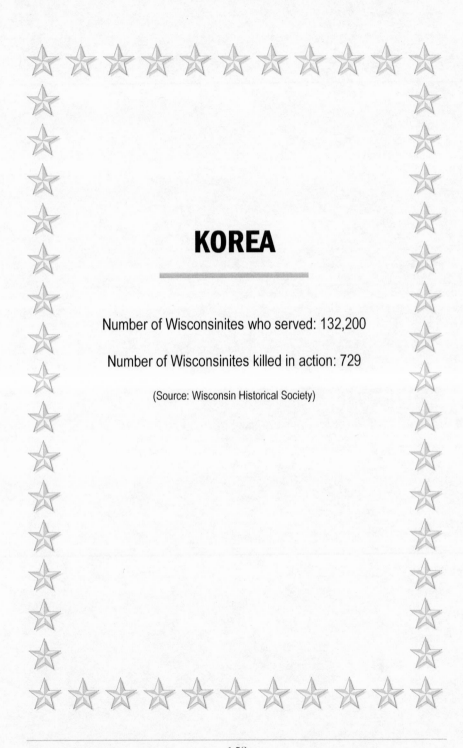

KOREA

Number of Wisconsinites who served: 132,200

Number of Wisconsinites killed in action: 729

(Source: Wisconsin Historical Society)

PAUL FINE

MANY VETERANS ARE afflicted by the psychological wounds of battle for the rest of their lives. Others also struggle to live with the physical damage they incurred in combat. Paul Fine, who was briefly in two branches of service at the same time, is a prime example of the latter group. He still has multiple pieces of shrapnel in his right eye from a battlefield blast from over 60 years ago.

You were in two branches of service at the same time?

"I have a story on that. In 1947, military came out that if you graduated from your junior year of high school, you could join the military and then they would send you back to finish your senior year in school. So in 1947, I joined the Navy on my mother's birthday, May 27th.

"And then I went down to Norfolk, Virginia for basic. And from there I came home and went to finish my senior year of high school. I was in the Navy. And then I happened to be out in New York for Christmas/New Year's fraternity brothers and that and while there, my dad called and told me, 'Paul, you got a letter of induction into the Army draft board.' I said, 'Dad, I'm in the Navy.' He said, 'No, I told them.'

"But I said I'll be home, and I had to come home and I got home and reported to Milwaukee on January 2nd and I was sworn in on January 3rd, 1951. So for January, February, March, April, I served in the Navy and the Army at the same time. And then one morning, my basic training was at Ft. Leonard Wood, while in formation, they called me out and gave me my Navy discharge and I finished basic at Ft. Leonard Wood and in May, I got my orders to ship to Korea.

"For me, it put a chip on my shoulder. Because I wasn't in favor of it, but yet I was drafted. As long as that went, my parents always taught us, you don't always take, you give as well. And I felt, as long as I could live here, I went and did my tour of duty. And when I got to Korea, I ended up in a front line unit. Love Company, 23rd Infantry, Graduate 2nd division.

"And I went in as a clerk/typist because not too many of the guys could type. And I had taken typing in high school. And I was there for a week and we took heavy casualties. And being low man on the totem pole, so to speak, I was transferred up to the line. And when I got to the line, they took my carbine away and gave be a .30-caliber, air-cooled machine gun for my weapon. And that's what I carried and manned my tour of combat time on line. I served on the line two and a half years on the line before .... Two-and a half months rather....before I was wounded on Heartbreak Ridge."

How were you wounded?

"When you're fighting in hills and mountains, you're always taking the high ground and taking next highest point to the next highest point. You work your way to the top. You work your way to the top. We were...we did that with Bloody Ridge and then I got through that. And then I got up on...we were lead unit going up Heartbreak Ridge and we got up to a certain point, we took that point and then we set up until everything caught up to us.

"And I was set up in a bomb crater with my machine gun and a couple BARs and fellas with those weapons. And up on that next point, I was fighting with my .30 caliber. I was matching fire with a .51-caliber North Korean weapon. North Korean and Chinese use .30- and .51-caliber weapons and ours were .30 and .50. You never wanted to leave our ammo behind because they could use it.

"We could not use theirs because it would jam our equipment. And in this battle, we'd use mortar rounds and that and we were surrounded. And we were running low on ammo. And due to weather, it was hard to get a ammo drop. Eventually, we got enough clearance we were able to sneak an ammo drop into us and by that time my .30 caliber was out of commission from overheating and I had a mortar round go off right in front of my...this bomb crater. And it bent the barrel.

"So then I went back to help sort the ammo and while we were sorting, I happened to look up from sorting the ammo to pass out ...to pass out to the different people that needed it. I looked up and all of a sudden I saw this North Korean step out from behind a tree and he threw a grenade in. The grenade landed right in front of me. I tried scooping it up my left hand to throw it out. Got it high enough and far enough away that it didn't explode the ammo. But I fell forward, I fell into the blast of the thing.

"And my helmet probably saved the biggest share of me. I ended up with wounds in my face with 11 pieces...12 pieces of shrapnel in my right eye. I still have nine left. And my hands took the biggest share of the blast. And so my hands were practically destroyed. And then I got back to the M.A.S.H. unit, behind the line, and from there they treated me and that and I was sent to Pusan to the hospital back there. And I guess you could say taken care and that and stabilized. Then I was shipped back to a hospital for treatment.

"I spent three months at the hospital fighting against having my fingers cut off. They didn't want to cut at the wrist. They wanted the fingers. And I wouldn't and I fought them. My hands are my own. They're full of shrapnel. Told me there's around 600 pieces of shrapnel in my hands. That small stuff. It affects my hands. They're partially numb. And unless I see it, I can't pick up small items. After three months of that, I was shipped back to Korea, still headquarters 2nd Division.

"And I was transferred to the quartermaster group and then I ended up in a place called Wan Zhu with food rationing...food rationing clerk, as they called it, issuing food, canned goods, meat, you know whatever for the various units around Wan Zhu. And then while I was at Wan Zhu, that's where I got the frozen hands and feet. We were always warned about drinking native alcohol. We didn't have too much in the ways of drugs, as alcohol. They told us stay away from the wood alcohol.

"If you drank too much in excess, you'd fry your brains. Well, there's always one out of the group that's not going to pay attention. He fried his brain. He became literally an animal in all sense of the word. And he was put in a tent out in an empty field with a shackle around his ankle and a chain to a post in the ground till they could do something, figure out what they were going to, because you couldn't bring him near people. It was almost like watching an individual change character.

"You could not give him food unless it was strictly finger food because you dare not give him a knife, fork, and spoon. And you could not get close to him. We used to put it down and he'd have to come and get it. And while we were there it was wintertime. Temperatures, for people that don't realize it, Korea gets pretty damn cold. And while there below zero, 5, 10, 15, 20 below, and while doing that...and then up there, I was put in a southern unit. And I used to fight the Mason-Dixon line in the Civil War, 24/7, all the time I was there. The North still won.

"And the end, I ended up being a northern boy in a southern unit. We did not gain a lot of benefit. So I ended up walking guard duty more than...there were four of us transferred in that were northern vets being returned. And so we pulled all these different guard duties. And I got put on 72 hours, a lot of walking, four hours on, two hours off. And your boots, you don't get a chance to dry out. You don't get warm. And over time, after almost 48 hours, I started to freeze up. My hands got so frozen, I couldn't take the weapon out of my hands. My feet and my socks froze right to the boots. Ears, nose.

I came off duty and I walked right out. Right up to the MPs and they took me over to the M.A.S.H. unit. It took four hours to thaw my hands to take the carbine out of it. Took eight hours to thaw my feet out. And then so you could remove the boots. And then they went down to the unit and there was a big change, commanding officer, everything like that.

"And then from there, I had transferred to a new supply point a mile and a half behind the front line. And while there, I did food rationing and was in charge of 245 South Korean labor disbursed to all the units around there for help and issue food to the different units. There were about 30 units that I had to issue their food. And then I used to issue Korean labor to the different areas of the supply point. And while doing it, because I could type, I got stuck with all kinds of assistance duties.

"And one of them was helping graves registration for eight months. And that's the part that's left me the worst. On patrols, we ran into problems like they did in Vietnam with people, the natives. Couple times on patrol walking to villages, we see children and old men and ladies, no young people. When you started to see that, the alertness increased. Couple times, we had to fight our way out. Fortunately, we didn't kill any children. A nine-year-old could kill you just as fast as a 40-year-old with a weapon.

"And when you walk in there, the women with all their long dresses and skirts and that, they could hide a weapon in the folds. We ran into that. And later that...that's before I was wounded. Naturally, it was that. And then I rotated home, after 14 months in Korea. My point system...in Korea, we had a point system. We was assigned 24 months duty.

"I went to R&R in Japan through a drawing as to who could go and when you could go. And then, I came home. I got my orders to ship home. It was September of 1952. I was released from the military. The Army in Ft. McCoy on October 5, of 1952. My wound date was September 19th of '51.

"Somebody said to me once when they were recalling people for Vietnam...I wasn't eligible for recall because I can't hold a weapon, and somebody said are 'They going to call you back. What's going to happen?'

"I said, 'There's going to be two people missing.'

"They said, 'What do you mean?'

"I said, 'Myself and the guy looking for me.'

"I had $2 million worth of fun and experience but I wouldn't give anybody two cents to do it over again. I served. I'm proud. I look back on it. It created a lot of change in my life. It changed a lot of outlook in my life. You service that part. You come home and little things drop by the wayside. You can't...little petty...drives you crazy.

"It took me 49 years to find out PTSD was. I fought it. I didn't know. Once I found out, I have worked with it. I've helped with it. I helped Dr. Bernstein of the Zablocki VA when he was there. And made trips to the high ground for therapy. In his therapy groups. I've been volunteering at Zablocki for 44 years, 31 years as a signed-up volunteer. Almost...it's over 14,000, almost 15,000 hours. Out of it, when Dr. Bernstein left, we wanted to put together a group for PTSD therapy.

"A group of some of us...some of us got together, Vietnam vets, myself, we put a group together. And I served on the board of Dry Hootch for a while. I was active with that group. From Dry Hootch, I and Dr. Bernstein and three others and two others, we were founders for a group called Veteran Quest to help veterans and their families. Up there on National Avenue. I'm not involved with them anymore. I have other issues that...health issues and different things.

"I have felt that I never went for drugs and I never went for alcohol. A lot of it I lay to the upbringing that I had out of my mother and dad. With my brother and sister. And they always volunteered to help. And like I said, they taught us that you can't always take, you have to give back. And that's what I go by. I'm active in veterans. They call up, I can't say no. Not to a veteran."

Paul was part of a group that founded Veterans Quest, an organization that helps veterans and their families.

ALFRED GONZALEZ

AMONG THE DOZENS OF interviews we conducted for the Veterans Story Project, we talked with some folks who exhibited great intestinal fortitude. But none were tougher than Alfred Gonzalez, who served in Korea, and then at an age where many are rocking grandchildren on their knees, signed up for duty in Desert Storm.

"Well, when I first got married, I received a letter. *Greetings and Salutations, Your Friends and Neighbors have volunteered your services into the military*," Gonzalez said. "So I came down to the Third Ward on Jackson Street. They sat us in bleachers. A Marine Corps came out and talked his part. And I was sitting right there and I told the sergeant 'I don't want to play God. Don't take me.'

"I went to Ft. Walton in Seattle, Washington, and got on a plane, er, ship. Took us two weeks. I got seasick from the first day from the Puget Sound. Got to Japan. We went to this room. They started talking to us. The sergeant came up and said 'Put everything to the side.' Gave us a jacket. Got on a ship and went to Pusan. In Korea. And they separated us and I was the only guy on this truck. And here we're driving up and down these towns. Finally got to Hill 747 on the East Coast of Korea.

"My commander, at a desk, opened up the shelf and said 'You want to play John Wayne? Here are all the medals.' And I looked at him. I thought he must be nuts. So it was nighttime. I slept in a tent. The next morning, I got up, ate, got my pack, and went up the hill. And I looked and the hills are outrageous. I mean they were asses. I got up there. I slept in a bunker. And I'm sleeping with my shoes on and I hear a horn. *Deet-deet-deet.* I said, 'What the hell is that?'

"Sarge says 'Get up. Get up. They're coming.' So I'm going through the trench and I got the bayonets on my rifle. I slipped and turned around and I caught a Chink right in the throat. And he puked all over me. Now when I go to a Chinese restaurant, I go to a Korean restaurant, I still have that smell. It's hard for me to forget that. And funny part, I married a Chinese girl. And she cooked but she steamed everything.

"Well, after that I couldn't sleep. I said, 'Christ, I don't believe this.' And how they come after you. Wave after wave after wave after wave after wave. And you're just knocking these people down. They're young people, you know. These Koreans. And they would, how would you say, they would have a diversion. At the right of me was the South Korean Army. The North Koreans, they just come around. They run right over them and come up on our hill.

"But in Korea, I couldn't sleep. It was hell. But you get into that. I was in 32-below-zero weather. My right ear is bent. That's frost. My M1 rifle, you used to have to operate it to put in oil, I used to pee on it so the handle would come open and the shells would be coming out. I cried and I used to say one thing: I used to say Michael, the Archangel, defend me in battle. I fought. And I fought. And then I stayed there for 3 months."

A friend of yours were killed in Korea?

"His name was Daniel Kirkland. He used to write...I have a clipping somewhere on it. He used to write the shortest letter at home. *"Hi Mom. Okay. Goodbye.'* That's all he said. On 6th and Mitchell, it used to be the South Side Armory Hall and you had that National Guard unit there and he joined it. And he knew they did half-assed training and he got up there and he got over and he got killed.

"I never thought that I was going to get killed. I never had that attitude. I learned a lot. I got an education. I'm the only one in the family that been in the military."

At the age of 59, Alfred also served his country in Saudi Arabia during Operation Desert Storm in the postal unit.

"This colonel asked, 'How old are you?'

"I said, '59.'

He says, "We gotta check your physical."

"They didn't have no doctors. I had to go to Chicago to a private doctor. And he put me on a treadmill and he put all these things on me and says, 'I can see you can't go.'

"And I says, 'I want to go.'"

"He says, 'Why?'"

"I says, 'I want my 20 years in the military.'"

"He looked at me and said, 'All right.'"

"I passed. Got up to the 440th, got on the biggest plane I ever saw, put our trucks on. Flew from there to Boston. From Boston to Spain. Stayed there in Spain, and then went to Saudi Arabia. Got off that plane and it was 95 and I thought, 'Oh, this is going to be hell.'

"A one-star general looked around and he says, 'Sergeant Al?'"

"And I said, 'Yes,' and I saluted.

"'I want you to be a liaison man for me.'

"I said, 'Why did you pick me? You got all these other sergeants.'"

"He says, 'I heard you're a Korean veteran.'"

"I says, 'Yes, I am.'"

"He says, 'You got a pair of balls, compared to the rest of these guys.'"

You're 84 years old and still look fit enough for active duty.

"Yup, 84 years old. I don't drink. I don't smoke. I'm a jock. I used to play a lot of handball at the Eagles Club. A lot of racquetball. I placed third in the state at racquetball in Oconomowoc in the Golden Masters there.

"I work out three times a week at the health club on Layton Avenue. A blast. And I meditate and I think a lot. And I'm always saying, why am I still kicking? My wife says because you take care of yourself. I didn't drink. I didn't smoke. I couldn't see that, you know."

When he wasn't in the military, Alfred worked for the Milwaukee County Sheriff's department and in the heating and air conditioning industry.

WALLY HART

WALLY HART JOINED THE Marines in January 1952. He was just 17 years old and his decision was not well received at home.

"Me and four of my childhood buddies decided to join the Marine Corps," Hart said. "We all decided to enlist in the Marines because eventually we didn't want to be drafted and we all wanted to be Marines. And so we all joined together.

"So my mother, when she found out, was totally against it. She was crying and everything and my dad was trying to settle her down and everything. And she went to our parish priest and told him the story. She said one of my sons just got home and now another one, I'm afraid he's going to, you know, get killed over there. And the priest, I think gave her some very good advice.

"He said, 'Mrs. Hart, you know, he's 17 but he's going to be 18 in a couple of months and he'll join the Marine Corps then. And he'll never forgive you for not letting him go when his buddies went, you know, because they...

"It was all kind of locked in, more or less, that that was when you're going and they joined and the whole ball got rolling.

"We all were sent to San Diego for boot camp and training and, well, you know, they split you up after that. One of them went to the Marine Air Wing and one, he was a cook. And I was chosen to be a rifleman so...it was like trench-line warfare when we got there and stuff and...we had to deal with a lot of you know it was not just the enemy we were dealing with. It was...the South Koreans were on our side. And we were fighting the North Koreans. And good luck trying to tell the difference between the two. Which made...We didn't know who we were firing at or what. It was kind of tough that way.

"And then I received my orders to go to Camp Pendleton for advanced combat training and then I was sent to Korea. And yeah, almost immediately, we were sent right in. We were like we call the draft replacement. We were the draft replacement. And it was tough. The conditions were just awful. In the summer, it was so hot you couldn't stand it. And in the winter, it was so cold. I mean I'm talking really cold. And we, when I got there, we had thermal boots also. But when your feet get cold, you're just cold.

"My daughter even says now I don't even want to go to a Brewers game when it's cold because my feet...I think I must have gotten frostbite when I was there.

"And then there were no roads so during the monsoon season; you were walking around in the mud up to your knees. I mean there was no place that you could go to bed and stuff like that. So later while we were there then, we were all so happy that we got to clean up with fresh water. Not shower, just clean up. Marine Corps shower.

"It's been 63 years. It's difficult for me to remember everything my whole day. But I do remember one thing: At night, I thought they were flies. I kept swatting flies away. They were mosquitos. I woke up the next day. I had mosquito bites all over my face and everything. It was...and I mean those mosquitos they wanted to not just take blood out of you, they wanted to carry you away, it seemed like. And here I'm thinking you hear the buzzing and the buzzing and the buzzing, I'm thinking they're flies. I kept swatting them away. And that's pretty much the highlight of the...what was happening and going on there. Like I said the conditions were difficult, very difficult to, you know, put up with.

"One time I got shrapnel in my leg and then they took me back...because it was difficult for me to walk with that leg. They were firing rounds and we was firing rounds and the shrapnel would go off and it hit my leg. They took me back to the hospital ship and that's where I received the Purple Heart, on the hospital ship somewhere in Korea. I was out of action for a month or so. Then I was fine and they took me back to my outfit."

They put you right back in the line of fire?

"Yeah. Yeah, that's the way they operated. I was very proud. A Marine would never leave another Marine behind. He's always got your back. No matter what. If the going gets really tough, he'll go back and drag you out of there. If he has to carry you off on his shoulders, he'll carry you off. The Marine Corps way."

Wally had a successful career as an insurance salesman after serving in Korea.

KEN HERMAN

KEN HERMAN WAS DRAFTED AND went to Milwaukee to sign up for duty when he was "volunteered" into the U.S. Marines Corps.

"Did the physical and while we was doing that, they made the announcement, they wanted, needed 15 guys to volunteer for the Marine Corps," Herman recalled.

"But of course, nobody volunteered. So then they read 15 names off and I was one of them. Put us on a train and went to California. Boot camp. It was a surprise.

"I thought it was kind of rough. Wasn't used to all that discipline and stuff. But after it was over, when I think of it now, it was important for them to treat us the way they did, you know? About the discipline. Follow orders.

"I thought everybody there, they were all tough. We laugh about it now when we talk about all that.

Food was good there. That was one thing. Always had plenty to eat. I didn't like the way we were treated once in a while.

"From boot camp, I went, they shipped me to North Carolina eight weeks of schooling, refrigeration repairmen. And from there, I went shipped to California and then I got in the replacement draft and sent to Korea. We went by boat from San Diego. A troop ship. We landed in Japan and from there, they flew us over to Korea. Because we got attached to the First Marine there we...a lot of replacement guys, a lot of those guys were flown over to different air strips in Korea."

What did you do there?

"I worked on the refrigeration. You know every mess hall had a couple big coolers for their food and the mess hall. Well, there were three mess halls there. And then they had the officer's mess hall, which had to have an ice machine. That was important to keep that running because they wanted their mixed drinks. And then we had a...we called it a 'slop chute'...it was the enlisted men's place where we had beer there. We had to keep that cold, too.

"It was busy in the summer. In the winter, it wasn't bad because the weather was a lot like Wisconsin except we didn't have as much snow there. But it got cold. In the winter, you didn't have as much trouble, they kept working pretty good."

"We had some hot weather. In the winter, we had cold, not too much snow. But it was cold and windy and damp because it was next to the ocean. I suppose that was the Japanese Sea. It was a little warmer than Lake Michigan here, I think. We didn't have the proper clothing neither for winter when I first got there. That was a big thing. We didn't have the arm boots and the arm coats and stuff like we had later on.

"When you're walking around guard duty, it's...get awful cold. When I was doing my regular work, I got a little tent with wood sides around it that we did our repair work in, kept our tools in, and had a little stove in there to keep us warmer in winter, so that was fine. We were next to the officer's mess hall and we'd go over and get ourselves a pot of coffee once in a while.

"I think the hardest part was that I didn't like the guard duty. I got that the first night I was over there. Or second night it was, yeah. I didn't hardly have finding my way to the mess hall. And then put us on guard duty. Dropped us off outside night watch, I think it was 10 'til 2. Four hours we had to...I got dropped off and they had a big bomb dump there, where they stored all the bombs and ammunition stuff. And there was three guards out there and they dropped us off. They other two guys had been there before. They knew where to go. So I had the middle section. It was so dark, I didn't know where I was. I didn't do too much walking around. I kind of stayed in one spot. But the next time I got into it, it was during light hours, so I walked around and found out what I was supposed to be watching.

"It was a little scary that first night, year. Right by the ocean. I could hear the waves and all that and I didn't know if it was boats coming in or what as going on. Guard duty and time went so slow. Couldn't smoke. Got me into chewing for a while. Tobacco."

Were you ever on front lines?

"No. I found out after I got back, because I was a sole surviving son, I was the only boy in our family, that the Marines tried to keep them out, off the front lines, you know, as much as they could. So really, I wasn't in danger or anything. It was always still a combat zone, you know. The only thing we seen, once in a while planes would come back in from making that run. They'd have a bomb hooked on the bottom that wouldn't release. And then when they'd come in, they'd hit the runway. They had a lot of that. It would bounce off. Scoot up the runway and off to the side and sooner or later it would blow up. But that about as much noise and that, outside of from the planes. We still had all prop-driven planes when I got there. And most of those were World War II planes. They brought them up from the islands. I was there about five or six months, I think, when they finally had jets come in."

What was the general atmosphere for your unit?

"You get to be like a family almost. You're glad to help each other and make the most of it. A lot of guys got a little homesick. Everybody was pretty busy always. We had all different trades in our outfit. We had mechanics for the airplanes, mechanics for the trucks and all that. We had carpenters. We had plumbers. We had all kinds of different trades there.

"We was told we were going to be over there a year. So when that year come close, I figured I'd be about home. It was kind of a schedule for when you got replaced. They told us a year. That was pretty much on time. I was back to Japan once for R&R for a week in the middle of my time over there so that kind of broke that up."

Happy to get home?

"You bet. I had a girlfriend waiting for me. We had plans to get married in November. But I got home in August so we had a lot of arrangements made already. We did that by mail. So I was glad when I was home. So was she.

"I don't feel like a hero or anything but I'm glad to have served and did my share."

After serving in Korea, Ken worked as a mason on commercial and residential projects.

FELIPE MONTANO

FELIPE MONTANO, WHO WAS born in Puerto Rico, was drafted into the Army right after his 18th birthday. He served heroically, dis-played extraordinary courage under fire in Korea, and established a military family legacy.

"I was in the Army," Montano said. "My rank was private and then PFC. Charlie Company, C Company, 65th Infantry Regiment. When you join, you are not afraid of nothing. And I like the Army. And I joined the Army because I like it.

"They send posts to a combat patrol, combat patrol, and we have to get contact with the enemy. And in the meantime, when they got close, we got down so many wounded, and I saved some of them and drag them to a safe place, and then go back again, to try to save some more. And that's what happened. And then they send me to the hospital in Japan.

"I was a real strong young...young guy and I grabbed him over my shoulder and I climbed the hill till I get them safe. And I run back again to the same place to save some more and put them on a side but saw they disappeared. I was on combat patrol."

How many soldiers did you save?

"I just remembered about one. His name is Leslie Moore and he was from Tennessee. That's the only one that I remember because I kind of put him there and then I carried others. Later around, they told me that I saved him and I saved all the other guys. I didn't have no names of the others ones. And that's why they gave me the Bronze Star medal."

You lost a family member in the war, someone who was in your unit and was nearby when he was hit?

"The husband of my niece. He was close to me because I told him, 'Don't get up. Don't get up.' He get up and he got shot and died."

You were also hit?

"Hit in the hand first and then the knee. See then I was coming with rifle and one bullet hit my rifle. That's why it got my finger because it got it in there."

But you kept fighting after you were wounded?

"Yeah. You kept fighting. Kept fighting and try to save my...my... friends.

"I remember that a helicopter come and pick me up from there and took me to a hospital in Pusan. And from Pusan, they sent me to Tokyo. In a hospital. Over there, I spent about two or three months. And then they sent back again to Korea. Two months later they send me back to Puerto Rico."

You were just 18 years old. Were you afraid?

"At the time, no. Not before. I was brave because I know that I have to protect my own life, too. So I was fighting like a man is supposed to do in combat in the war. I have to think of myself, too. I didn't care. I wasn't afraid. At that time, I wasn't afraid. When I was there I really was not afraid. I asked for combat patrol. I tell my lieutenant, 'I want to go.' Really, I never feel afraid. Never. I was always in good shape and even when I was wounded, it was like nothing."

Your son and daughter served in the military?

"Yes, in the Persian Gulf war. My daughter I think she was in a... like a nurse. And my son one was like in communications and he serve 20 years in the Army. He's a computer expert."

Are you glad you served?

"Oh, yeah. Because I'm fighting for my country. And the United States of America, that's my country. And I have to fight against the enemy for my people. Even if I don't know my people. But it's my country. It's where I born, where I raised, when I went to school and so I have to fight for my country. Because this is my country."

Felipe's son and daughter both served in Vietnam.

RON ZIOLECKI

RON ZIOLECKI FOUGHT IN Korea as a member of the U.S. Marines Corps. For those who have only experienced war from reading books or watching it unfold with a Hollywood flourish on the big screen, Ziolecki offers a powerful reality check

"So all wasn't glorious. Nothing was glorious," Ziolecki said. "You were fighting for your life. You were fighting for your country. And scared? If any one of these guys come in here and say they weren't scared, I don't think they're telling the truth. I was scared the day I got there and I was scared the day I was left. And I was happy to leave.

"I was 17 years old. November 30th, 1932 I was born. And November 30th, 1949, I joined the Marine Corps. And December 1st, I left for Chicago. I was sworn in Chicago.

"I hated school. I hated school. Long as I was able to play football, it was fine. But when I went in the Marine Corps, I went to school. I went to school with a tie on and everything. You learn. You make mistakes in life and you benefit by them. And I'm proud that I was a Marine. I'm still proud. I still say I was a Marine. I'm proud. They indoctrinate that into your head that...to have pride and you do. And I've never been sorry.

"I was in Korea from '51 to '52. I was with Ida Company, First Battalion, First Marines. And it was...it was miserable. I was only 18 years old and I seen a lot of things that you don't ever see again, you know, because it just brings back awful memories. When you'd come home from that war, you just...it was on your mind all the time.

"And you know, I'm going to be 83 years old, I still remember so many of those things. So many. I can hear them playing the bugle on the mountain across and holler, 'Marines, you'll die tonight.' And that just wasn't in the movies. That was for real. And when the Chinese came in, well, they pushed all the way back to Pusan. And it was cold. And we had had nothing to eat. C-Rations were gone and everything. We'd sleep in the road. And we'd hear, 'C'mon. C'mon. You got to keep going.' And we marched for three days and three nights until we got reinforcements and we pushed them all the way back again."

Did you see action right away?

"That night, you're already brought up to the front line by trucks. You get off and you put up your pup tent and...and it snowed that night and the damn pup tent caved in. But the next morning, you start walking up the mountain. And it was kind of a steep one and you got up there and the guy that we were replacing, he said, 'Don't stand here because at 4:30, they try and bomb this bunker every day.' Sure as God, that's the first ounce of combat that I heard was when they tried to blow up our bunker. Then you got to rebuild it that night. But from that time on, you get seasoned, harder and harder and harder.

"My good friend was Ross Hartwick. He was from Iowa and he was 19 and I was 18. And they always told us, 'You two guys are too close. You two guys are too close.' Ah, baloney. Well, the artillery came in and they had a tent below the mountain and that was our mess tent. And he said, 'You want to eat first, Ron, or do I?' He says, 'I'm hungry.' I said, 'No, you can go.' I wasn't that hungry.

"And when there was about 40 guys down there, the artillery came in. The Koreans knew that that tent was there. And I knew my buddy was there. And I ran down the mountain down to him. And he hollered, 'Ron, Ron. Help me.' He says, 'It's my back.' And when I turned him over and felt up his jacket, it was just like if you picked up you skin and threw a bunch of rocks under it. And part of his head was gone and we got a helicopter right away and we put him in a chopper and I closed the cover on there and I says, 'Well, I'll see you when I get back for a rest.'

"When I got back, I asked them guys, 'Where's Ross?'"

"They said, 'Well, he's not here.'"

"I said, 'Where'd they take him? The hospital ship?' Because the *USS Hope* was out in the harbor. 'They go to Japan, huh?'"

"They said, 'No. He's not here.'

"He died two days later. He had a daughter that he hadn't seen. Because his wife was pregnant when he came over.

"And we made a promise to one another that if something happened to me, I would...he would tell my folks. Or if something happened to him, I would tell his folks. Well, I forgot what town he was from. I knew he was from Iowa. And 60-some years later, on the Honor Flight, the flight attendant and my neighbor was with me. And he says, 'I'll find him for you.' He works for an insurance company or something like that. A month later, he did. He found Ross's brother and his brother gave him all the right directions to Ross's daughter.

"So when she called me, she was beside herself. She says, 'I had no contact at all with anybody and I just wanted to know what happened to my dad.' And she says, 'Can we come down and visit you?'

"I says, Sure. So they came down. They visited with me and she brought homemade bread and cookies. I didn't want to tell her what happened to her dad, you know because. I told her at the beginning, I don't want to tell you how he got killed. That is...it's just too hard.

"But by the time she left, she got it out of me. I told her how he died. And she said, 'At least I got peace. I got comfort in my life. All my life, I wanted to know about my dad. My dad was my hero.' And that's some of the things that you remember.

"I never got close to anybody else after that. Never. It just wasn't meant to be. You slept with people but if something happened to them or happened to you, I know they'd take care of you because you're a Marine. You always took care of your own. But when you get so close to somebody, that you did everything together, something happens, it hits you. I never forgot. I never forgot that man. It was always in my head. And my soul. And I knew his name—Ross Hartwick—and I knew he was from Iowa.

"I had senators. I had congressmen and everybody you can imagine find that man. Nobody could find him. And they finally found him. My neighbor and I'm happy for that. I always mention his name in a lot of interviews because he was part of my life then. He saved me. I saved him. The Chinese had me pinned down behind a tree and he just stood right up and he shot both of them. And he says, 'You OK, Ron?' and I says, 'Yeah.'

"Friends like that you never forget. Never. They're valuable. So, the family still come down and see me. And I communicate with the family quite a bit. And that was all part of the life.

"The weather there was just horrible. Just horrible. Your hands are freezing. Your feet are freezing. Everything about you, you're cold. And then when they come in with them Mickey Mouse boots, that saved us. Those were the ones that were filled with air. And your feet never got cold in them. We called them Mickey Mouse boots because they were so big. And then they come through with new...we had new ponchos. They came through with different coats. They'd start getting better material for the guys. For the weather. So they made it better for us.

Were you wounded?

"No, come close. No, don't wish that on me. Sometimes I was wondering if I'd be alive, you know? Because you got so many things that are coming at you. You got artillery. You got planes. You got mortars. You know, everything is flying and when hell breaks loose, I mean, when you start going up the mountain and they're coming after you, I mean you knew who they were. They were in front of you when you were pushing them and thank God, we had the better weapons and the more intelligent people running and guiding us. Because I seen a lot of them get killed. Pork Chop Hill, you could walk over the guys there were so many dead ones. A lot of hills had names but I forgot a lot of those names, you know. I didn't want to remember them. A lot of things I didn't want to remember. I still don't want to remember.

"Too many things come back into your life that you don't want in your life. And you seen guys, when you're going home on a ship, and the guys would be talking. *Oh, yeah, he's gone. This guy is gone. This guy was wounded.* They were talking about all the guys, you know. But that's what you went there for. You knew it before you got there. That's what you were going there. You were going there to make our country safer and benefit our people and I think that that's what was important to benefit people.

"I took care of three little boys, Korean boys. They had no food. No clothes. I had clothes for them. I got...we'd bring food back form the mess hall and let them sleep in our tent. I got them some sleeping bags and they never could pronounce Ziolecki. They always used to call me 'Lecki.' So they always wanted to go on the line with us and I was, 'No, no. You stay right here. I'll be back.'

"'No, no, we'll go.'

"'No, no.' They were little guys, you know. About 10 years old.

"And I says, 'When my friends come back, they'll take care of you.'

"They said, 'OK. We wait for you.'

"So it was my time to go home. And I was starting to put stuff in my bag and the little guy says, 'Where are you going?'

"I says, 'I am going home.'"

"Oh, we go with you. We go with you.'"

"No, you can't go with me.'

"They said, 'Where are you going?'"

"I said, 'I'm going to Pusan.'"

"'No, no, no, we go with you.'

"I said, 'I can't take you with me. I'm sorry.'"

"But they wanted to come to America with me. And I felt sorry. They had no mother. They had no father. They just lived off of nothing. And they were always so grateful for what you did for them. And you look back at those things and you say, yeah, we made a difference. We made a difference in people. And I understand today if you went to Seoul, you wouldn't even know it. We built that part of the country. Other than that, I don't miss it. I don't miss it."

Were you a different person after the war?

"No, it wasn't hard to readjust. I think because I was so young. You know, I was 19 years old and I was out of a war. No, it wasn't hard to adjust because you got back with your old buddies again that you go to school with. And they kind of made you forget what you were doing, or where you were at because you were playing baseball and all that, see?

"So, no it wasn't hard to adjust. But the memories never go away. Never. You go to bed at night and lots of nights you think about what you did and how you did it. Why did you do it, you know. It's hard. I'll never forget my uncle was in the Second World War and he wrote me a letter. He said, 'Now listen, son, there's going to come a time when you're going to have to shoot somebody. He always put it in your head, it's either you or him. And if you don't get him, he will get you.' And that always stuck with me.

"I think the first time that I had to shoot somebody, I closed my eyes. It's so horrible. It's just a kid. But I don't care how old you are, it's got to be horrible. It's got to be horrible.

"But I made it and I'm happy for it. And I'm happy for my family. And I'm happy for the people that I'm surrounded with now. I get more recognition now from people than I ever got when I first come home. Mainly doctors. Doctors will always congratulate you. Professional people will thank you for your service. At the football game last week, all the referees, they came up and shook my hand. And they said thank you. Makes you feel good. And I know, I felt awful good."

After returning home, Ron worked for 40 years as a foreman at Unit Drop Forge in Milwaukee.

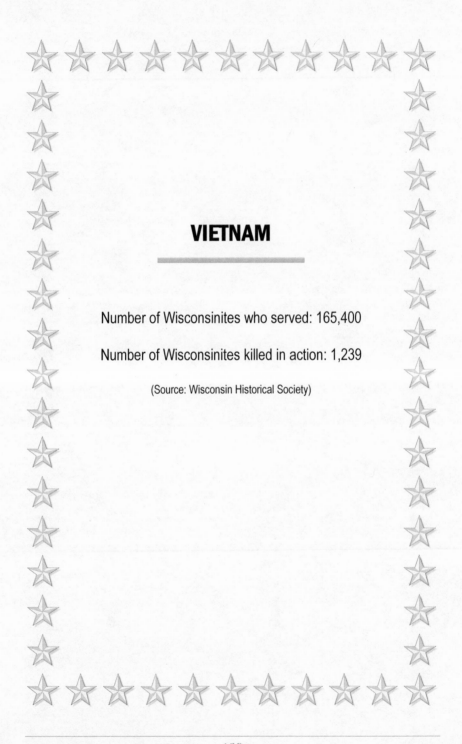

VIETNAM

Number of Wisconsinites who served: 165,400

Number of Wisconsinites killed in action: 1,239

(Source: Wisconsin Historical Society)

RUSTY ARMSTRONG

FOR GLENN "RUSTY" ARM-STRONG, 1968 was a red-letter year. He got married, joined the Army, and was sent to Vietnam.

"The war was still going on obviously, in 1968. So the needs of the services, they're always proud to say. I was commissioned as a 2nd Lt. Infantry. I was newly married. We knew where I'd be going. So went to Ft. Benning, GA, which is fondly called the Benning School for Boys. Went through the Infantry Officer Basic course, which at that time, I think it was like a 10-week course because there were lots of soldiers in the army who were going to be going downrange.

"Ft. Benning was a very crowded place then. After that, was sent to Ft. Ord as a training officer. Worked on the basic training brigade for about six months. Got my orders to go overseas. And on my way overseas, I went to Panama for two weeks of general training. And then directly overseas."

What was it like when you got to Vietnam?

"When I was in the service, you know, there were plenty of guys who'd gone and done their second tour and some of the career people were on their third tours. Much like, unfortunately, some of our Iraqi and Afghanistan vets now. So we had rumors and we knew stories; people would tell what would happen. So I arrived there in August which is probably the hottest time of the year there. And so it's true what they say. When that door opens of that airplane, you were just hit by a blast of hot, humid air. So it was pretty well organized without any shocks as far as being shot at getting off the plane. That was all rumor control.

"But you got off the plane, and you went to a repo depot, which is basically a replacement depot. And you stayed there for two or three days. Rosters came out every day telling people where you're going to be assigned. So I was assigned to the 4th Infantry Division, which is up in the 2 Corps, which is in north-central part of Vietnam, up in the highlands.

"So by the—oh, my gosh—by the end of August 1969, I was in the 4th Infantry Division. They sent me to my battalion which was the 12th Infantry, which was operating way up north where they had some pretty difficult battles a year, year and a half before. So my first assignment was to a rifle company at a company patrol base way out in the mountains in nowhere land where we could actually see Cambodia from our...from our patrol base. So that was my initiation."

What was your job?

"Second Lt. in Infantry, typically you're a platoon leader. So when I arrived there, the guy I had replaced had actually just left. So I was assigned the Table of Organization Equipment; said at that time I should have had 44 soldiers. I rarely had more than 30 or 32 in the field. So when I got there, I was supposed to be in charge of these guys. And our job was to seek out the enemy if we could find them and more often than not, at that time, the 4th ID covered more geography than I think any other division in Vietnam.

"So all the battalions were spread out, different bases on different hilltops. And the companies were further spread out. And so most of the time, it was just me and my platoon walking through the jungle going where we were told, looking for who we thought we were looking for. Pretty awesome responsibility, when you look back now because I was probably older than most guys in my platoon, because I was...let's see...I was 23, and I had four years of college under my belt.

"Most of my guys were draftees or a lot of them had enlisted. And we had, by that time, I'm really struck today that we just did not have a lot of experience at the CO level. There had been casualties. Or on second tours, or their third tours. So technically, I was supposed to have four qualified squad leaders and a platoon sergeant with me. And I had a platoon sergeant, but everybody else had been in country probably a year or less. So these young guys accepted a lot of responsibility early to get their job done."

Was it difficult to fight the enemy on terrain they knew so well?

"I don't know. I think my guys did pretty well to account for themselves. But you're correct. Most of these guys were either natives to the area or they'd taken I don't know how long to walk down the Ho Chi Minh trail to get into the area we were in. So their...their life skills in the jungle, I think, far exceeded ours. They were also smaller. They didn't carry as much stuff as we did. So yeah, they were a different...they were a different enemy to get along with. But fortunately, I didn't run into any large contact like a lot of people did. But we had some short firefights. It was usually pretty quick and it was usually over quickly.

"There's always close calls. It's kind of like what you hear pilots say...you have hours and hours and hours of boredom spike by absolute seconds of terror. Because you are marching through, you know, the jungle...three months out of the year the heat is just unbearable, three months out of the year it's a monsoon and you're never dry. You're constantly being rained on. You're walking through terrain, up and down hills, through rivers, constantly going up and down a mountain, tired, exhausted, carrying all your gear.

"And then at the same time, you're always anticipating you might run into someone who might do you harm. So it became really an exhausting endeavor, I would say, because move all day, set up at night and then even at night you had to have security, or we'd send out ambush patrols. So I don't think anybody got more than three or four hours of sleep a night. And then you get up the next day and do it all over again. It was pretty tough, as far as that goes, for folks who were truly infantry-type guys like I was. I was never wounded. No Purple Hearts here."

Was it tough knowing that many Americans were against the war?

"Not in my experience. Not with my folks. GIs gripe and bitch a lot but that's their nature. If they're not, I would be worried. We knew that was going on, you know, because of the letters you got from home. A lot of guys had read their subscriptions from their hometown newspaper. We would get that when mail would be brought on. So we knew what was in the headlines. We knew the political situation.

"Nixon was president when I was over there. Guys would talk about it and complain and moan and groan. But the next morning, they'd get up and we'd go out and do what we had to do. But a lot of them were looking forward to getting home. And they were going to...and many of them, I'm sure, were going to join those protestors when they did get home. But it was not really an issue for me."

What was it like when you got back home?

"I think I've survived pretty well. I probably have a little PTSD. We all do. But I haven't had a claim in that direction. Different perspective on things. Perspective. I came home a little more serious. A lot of us were a little more anxious when we got home. Loud noises bother us. Surprises bother us. But—my wife might disagree—but I don't think I had a seismic change. More mature obviously. Saw a lot of things that other people haven't seen. But I treasure those memories."

You served in the Army Reserves until you retired in 1996.

"When I first got back, I went back...I started teaching school. It was an opportunity that the Army provided that if you wanted to, included your professional education so you could eventually get promoted. So occasionally during the summer, I'd go to the two-week schools for my career course and things like that.

But it's just a case that I kind of missed the camaraderie of people that were in the service. You know, we think somewhat similarly. We had similar experiences. So I kind of like that camaraderie. So I did that for two, three, or four years. Then, like I said, when we moved to Wisconsin. It was an opportunity to come into an Army Reserve unit. And same thing there. It was a training unit right here in Milwaukee. So it was close by, fortunately for me. And there again, I liked putting on the uniform. I like serving my country and being with people who felt similarly. So that sort of perpetuated a military career while still being a civilian job. So I enjoyed that until it was time to go.

"I was teaching initially, and then I got a job transitioning into sales and it was a nice transition because I was actually selling textbooks to public schools. So that was a nice transition. Then when we moved up to Wisconsin, I got caught in a couple of corporate situations, so I stayed in sales for a while, being a salesman in the road, basically, stayed in Wisconsin, initially selling office supplies and then wholesale. Then later on got involved in a market research firm.

"I'm a big believer in service and nowadays, I believe I am trying to give back, so I'm involved in various veterans' organizations. Serve on a couple of boards of some veterans groups, still. And trying to, I guess, help provide as much benefits, and positives for those who are still serving in uniform."

After coming home from Vietnam, Rusty worked as a teacher, textbook salesman, and with a market research firm.

GEORGE BANDA

WHEN YOUR JOB IS TO treat wounded soldiers to keep them from dying, what happens when you are hit by enemy fire? George Banda will tell you—you just keep doing the job you were trained to do.

"When I got to the 101st, and reported in, I said, 'Here I am.' And they said. 'Why are you here?'"

"They don't know. They don't know. I mean you're on your own actually. So I get there and I said, 'Well, they sent me here. They said you needed a medic.'

"'Yeah, well, we do need that. C'mon on.'

"They said, 'We're going to send you even further north.'

"Further north? Gee, much further north than here?

"They said, 'Well, we got some firebases, artillery bases, and that's where we need you. We'll send you to Echo Company, 2nd of the 101st Airborne Division.'"

"So they sent me up there and when I got up there, I reported to the captain. Two captains. One said, 'Well, we need somebody in Echo Company; they're a Recon unit. And they need a medic. Their medic was just injured and he had to be medevaced down. So they're short a medic.'

"I was scared the moment I landed in Vietnam. I never stopped being scared. I was terrified because you're in a...it's a whole diff...it's surrealistic. One moment, I was home for a while. And all of a sudden, you know, I'm in Vietnam. And all the things you hear about Vietnam. You know, watching it on TV because it was always on TV about the fighting and this and that. POWS and Missing in Action and all the wounded and all the killed Americans. And here I am right there. In that Vietnam. And so I was... you know, we were all scared. Every one of us.

"We didn't know what to expect. You're thinking, 'Oh, I got a year to go. I just got here. On my first day. Got 364 days to go yet. Ok, well, just take it one day at a time.' That's all you can do.

"I got assigned to the 2nd 101st Recon unit. And they were happy to see me. and they, the first thing you do when you get to a unit or a platoon, the people that are already there, ask you where you're from. They always want to know where you're from. Just in case you're from where they're from. And at the time, there wasn't anybody there from Wisconsin. There was some people from Minnesota, Michigan, you know, Illinois, Brooklyn, Texas, California, and nobody from Wisconsin. Ah, no problem.

"Make friends. So I made friends with the guys, you know, and you kind of have to prove yourself. Because you're a new guy and how is this person going to react in combat. You know, he's a medic. You trust...we need to trust a medic. We need to know that the guy can do what he has trained to do. And when the shit hits the fan, he needs to, you know, what's he going to do? Hide or take care of us?

"From day one, we went out and made what they call contact, you know, in an ambush. We got ambushed. One of the guys got hurt. He got shot in the arm. And then you realize, how this is real. Because they are people actually shooting real live bullets. You know, high-powered rifles they're using. AK-47s. And it's like a slap in the face.

"Like, wow, OK. Let's do what you were trained to do. And you know, when you first get there, you start knowing all these guys and they become friends and buddies, you know? A brotherhood. It's a brotherhood. You rely on them. They rely on you. So what I did to kind of protect myself is I kind of blocked the emotion off as far as feeling really, really bad about this person that I know that just got injured or shot or hurt or blown up. And not to get too emotionally involved with anybody. Because you would go crazy.

"You see all your buddies, I mean, wounded or killed and you're treating them and trying to save their lives. And sometimes you can't. But you deal with it. Do you let it get to you or just block it out? And for me, I just blocked that emotion out. Feeling sadness and remorse and you know, hurt. I got to do my job. That's it. Just think about what you're doing. Stop the bleeding. Start breath...start the person to breathe again. Start an IV solution. Give them plasma. Whatever I have to do, just do your training. And just try to save that person and get them out of there by calling a medevac helicopter to get them out.

"But unfortunately, once they left, we never saw them again. You don't know if they lived or died. You know...you never heard about...because you're out in the jungle...I mean, they're not going to call you up and say well, this person lived or this person died.

"I had two real good friends of mine. One, well, with Tommy Turan. He was from West Lynn, Michigan, that's right across the lake here. And we got to be really good friends. We met in around January of '70 and he had come in country. And again, you ask people, hey, where you from? And he was from Michigan, and hey, that's pretty close. You know, we could be friends. And same thing with the guy from Minnesota. We...you know some guys were Vikings. Tommy was a Detroit Lions fan. But we got along. We always kidded each other. You know, he had Alex Karras and the Detroit Lions. Is that all you got?

"So it was...he was a great guy, obviously. They were all great guys but I got to know Tommy pretty well. You know, we just kind of like each other and you know, we hung out together and became real good buddies. He watched my back. I watched his. And so we would go out in teams because being a recon unit, we'd go out with just a seven-man team, you know compared to the infantry-aligned units. They would go out in platoon size, which was about 30 men. And we would do that because we wanted to be quiet and not give our positions away from the enemy.

"So we kind of snuck in and did a reconnaissance. You know, how many enemy is there? What kind of supplies do they have? What kind of weapons, you know, do they carry? What trails are they using? And that's how we would report back. And so me and Tommy would go on...not always together because, depending on the sergeant, he would assign you a team. And half the time, we would be on the same team. And we would go out together and we hung out together and talked about, you know, home. Family and friends and what are we going to do when we get back. And so we got pretty close.

And on May 6th, 1970, he was one of the guys...he was about 20 yards away from me. He was positioned in a bunker. I was in one bunker. It was a perimeter around a mountain top and we had been assigned to a...secure an artillery base near a mountain top near the Quang Tri province, which is about 30 miles from the DMZ in what they called the A Shau Valley. The A Shau Valley is a real bad place. A lot of enemy activity. A lot of them there. And some people called it the Valley of Death. And for good reason.

"So there we were. We had been assigned there and we got there on May 5th. About five days before Mother's Day on that day in the year 1970. And when we got there, we could...we looked around at the artillery base and it was like, this is not a good base. They did not have enough perimeter wiring as far as concertina wire and razor wire and protection. To protect the perimeter. It was just kind of like actually a temporary base so...and the jungle was right there. I mean it was...usually, you want at least 100 yards or more of clearance before you see the jungle. And there it was...it might have been 50 yards and then the jungle was there and that's not enough. And so we got there on the 5th and Lt. Hawley, Richard Hawley, West Point Grad, good guy. He said...he saw it right away.

"He said, 'This is not good here. We're going to have to get more sandbags, dig deeper foxholes, and in the morning, we're going to have to clear all this brush off and lay more wire. And get that done because this is...this jungle is too close. You know, the enemy could come sneak right up on you before you know it.'

"And he was right. The next day, that next morning, we hadn't even been there, been there one night and the next morning at 5 a.m...I remember that because I was on guard and I was looking up and it was still dark. And I said, 'I can't wait until the light comes, until it gets daylight. You know, I don't like this. You know, I'm getting a bad feeling.'

"I looked at my watch and it was 5 a.m. exactly and all of a sudden, an explosion goes off. Then more explosions go off. Then the shooting starts. Then, you know, I'm shooting, my buddies are shooting in my bunker and I look to my right and Tommy Turan is over in the next bunker. And he's shooting and we're fighting for our lives.

"We got hit with a battalion-sized North Vietnamese army. These guys are regular army, lots of training like we had. And they were breaching the wire. And they were coming up the breach. And I could see Tommy, he's got out of his bunker and started moving forward to get a better shot to stop that breach that was coming up. And I remember he got hit once but he got up and he kept moving forward and shooting some more.

"And then there was more explosions, more smoke, more chaos, and that's about three or four hours at battle. And once the smoke cleared and everything got quiet and we went around treating the wounded. And 33 Americans were killed that day. 33 American soldiers were killed.

So we went around, like I say, treating the wounded, taking care of the dead, praying over the dead. Guess we were all in shock. Then we went around—you still look for more wounded, more dead and no Tommy. Couldn't find Tommy Turan. I remember seeing him, you know, moving forward. So we looked all day, all that morning, all that afternoon. And still nothing. And we looked under all...everything we could look under, sandbags, dirt, in-bunkers, all into the jungle. And we sent teams into the jungle, but they were being ambushed because the enemy was still there. So they couldn't really do a good search for Tommy.

"But they did for all day, the next day and for about three or four days and then for about a week. They sent out teams looking for...for his remains. And not just him, but there was a Sgt. Cryer from Alpha Company was also missing. But I didn't hardly know Cryer. But I did know Tommy and nothing about Tommy turned up.

"After a while, they just listed him as Missing in Action. There was rumors going around that they saw him in a POW camp, or somebody saw him here or there and we kept the hopes alive. I can't even imagine what his parents were going through when they got a letter or a phone call saying that he was missing in action.

"I remember his girlfriend because he showed me a picture of her, a very pretty young lady. She had sent a letter to us, very... angry and...sad. Disbelieving letter that she couldn't understand why we could not find Tommy and how did it become that he became missing. You know, didn't we keep track of our people? And she just couldn't understand it and she wanted us to continue looking and that he must be there somewhere because, I mean, where else could he be?

"You know, but...you, and I understand it, that feeling from her. Because when you know what, I think about it now and I think, man, he was right there. Where is he? What happened to him? But, yeah, he was listed in Missing in Action. Parents never knew anything until around 1993. A farmer was digging around... we been gone...we left Vietnam in '75. All the troops were gone. So in '93, a farmer was digging around and tried to plant whatever he was planting and came upon some remains. And he was smart enough to report it to his higher-ups, the village president, whoever it was, the village leader, elder and they, you know, contacted the government. There's a coalition between the Vietnamese government and the U.S government and if they find any remains, they have to investigate and search. So that's what they did and they did find some remains.

"And then those remains were sent to Hawaii. There's a research center and a...there in Hawaii that does all this and do a DNA testing and they keep remains from all wars. And so in '93, they found some remains and had to do more testing and it wasn't...I guess the remains weren't enough to have a conclusion and then they went to the parents and got some DNA samples from them and I think his sister. And then they went through that process.

"So finally, finally they said, 'Yeah, this...you know we found some teeth and some other samples, you know, I mean just a handful of Tommy Turan and they determined that it was his remains.' Was Tommy Turan. So he was buried, finally, brought back, repatriated to the U.S. and April 19th, 2002, he was buried with full military honors at Arlington, VA. Arlington National Cemetery. And I went to visit him. And I go to visit him at least once a year, Memorial Day or Veteran's Day. He's buried right there so...It's good that he finally made it home."

Were you ever hit?

"Yes, I was wounded on that day, May 6th, 1970, same time we lost...that same day, that same morning we lost Tommy. I was wounded. I got shot, grazed, left side of my head, it grazed, you know, it severed an artery but I was smart enough and being a medic, you know, knew how to stop the bleeding. I had run out of trauma dressings and bandages because there were so many wounded that morning. But I was smart enough that I had my T-shirt and I just ripped a piece of my T-shirt and I put it into a little ball and I pushed it into the hole. And I stopped the bleeding. And I took another long strip and just tied it into a band, real tight, to keep the blood from squirting out. Because I had lost a lot of blood.

"Didn't realize how much blood I lost. But I was transferred to a...interesting because the hospitals we so full that day, there was just so much going on. Not only with us but with other firebases around in other areas around Vietnam. There were taking a lot of wounded Americans, American wounded. So they sent me to a Army Marine hospital and that's where I recovered. I spent a couple of weeks in recovery at...in Da Nang. The Marine Navy Hospital there and they treated me pretty well."

After you were hit, did you keep on treating the wounded?

"Oh, absolutely, a year. Because when I got hit, I felt OK. I mean, I wasn't passing out. I took...later on, as I took...you know, the hours went by and, you know, and then I started getting weaker and weaker. But I kept treating. I mean these are...these are people I know. These are my buddies and I wasn't going to let...let that stop me. And that's why I did what I did.

"You know, I didn't think about it. Just so I could stop the bleeding. I put my hand out this far and the blood was hitting my hand from this far out. So, I mean, it was just squirting out. I knew, you know, this blood was coming out like this and I'm going to be dead in a couple of minutes. So I knew it would work, push that ball in there. It hurt a little bit, of course. But that was nothing compared to, you know...I'd rather hurt a little bit than be dead. So covered that up and took care of the rest of the guys.

"I feel very fortunate coming back. You know, because I saw a lot of my buddies did not. You know, that May 6th. Thirty-three Americans were killed. And that was just that day. And I saw a lot of death over there.

"And I come back and I think to myself, 'Man, George, you were very fortunate. You're back. You're back home with your mother and father and your sisters and brothers. And you're sitting at the dining table having Thanksgiving dinner or Christmas dinner with my family and there's other families not having that opportunity. They lost their son. So I got to do something to make my life worthwhile. I shouldn't waste it. So I started...I started...I joined different organizations. VFW. The Disabled American Veterans. American Legion. And I started getting involved with them because I wanted to give back. Because I'm here. I'm fortunate enough to get home. I want to do...I want to do something positive. I didn't want to waste that time.

"So I got involved with the POW-MIA causes. Joe Campbell, a dear friend of mine, is very involved so I started doing it too.

"And he said, 'Hey, I need someone to do the POW-MIA table at the ceremony.'

"And I said, 'Absolutely. I'd be honored to do that.'

"And so I started doing the ceremony for the POW-MIA missing man table. And volunteering at the VA. And doing as much as I can for the veteran's community. You know, make sure that veterans know their benefits, the education benefits, health benefits. You know, loan programs and things like that. So whenever I run into a veteran, I'll say, 'Hey, or you know about this program? Or do you know about that program? And you know where....here's a card. Call these people up and if you're not sure, call me up and I'll drive you there. We'll sit down together. These people will help you, you know.'

"And the VA is a little different than it was when I first got out. I went to the VA, it was 1971. And there was issues with the VA back then. It was overwhelming. I remember going to the VA back then in '71. And I wanted to register with the VA; I'm a veteran. I want to register. So if I'm eligible for health benefits, I want to be able to use them. And there was so much chaos at that hospital and people weren't paying attention to you and walking around asking people, you know, hey, where is this office? Well, we don't know. Maybe go down that way. What?

"I'm outta here. So I turned around and walked out and I went back. So I understand that feeling, you know, for veteran's coming out of a...just getting out of the military and going to the VA because it's overwhelming. There's lot...it's...there's a lot of people down there. There's a lot of patients. A lot of veterans. There's a lot going on. So when you first walk in there, it can be ....it can just overtake you and say, no I don't want...I'm turning around and walking out of here. I don't know where to go."

George became a Milwaukee County Firefighter after he finished his Army service. He participates in many activities in the veterans community, including the POW/MIA remembrance table ceremony.

TIM BARANZYK

TIM BARANZYK FOUGHT THE Vietnam war on two fronts, with the U.S. Marines in Asia and back in the Midwestern United States, where his reception was less than friendly when he returned home.

"I was in the true branch. The Marine Corps," Baranzyk said. "There for three years. I enlisted in '66 from Milwaukee. Was sent to San Diego for boot camp training. Sometimes you go to San Diego, it's more like being a Hollywood Marine. I had a good time when I was there. And after boot camp, I went up to ITR, which is Infantry Training, up in Camp Pendleton. Got sick after, oh, six weeks with bronchial pneumonia. Was put in the hospital for two weeks, three weeks, I forgot what.

"And then resumed my training and was assigned to a cadre for 8-inch artillery. So 8-inch artillery was stationed in Camp Lejeune, North Carolina. I was there for several weeks with the training. And then we took our 30-day leave and then met in San Bernardino, California, and from there we flew over to Vietnam.

"My unit left out of Da Nang. From there they went to provide support for the Battle of Hue. And I also volunteered to go to what they called Gao Lin, which is right on the DMZ, the far northeastern part of Vietnam. Then we did support missions for artillery missions, 8-inch, as well as support for the *USS New Jersey*, and another unit of 155s and 105s, for support running the entire area. Which was pretty interesting. We had...we got hit several times by Red Chinese, not North Vietnamese, Red Chinese. I was never wounded. Never received a Purple Heart.

"We got there, they had what we called sea rats. If we needed any food, we had to steal it from the Army. If we needed any beer, we had to steal it from the Air Force. We didn't have any of that stuff. We lived in...in holes, were bunkers. And fire direction control, you were protected big time, because the biggest thing we found out of the beginning, when we got into 8-inch artillery, you do not want the enemy to get ahold of these guns. 8-inch are large.

"They're half the size of the *USS New Jersey*. These are big artillery pieces. Your bullet or round of about 245 pounds. So we were protected very well. Had enough security around our perimeter to make sure that nobody got in. And we did have one hit up by June when three Red Chinese came in, but they didn't make it through the wire. Other than that, it was...we get hit, but not near us because the main thing was to keep activity away from the guns. Because the guns were so important. And with us, we had the 28-inch, we had 155, and I think it was a 105, the Army, a real long barrel that would shoot a projectile faster than the speed of sound.

"But again, with the whole...with the whole area, it was you had to maintain the integrity of this unit. You could not have anything happen to it. If it got into the enemy's hands, it would be big problems all over the place. Especially on a DMZ. But the fire direction control living in bunkers, deep. We'd have like two chart operators. When we'd get a fire mission, you'd have some...some officer, I don't know which branch, flying around in the air, they have what you call aerial observer. And they'd report a fire mission. We had about seven radios, nothing else, pretty quiet. We didn't have TV during the time. We'd have several radios all synchronized with the different aerial observers so when they were talking about any activity, we'd have that stud plotted on our maps so by the time the...the OK came down for us to fire, we already had it. And we just let the guns know and away we went.

"When we first got there, it was what you would call maybe in the 80s. And then it would start to warm up a little bit and then when you're driving in the convoy, you see this big old cloud come over, you get drenched with like maybe two or three inches of rain. And in about maybe 15 minutes later then sun would come out so you'd be able to dry off real quick. In the fall, when the rains would come, it was mud. I mean it rained and rained and rained. It's worse than playing in the mud because you were in the mud. It was a mess. But that's why a lot of the guns didn't move when the rains came. They stuck. They stayed right there. It would have been very difficult for them to move.

"I had a good time. I had a good time. Very memorable. Met some Vietnamese people, which was good. Had a chance to visit some of the cities and I went on R&R, once to Singapore, and the other one to Taiwan. And did a lot of sightseeing and filming. I carried my camera recorder wherever I could. Yes, they were all good pictures. Nothing below the table, as some people would think. And so on, but it was all good. It was all good. And completed my training one year, 26 days, we came home. And when I came home, that's when everything else changed.

"I had an aunt and uncle who lived up in Marquette, Michigan, and one of them was just taking a bus where you got everybody sitting at the back and you're in the front because people could tell whether or not if you were in the military. I mean that's kind of subtle. Because of your haircut, they could tell. Whether you're losing your baggage in the airport. Or you're being treated differently when you go to the store. A lot of different things. A lot of different things. And I know, dealt with lot of ignorance. A lot of ignorance. That's why I went back to school, to try to educate a lot of these people. Try to help...education is one thing that nobody can take away from you. Education is very important. Big time.

"You had difference of opinion with people in locality. Different sorts of treatments and so on. And I just went back to trying to live, trying to fit in with everything. It was...it was...I got married and then things changed drastically. So I went to school, you know, and that was OK. But I always had a thing in the back of my mind about, you know, trying to help a lot of the vets.

"Just the way a lot of them were treated when we came home. Not again. Because when we came...after several years happened, and them I became...I got involved in military organizations, the Marine Corps League was probably the big one that helped me get to a lot of different areas when I met Gov. Dreyfuss and a lot of other officials from Madison, as well as from the national government. And also got involved in the Vietnam Vets, the American Legion, volunteering at the VA at Zablocki. Also also of that got me further involved in politics, more actually veterans' affairs, the more concern than politics. Trying to keep the politics out of everything. So trying to take care of the veterans and their needs.

"Because right now, the Legion has me as the Homeless Task Force Chairman, working with homeless veterans. And I got, they call me up all over the place. All the time. Even today. Trying to help them out with security deposits, rent, moving, whatever. You wouldn't believe some of the stuff that comes up. And a lot of them are legit but a lot of them are not. So being a volunteer, I have to go out and investigate and see whether or not these people are telling me the truth. What do they really need. Also direct them to other sources.

"Resources around the state. Which would save us a lot of money. And a lot of the other not-for-profits around the states help them out quite a bit. Veteran organizations in Oshkosh and Eau Claire and so on. So that has worked out pretty well. And through all of this time, I've had the opportunity to get to the limelight a few times. Not that I look for it. I don't. It's just that I like to do things behind the scenes. I'm not one to be sitting behind all these cameras. That doesn't really...I know it's nice but that's not my bag. I just feel guilty sometimes when I do this, that's all."

Are Vietnam veterans getting enough respect?

"Well, enough respect, in the past, no. Now? To me, in my own honest opinion, I think the Vietnam veterans should be taking more of a lead in the everyday affairs of what's going on in this country. I know some in some areas they may do that. But you're dealing with homeless vets. There's the job of helping the brothers and sisters is not done. They still have to watch the ones that have...even these vets that are in Iraq and Afghanistan. Taking care of their brothers and their sisters. This is a job that they have to do. This is not a gimme. It's a have-to. They have to...have to do this. And I think that a lot of them have not done that. I think that some of them believe that now the world owes them. I don't care what people think. I think that they think that people owe them something and I don't believe that's true.

"We have a lot to help this country with. We have a lot to be thankful for. And I think these men and women are the ones that have to take the lead to get this country back on track as to what's right, what's wrong, and not have our future generations of service people, as well as the common person, suffer a lot of this disgrace and anything else that would relate to the country."

After the war, Tim became a corporate trainer for Allen Bradley, Cousins Subs, and Holiday Inn.

JOE CAMPBELL

IT IS NOT UNCOMMON FOR veterans who survive war to return home with decidedly mixed emotions; thrilled to be back in a safe place surrounded by loved ones, but wracked with guilt wondering why they weren't killed in action along with many soldiers in their units who lost their lives. Joe Campbell understands that psychological dichotomy all too well.

How did you get in the service?

"Well, I was going to school, technology school, in Chicago and the Vietnam war was getting more and more active and it was obviously a draft back in my generation and I just felt that I'd go in the service and maybe pick up the auto technology that I was studying in Chicago through the service. That was, of course, a very big mistake. But nonetheless, I went in and enlisted for three years and that got me to Aberdeen for automotive and artillery.

"I was in Vietnam for a year. When I went to Germany, that was in August of '66, and I wound up....when I volunteered right away, requested it right after I got to my unit, that was....then in December, before Christmas, I think it was December 20th, I got a call from the company commander that my request was granted. And at that time, I kind of had another second thought, because Vietnam was a little bit more, on the surface, but nonetheless I got to go home for Christmas and I went over to Vietnam in February of '67.

"And I was with the 1st Logistical Command and Artillery and Automotive Service. And I start out being attached to the 25th Infantry Division in Cu Chi. I wound up getting transferred to the 101st Airborne when they came with a new brigade and then just before I left, they transferred me down to the 1st Infantry Division. And left right after the Tet Offensive of '68. My primary responsibility was servicing artillery and automotive repair and service and guard duty."

What was like when you stepped off the plane in Vietnam?

"Well, I can tell you, coming from Chicago, in...January of '67 when I left, it was the worst snowstorm they ever had. And I was lucky to even get out of Chicago at that time. So we're probably dealing with about 10 degrees above zero and a helluva snowstorm and then two days later, I'm sitting in about 110 degrees. And when we landed, just before we flew in to Vietnam, there was all kinds of black smoke. It was early in the morning and fire everywhere and I'm like, 'Oh, my God. What are we getting into?'

"And we have no weapons. We're in our khaki uniforms. Turns out, that was the time they...excuse my French, they burned shit. So they light it with kerosene and that's what was going on. And I looked and the smell and I thought, 'Oh, what did I do?' But shortly thereafter, they...once we got assigned to a unit, things settled down.

"Right after I got there, in the replacement depot, there was incoming mortar attack. And probably the thing that helped me as far as being a sober soldier was...we had no weapons, and we were told to go into a bunker. And in between bunkers, there big ditches or trenches that were used to let the monsoons rains flow. Lot of the vets...lot of the GIs used to piss in it and it was pretty raunchy.

"And while I'm in this bunker, a guy falls in the ditch crying for help and I'm going to go out of the bunker to help him. And I don't know who this was, some big sergeant grabbed me, threw me upside the bunker and said, 'Let the son of a bitch die. If he wants to drink and drug, you ain't risking your life for that.'

"And that just shocked the living Hell out of me. And it probably helped me from the standpoint of not indulging in alcohol and drugs while was over there. That was my first experience. Doing guard duty in the villages where the medics performed medical civic action program for the villagers, I would say was very, very scary because of the eyes and what have you, the people.

"There were few of us looking over where the doctors and nurses did their thing. But I would probably say the biggest thing, because I was basically in camp, not out on patrols, was the incoming, which we had no control of. Another situation was putting Claymore mines out when we did guard duty. Generally, we would work from say six in the morning until six at night and then we'd be on guard duty from six at night until six in the morning. Two hours on. Two hours off. Situation: you'd put the Claymore mine out, which obviously has a sign on it which says "front" and you put that out and you back in your guard post and a couple bunkers down, these guys get drugged up or whatever and the Viet Cong would escape through the barbed wire and turn the Claymore mine around and they were blown away.

"And again, that was just another situation where it just took luck. I want to be alert, no matter what. And probably one of the other experiences was minor to most of the guys over there, but it was on guard duty at the Long Bin ammo dump, which was the largest ammo dump in the country at that time. And so two hours on. And two hours off. You get pretty tired, but I saw this huge rat, which was not uncommon. We'd lay on the...actually the artillery casings boxes off the ground and they're about 100 yards apart between one ammo pad and another.

"And so we'd sleep on the artillery box and back down, we used .12-gauge, sawed-off shotguns so obviously, if we did have to fire, we'd wouldn't blow out another ammo dump. So I had the .12 gauge on my stomach and I'm sleeping on my back and this thing, and my partner—there were two on each pad—squeezed my elbow to wake me up, it's my time to be on guard duty. I thought it was the rat. I almost blew his head off. So it was a unique situation.

"There was another situation and we were filling sandbags. There was a massive big sand pile and the little Vietnamese kids would come and play by us and there was an avalanche. The sand had covered up this little boy and I and three others tried to dig with our hands to save this poor young lad. And as it turned out, by the time we got to him, he was dead. And so we carried him up to the village and I just couldn't believe it. Nobody really wanted to claim him. And it was a very hard thing. I come from a family of nine. I'm eighth of nine kids, and my sisters married and had kids and still we start seeing this with the children.

"Another situation was with the village and it was at in Phuoc Vinh. I was very fortunate to be able to be around children and one of the young lads—Chi was his name, probably about 8 to 10 years old and just a great little guy and they called him 'Cowboy' and I'd bring candy or stuff that we got from home—and the next day I couldn't find Chi. It turned out that his father was beheaded and it was put on a stake outside the village to let the people know that you're not to cooperate or help our U.S. Army.

"Those were things like that. So taking all this stuff in, and coming home quickly. I was due to come home on Feb. 12th. We all knew what our discharge date of return was. And this was right after the Tet Offensive had started.

"And on Feb. 7th, I get a call from my company commander. 'You've got two hours. You're going home.' And I thought this is, in one breath, this is absolutely wonderful. And as life progressed after Vietnam, and I know I'm jumping the gun, but it was years later when one of my son's friends went to the Vietnam Wall in Port Washington, and that particular wall was the first time that it was at in the Milwaukee area.

"I knew where it was at and I could afford to go, at the time go, but I couldn't go. And that really, really bothered me. My son's friend, about 12, 14 years old, comes back with an etching and he said, 'Oh, Mr. Campbell, I'm so proud of you.' For what? 'I brought this etching from the wall for you.' The only thing is that there were two Joseph Campbells and I wasn't sure which one was you. I'm thinking, 'Young man, this is not a wall about the living.' and so that was the first time that I went on the Internet and to the virtual wall to take a look. I found Joseph Campbell. He was killed the day before I left. And the reason I went home, is because of guys like him that gave their life, that went home in a casket."

How did you deal with all of those emotions?

"At first, it was really tough. I never wanted to talk about Vietnam. I had a brother went to Vietnam two years after I did. We never discussed it. And I became an alcoholic. And it was not good. And I finally went in for help, and I got help. And I would say all that terrible, terrible experience that I could never talk about started to become my best friend because it allowed me to help other vets. Sobered up and I've been sober for over 16 years.

"Work at the VA every Sunday morning, running an AA meeting with all the vets. And it's things like that that I look on, while it was bad, I successfully proved how not to do things. So my experience, while it was not good, and I don't think it was good for anyone to go from an environment where we might get in trouble for hitting our brother or hitting a neighborhood kid, to an area where it was life or death. And I would just say that it, looking back that the experience had become my best ally."

Joe organized the construction of the 9/11 Memorial at Milwaukee's War Memorial Center, which features an 1,800-pound piece of steel from the Twin Towers.

JANICE DAHLKE

JANICE DAHLKE DIDN'T FIGHT in the Vietnam War but was a victim of the conflict's consequences. Her son Randy was killed in action, which shattered her life and divided her family.

What was Randy like?

"He was good natured. He was kind. Considerate. I wish I was there working...I wish I was there more for him. But he was a happy soul."

"After school, he had a paper route. And one person was trying to collect his...the weekly money. And one person was smart enough to invite the kid in and took his picture. So much for that one. And then he worked at a garden center on 55th and Silver Spring. And he brought home a plant, a bush, that's still in my front yard after all these years. It's unbelievable. Christmas he bought me a cameo and earrings. Said it was from him and his two sisters. But that was stolen from me when I was broken into.

"Yeah, it's...people don't understand and it's not the price of things. It's the sentimental thing behind it. And it doesn't make sense that these kids could do such a thing, you know?"

How did Randy get involved in the military?

"I really didn't realize there was this war going on. And...I don't know how it came about, that...that the Army came up. I really don't remember, to tell you the truth. If I knew there was such a bad war going on, I wouldn't...I wouldn't have signed up for him.

"He enlisted. He was 17. Signed up in February and March 14 was his birthday and I signed up for him *(since Randy was not 18, he needed a parent to sign up for him)*. March 3rd of '69, he was killed in Vietnam.

"I was packing a present, a package for Randy for his birthday. And I looked out the window and saw these two servicemen coming up the driveway. My husband wasn't too...that was my second husband, wasn't too supportive. He thought I was grieving too much. Shouldn't even say this but...he wanted one of my close friends to sign a slip to commit me. He was a gem. Needless to say, that's when I got a divorce. That year.

"See, I was married twice. And the first husband's third wife came up to the casket and said I killed him. So, you know, if I hadn't my faculties about me, I would have slugged her. (laugh)

She can't do that. That's...doesn't show respect for Randy. So what are you going to say? You can brain...brainwash your children and ...that's another subject.

"I think that's why I joined the Gold Star Mothers, because you're able to talk to people, to women who are going through the same thing. And I think that was more comfort to me, to be able to talk to someone that...you get the crazy comments...'Oh, you're grieving too much, get over it.' You get crazy statements like that, you know? What are you going to say? And it's people that should have understood you. I think that's what hurts more than anything."

Janice worked at Badger Meter, Briggs & Stratton, and Zenith before she retired. She remains active with the local chapter of Gold Star Mothers.

MIKE GREBE

SOME MEMBERS OF THE military from Wisconsin were deployed to Vietnam even before America became formally involved in combat there.

Mike Grebe from the 81st Airborne arrived in Vietnam in November 1964, where he was an advisor for a Vietnamese infantry battalion. Even at that early stage of the conflict, Mike could see it would be an uphill battle.

"I went to Ft. Benning for Airborne school," Grebe recalled. "Learned how to jump out of airplanes. My first unit was the 81st Airborne Division at Ft. Bragg. I spent a little over two years there. Then I was assigned to Vietnam, where I was an advisor to a Vietnamese Infantry Battalion. On my way to Vietnam, I spent three or four months in California learning to speak Vietnamese."

How tough was that?

"Actually, Vietnamese is a rather simple language. During the course of a century or two, the French converted the Vietnamese, the written language, from characters to our Western alphabet. So you don't have to learn the characters. And all the words in Vietnamese are one syllable. And the verb conjugation is very simple. Just present future and past. The Vietnamese word for go is '*di.*' Will go is '*se di.*' So the verb conjugations are very simple. All you need to learn in order to speak Vietnamese is the intonation, because the same words are spelled two or three different ways, pronounced two or three different ways, can mean very different things.

"The language barrier, even though it wasn't as difficult for me as it might have been since I did learn some Vietnamese, was an obstacle in doing my job. I worked mostly with the officers who commanded the infantry battalion that I was assigned to. One fortunate thing for me is that they had all fought with the French, and as a result, they have a pretty good grasp of French. And I studied French at West Point. So every once in a while, we'd lapse into French. But yes, it was very challenging.

"We did have an interpreter who helped a great deal. Unfortunately, just a couple months into my tour of Vietnam, he was wounded. And so we went out without an interpreter for about six months and that was challenging."

What were your first impressions of Vietnam?

"Well, I had never been in Asia before. And I remember when I got to Tan Son Nhat, when I arrived there, being overwhelmed with the change in culture. Everything was different. The sights. The sounds. The odors. Everything was different. I remember during a time I was being processed in to the country, in Saigon, they put us up in hotels. I remember the first time I went to turn on a water faucet, a lizard came out of the faucet. So there was an incredible culture shock. And it took me a while. It took me a while. And then when I got to my unit, I was living with the Vietnamese out in the countryside, moving every day or two or three, eating Vietnamese food, living like a Vietnamese. And it took some getting used to."

How were the troops in your unit?

"Actually, I came away with a good respect for the Vietnamese soldiers. I think they were dedicated to the cause and God knows, they suffered for it. And I thought the officers were quite good. The problem with the Vietnamese Army involved a lack of non-commissioned officers. Unlike our own Army, there were no sergeants that basically run the Army. As a 2nd Lt., in the 82nd Airborne Division, I understood that the sergeant was actually running things. I got that. But they didn't have non-commissioned officers that did anything. And so that was the problem I had with the Vietnamese Army. They were courageous people.

"When I got to Vietnam, there were no American troops in the country. That was in...I was there quite early in the war. I arrived in November of 1964. There were no American units, except for some support units. And I was sent to the Mekong Delta and that's where the war was at the time. And I was in a fair amount of action.

"Now during the course of the year I was there, the war changed completely. That was the year we began bringing American fighting units into Vietnam. So when I got there in November of '64, there less than 20,000 in the country. When I left a year later, there were almost 300,000. So the war changed and the war also moved north. Whereas when I got there, the war was in the south where I was stationed.

"We were involved in close combat. I was never wounded. I was shot at but I was never wounded. And we had three or four situations where many of our soldiers killed or wounded.

"It was very, very difficult to fight the enemy on their own terrain and it was a tough environment for us. We were...the Vietnamese were losing the battle for the people. The Viet Cong truly were terrorists. They systematically killed off most of the civilian leaders. Village and provincial chiefs. I saw the aftermath of several of those murders. Usually they would disembowel the village leader and leave him out in the village square or market for civilians to see. So we were losing the battle for the people. And the Viet Cong controlled the countryside at might. That's when they did all their moving. And we would be sent out some ambushes at night but we did not control the countryside at all."

Were you scared?

"Sure. Yes, I was frightened. Less so the longer I was in the country. I think you become a bit immune to that after a while, when your senses get dulled. But sure, it's a...it's a frightening experience.

"I was different after my service. I would say more than anything else, I learned to appreciate life and the randomness of the combat experience reinforced that. You can be standing next to another person and they're shot and maybe killed and you aren't. And so you ask yourself why him and not me? So I just came to have a deeper appreciation for life. It also changed me when I saw how people, particularly the Americans in the country, cared for each other. You know, there's a bond that develops in any unit and the level of care that people have for each other. Having somebody else's back or having your back is just an incredible experience.

"When I was there, when I first got 'in country,' as we used to say, there were very few people who were there who were draftees or didn't want to be there. Most of us were career military. I think that probably came later in the war. I didn't...I didn't experience the dissatisfaction that the American people had for the war until I left the Army and went to law school. I was first of all older than much of the other people in law school. The war was unpopular. There were very few of us who had served. And while I got along well with my fellow students, it was clear that most of the faculty did not like me and the fact that I was a veteran. And the fact that I had been in Vietnam.

"It's very difficult to have your service disrespected. I never when through some of the ordeals that other Vietnam vets did. I never had personal confrontations. Physical confrontations with people. But it was clear that most of my law school teachers did not respect my service. It was obvious from the way that I was being treated and things that would be said in class.

"They would make light of my age or my service, 'Gee, where were you?' That was at a time when most law students went directly from undergraduate school to graduate school. That's no longer the case. Most people now will do something else for a year or two. It was mostly innuendo. I wasn't embittered by it. It was fine. It was what it was. I got through it.

"To the extent I've been successful in my life, I attribute much of it to my military education and my training. I think I'm a relatively disciplined person and I wasn't born with that. I learned it in my military service. I think...I think Vietnam in one respect helped me. I think everyone who is injected for the first time in a combat situation wonders how they're going to react. Will they turn around and run? It's actually reassuring to know that you don't. It's a very, in some ways, inspiring experience to know that you're up to it.

"I was very proud to have served. And that's another thing that I think comes from my military service. I try to be active in community and civic activities. That's another way of serving."

Mike was awarded the Combat Infantryman's badge and two Bronze Stars for his service in Vietnam. He became an attorney and was Chairman and CEO of the Milwaukee law firm Foley and Lardner, as well as CEO of the Bradley Foundation.

RICHARD KALASHIAN

LIKE MANY WHO FOUGHT in Vietnam, Richard Kalashian had a difficult time telling the difference between the enemy soldiers zealously dedicated to killing him and innocent civilians caught up in a conflict they didn't understand. Kalashian had emotional encounters with both groups serving as a staff sergeant in the U.S. Army.

What was your primary assignment?

"Search and destroy. We had a lot of intense fights. My first contact, I was a platoon sergeant because I had rank. So being new 'in country,' when you place yourself in a platoon, the members of that platoon have been there maybe six months, nine months, whatever. So you have to work with them. And they train you. And teach you the ropes, as they say. My first contact that I had in Vietnam was we were crossing one of the major rivers. And each person had his own responsibility. Hanson was our rubber man. He also carried our 160 machine gun.

"So he would be first to go across the river. And he would tie down to a tree. And one by one, we would come over. When the last person crossed, which was me, the NVA *(North Vietnamese Army)* opened up on us on the beach. So we were kind of pinned down. And at that time, I thought I was going to die because the bullets were very close to us and it was late in the afternoon. So there was about 13 of us.

"Our platoon wasn't very large. We kept the men in small groups because the more people you have, the more you're noticed and the more noise you make. So we couldn't move. We were pinned down. And I remember having my face in the mud, trying to get as low as I could. So we called the Air Force for air power. And they dropped 500 seven-pound bombs on that area. They were pretty much dug in. The delta was pretty flat and there was a lot of water. But this area we had was kind of hilly so they probably bombed that for a good half hour. And then we were able to move forward. And took a body count and retrieved any weapons that were there and stuff like that. That was the first time. That was kind of an icebreaker for me. We had to adjust everything.

"The worst moment would be Tet, 1968, the Tet Offensive. They were expecting a huge amount of NVA, four to five battalions. So they flew us in an area. It was during dry season now, that's when that usually takes place, because if they're going to attack you, they're going to do it during dry season. Otherwise, it's too hard to move through the mud and the water and everything else. So we went into a huge rice paddy and I happened to learn Vietnamese. Wasn't real proficient.

"But I probably was 40-percent proficient. And I have to tell you this because this kind of ties in with the story. I heard crying in the distance. So I told the platoon that I would be back shortly, because there was other Army and US Marines out there too. We were getting ready to go to Saigon. And I went over there and there was a grandmother and a mother who were crying and they spoke to me in Vietnamese. They said that their children—they had three children, three girls in the bunker. And the GIs started throwing hand grenades in there. And that really bothered me.

"So I decided I was going to go into the bunker. I was also a tunnel rat, too, so I was kind of used to that. So the grandmother said, 'Are you really going to go in there?'

"And I said, 'Yes, we have to bring them out.'

"So we brought them out and one girl was 12 years old and she had died. And then there was a five-year-old girl and I think a three-year-old girl. Both those were pretty well wounded. Fragmentation just kind of tore their skins off. I actually cried there. It was pretty bad. Grandmother, in respect for me, said that there was a huge amount of NVA in the area. And I thanked her for the information. I found that in knowing the language and approaching them and talking to them, it helped. People trusted you more than they would the average GI, let's say.

"So I went back to my unit and I told them what she had told me and then our orders changed. They were going to take us out and move us into a more hot spot, the way it was. There were two companies of Army units that were pinned down and they needed support. So the helicopters came in. We called them choppers, picked us up and there was only about 13 of us, in for support. So they flew us in and we landed into another rice paddy that was hot. We were receiving fire and I had two brand-new soldiers with me. They had been 'in country'—that would mean Vietnam—a week.

"So they had no experience whatsoever. And I kept them by my side and I had a 90-millimeter and their job was to load me up in case we needed to return fire. In this case, we had to return fire because we were behind a dike. Dikes are higher above ground during the dry season because the water seeps all the way down. So we were hiding behind the dikes and they were shooting mortars at us and they were shooting automatic weapons at us and I asked the two young men to load me us and I looked over there and they were crying and it brought everything back to me when I was crying.

"So I had to load myself up. And I returned fire and I must have shot maybe 20 rounds or so. And it was getting dark and I could see in the distance, the movement, a huge amount of military movement out in the distance. And I knew there was going to be a human wave attack. My unit was by itself somewhat. We weren't really with a main group of men. We were flanking them basically. We ran out of ammunition for the 90-millimeter so we couldn't use that any more. And we were getting low, trying to return fire.

"So what happened was when you get pinned down like that there's a code and I don't remember the code anymore, it means that were going to be annihilated if someone doesn't help us. And that's all it was. So at that time, shooting all those rounds, I didn't have earplugs. So I was pretty well deaf. So we used hand signals to the radio man and we called in napalm. We had no choice. So there was a number of jets came over and if you've ever seen napalm come out of a jet or a plane, it tumbles. And it hit fairly close to us but not close enough to hurt us. And you could just see the smoke and flames.

"You could see people running on fire. And that suppressed them. They retreated. It was dark at that time now. And there's some C-133 transfer planes, those are pretty heavy planes. And they had two galley guns on it. We call them 'Puff the Magic Dragon.' And they covered about every square inch around, one round every 3,000 rounds came out. If not more.

"And all night long, the Air Force flew and protected us and the other companies as well. And they dropped parachutes, flare parachutes. They last about maybe five minutes max. Dropped those all night long. And they kept firing and firing and firing. That was really, really a wonderful feeling that we would survive hopefully. So they did that all night long and then in the distance I could hear moaning and crying. It was the enemy. And you think about it, it could be you. They're human beings too, you know. You feel bad.

"Yet it's a war. So you're kind of torn between being compassionate and being hateful. And I'm kind of the compassionate person. So I felt bad for them. That morning, we had to pick up bodies and weapons and stuff like that so we survived that ordeal. Thank God."

Were you wounded in action?

"I just lost my hearing. I had a graze here, pretty much gone. And that's about it, thank the Lord. The last contact I had before I was out, was a river crossing. And being the rank I had, I always made sure I was the last person to cross. And we had a medic with us that day, too. We called him Doc. And there was about 12 of us at that time. And I wrapped myself with the rope, put on the hook and everything. And I had the rifle on my back and they pulled me across.

"The river was pretty swift. You really couldn't swim across at all. And when I got across, the NVA opened up on us. That's when they do it. When you don't expect it. They wait for you until you're a sitting duck and open up on us. And I could remember diving below the surface of the water and you could hear the bullets zinging by you. You can't describe the sound of how that bullet sounds in the water when you're underneath the water. And they kept pulling and pulling me and I thought nothing of it. I just thought, 'Am I going to get hit? Am I going to make it to the other side?' And they kept pulling the rope and pulling the rope, and the enemy was still shooting.

"And I finally got out of the water and then they more of less stopped shooting so I looked up at Doc. He had a blank expression and he took a bullet in his chest. That was tough. Because he sacrificed his life for me."

Did the war change you?

"Well, I came back home. You know, it's so hard because here you're in a war zone, on the other side of the world and I had a fiancé at the time. And they're going to parties. They're going to school. It's like nothing's happening over there. Here you're in a war zone. So that stays with you all that time while you're in Vietnam. And I remember coming off the airplane at O'Hare Field and at that time she was my fiancé and my mom with me had the suitcase and the suitcase had my civilian clothes in it. And I went to the men's room and actually changed my clothes.

"And they didn't want any confrontation because back then the war was very unpopular and there was no welcoming committee or people to welcome you off the airplane. Other than your family. So I kind of stayed to myself for maybe five, seven, eight years. And I just kind of buried myself back in school again. And finding a job and going that route.

"It's not easy. Even the World War II veterans were not compassionate for us. I remember going to a VFW post, thinking that if I joined, that might help. And they kind of looked at you. They always talk about The Big War. Well, it's really not the Big War because I did some research. The actual World War II warrior in a year's time had ten contacts with the enemy. The Vietnam veteran had 240 enemy contacts in a year's time. So that shows you the difference. And in World War I and World War II, you had a front line and you had a rear, and that's where your base camp would be.

"In Vietnam, you didn't have that. You're out there by yourself. And you didn't know where the enemy was. So there was a big difference, you know? But when I walked in there, they looked at me. It's like oh, oh. What war was that? And that hurt me. So I left and for the next 15 years, I didn't have nothing to do with anybody, any organization.

"My wife is very supportive. She's gone through hell with me. And about five years ago, I remember going up to a gentleman who was handing out poppies and I just yelled at him. 'You guys, you know, you don't know what it's all about. Half of you guys haven't even seen combat at all.' And then I felt bad. *What the hell's wrong with you, talking like that?* You know. So I went and found a post in Hartland and I joined up. And I've been raising a lot of money to help our current troops and our veterans. And that was kind of like closure. So I feel good about that.

Do you ever have flashbacks to your combat experience?

"You still think about it. Last night, I was watching on YouTube the 9th Infantry Division. They had two clips, five clips about it and it was pretty realistic and it covered pretty much all the areas that I experienced. And then my wife came in and said, 'Turn that off. Why are you watching for? You're going to get depressed.'

"And I said, 'No. This is part of healing.' So that's how it goes. Little by little, you heal more and more, you know."

In 2013, Richard, who works at SNS Research in suburban Milwaukee, designed a special cart for Southwest Airlines to transport caskets carrying fallen soldiers upon their return to the U.S.

JOHN KOEPPEN

SOME VETERANS EMERGE FROM war unscathed physically or emotionally. Others suffer the aftereffects from their experiences with the repetitive nature of combat, days, weeks and months of being in harm's way. But for still others, such as John Koeppen, a single incident makes an indelible mark that impacts their view of life for the rest of their days.

"I was 18. I graduated with a whopping 1.8 grade-point average out of Custer High School," Koeppen said. "So at that time, most men either had the option of being married, going to college, going into the service, or just taking your chances with draft, or you could go to Canada. Canada was not an option at the time.

"I grew up, I was raised Catholic. I went to a Catholic grade school. So at that time, the Communists were the evil people, the Godless Communists. So that was one of the reasons the Vietnam war was conducted, to fight the anti-Christ. And so I had taken my draft deferment—I was 1A—and I applied to go to college. At that time, they had a college entrance exam. And I was slightly dyslexic and they had a lot of multiple-choice questions because they called and said you really scored high on this. We'd like you to go to UWM. But you can only take 9 credits. You had to take three remedial credits. And I got a draft deferment for the first season I went, which was in the spring of '69.

"It was run by Gerald Spates for poor, underprivileged kids. My dad worked for the city of Milwaukee. He was basically a garbage collector. And after that year, they pulled my draft deferment and so then I was working at a can factory. I was a blue-collar worker, working at American Can Company over on Teutonia Avenue.

"And so I got called for my second physical. I was 1A again. That was after '69 after the mini-Tet. And the Army's was drafting I think about 50,000 guys per month at that time. Or the services were. So I went to the recruiter and I said, 'You know, I'd like to become a helicopter pilot. That really looks exciting.' Took some tests. He said I qualified.

"And so I quit my job at the can company. Went down on the day I was supposed to, which was September 19, 1969. And when I got there, the sergeant says, 'Well, the helicopter class isn't until November.'

"I said, 'Ok, I'll just go back home.'

"He said, 'Well wait a minute. Let me check with the draft board.' And he came back in and said, 'You'll be drafted next month.'

"Being young and impressionable, I kind of believed him.

"And so he said, 'Why don't you sign up now?' and I said, 'I'm not signing up for three years.' He gave me the two-year program. Turned out to be part of the program called Project 100,000 that was started by LBJ during the riots and so I called my mom and dad and said I wasn't coming home for supper and I went to the service that day.

"I didn't become a helicopter pilot; didn't work out. What he said was, I could get into the service and you just tell them you signed up to be helicopter pilot. And then they'll direct you. So when we got on an airplane, we were flying North Central Airlines at that time, went down to Ft. Campbell, Kentucky and the first thing they did was hustle us out of these busses and I handed my papers to one of the people that was processing me in and I said 'I'm supposed to let you know that I'm qualified to be a helicopter pilot. You guys would me direct to what school.'

"Needless to say, they all kind of got a big chuckle out of that. Told me to go over there and I ended up in basic training in Ft. Campbell and I spent my basic training there. And in September, that ended just after Thanksgiving and from there you took tests to do your MLSs and so I qualified to be a military policeman, a medic, and then the third one was combat infantryman.

"So my next step, I was sent to Ft. Pope, Louisiana and that was my next step of training. We all went down on a bus because we were young and full of piss and vinegar at that time, feeling fearless. And I remember when we were on the bus going down south, a couple things I remember...First off, I'd never been south so I was shocked at the poverty because there was still a lot of poverty, especially for the African-Americans. We went along the Mississippi River and then as soon as we were getting into Ft. Polk, it was dark and we were all kidding around, and when we got into Ft. Polk, there was a huge billboard sign of an American soldier bayonetting a Viet Cong in the chest and it said 'Home with the combat infantrymen for Vietnam.' And the bus totally got quiet.

"Then we went to the next station. We got out at midnight and they came in and started hustling us out the bus. I remember I had a fierce drill sergeant. He was black as coal. He had piercing eyes. And he came in and read us the riot act and we got off as fast as we could. So I got to my next training session but what happened was, I must have done something right because instead of it being what we called 11 Bravo, a straight-leg run, I was 11 Charlie, which was a mortar man. You had to do some math for fire direction. And so I became a member of that company which was the mortar company. And they always told us we were smarter than the combat infantrymen. And that's why we were there. So then I did my training. Went home for Christmas. Graduated. And then at the end of January, I had a week's leave.

"And then on February 7th, I flew over to Vietnam. And I got to Vietnam and I was attached to the 9th Infantry and this was in February 1970. And the month before, *Time Magazine* had put out a wonderful article that there were no combat troops south of Saigon. The 9th Infantry was located south of Saigon. So when I got there, that was one of the first things they told you was 'OK. I don't care what you read in the papers back home, you're going to be long-end privates and you're going to be south of Saigon. You're going to be on the plane and you're going to be fighting the VC and the enemy there.'

"So it was kind of an impressionable time when I got there because you get into what we call TDI, which is where you kind of get your assignments. And so I got to the 3rd brigade. They were in a town called Dien Luc, which was along a river and one of the first things we had to do was pull our perimeter guard. And so they blasted out and then right behind us was the medical center and the morgue.

"And so we heard the medevacs coming in and hear the guys screaming as they got off the helicopters wounded. And then Roger and I would walk down that ladder and walk that line again and check that gate to make sure that nobody had broke the lock. That was pretty much my first couple of days. And I ended up flying out to a base a little further down with the 9th Infantry and I became an infantryman. We had a mortar but we never carried it out in the field. It was in the swampy areas. We had a firebase Chamberlain, Gettysburg and Tan Ad was along. It was an old French along the canal. So what we conducted was a lot of rice paddies, swamps, what we called nipa palm and mangrove trees. We conducted search-and-destroy and ambushes out there.

"The other unique thing is that we became part of the Brown Water Navy, because 9th Infantry worked with the Navy up and down the river canals. So in my experience one of the things that I always felt when I talked with the guys is that I got to do a lot of things because I rode on tango boats, rode on landing craft. We had artillery barges, so we had all this equipment that we just really got to touch. We had air-cushioned vehicles. There was a vehicle that was went on water and that...and what they used to do was run over the VC with it. Try to crush them all.

"And Firebase Gettysburg was in the Plain of Reeds, which was along the Cambodian border and it was 'in country,' but the unique part about it was when the South China Sea went out, the water would just drain out and there would be mud and some occasional muck and some water.

"And when the South China Sea came in, the water would rise up to six inches. So this is like 40 or 50 miles 'in country.' And it was flat and they had some old French forts, so when the NVA and the VC used to come, it was one of their supply routes to Saigon. And so what we did was pull squad ambushes along the route canals for sampans and things like that.

"My first hot LZ, *(Landing Zone, a military term for an area where aircraft can land)* what we had was Eagle flights. Since we were in an area that was really wet, you only went out for three or four days because your feet would basically get rotten. Your toenails would fall off. You skin would peel. You never took off your boots. You only had your one change of clothes. You would try and go ambush them and lay down. Sometimes you'd be in water all the way up to your neck at the what we called the berm line, where the rice paddies were. But at this time it was free fire, since there were no villages around there at that time.

"I remember the first time I went into a hot LZ, we went in and I was sitting next to the machine gun. And didn't know that. The new guys, they didn't tell too much about. So as soon as we headed over to the hot LZ, tracers started coming out and the machine gunner next to me opened up and I about jumped out of my skin.

"First, off, it was so loud. The thing was these hot shells were going down the back of my neck and they were ejecting and I couldn't get out of the way. And so as we went in for the hot LZ, they kind of strafe rocketed it. We got down and we got in there and I was just really shaking in my boots. You know at that time we had a brief contact. They broke off contact. We had some equipment and some blood trails. Because mainly we would find blood trails. But that was my first experience off the helicopter. That was just... heart was pounding. I was 19 years old. You're starting to think like 'Oh, my God. I hope I get out of here. All I got to do in one year.' And so that was it.

"We did a lot of those little things. You know, there were some times when we had some pretty hairy firefights. But we never really hit any really big company-sized things. And the only times is really changed is when we went in Cambodia, on part of the Cambodian invasion. So what happened is just before Cambodia in May, when the ARVNs *(Army of the Republic of Vietnam, the South Vietnamese Army)* went in, we were what we were calling trip wires along the Cambodia border.

"And so at the Cambodia border, it's flat and level and so as Cambodia started to heat up, we'd see and feel the B-52 strikes. We could see them because at night it was totally dark. You'd sit there and all of a sudden, you'd just hear this rumble. You could actually feel the concussion. It was like a little earthquake. And you'd look off in the distance, and you'd just see boom, boom, boom, boom. The flashes.

"And about a week later, we got orders to go in and the unique thing about that is when we went in, as soon as you cross from Vietnam to Cambodia, you could tell from the air because

Vietnam looked like the moon. The whole border had been shelled and bombed, and it had all these craters. We went in to Cambodia and you'd see villages when you had hardly saw any.

"And so we went in and hit the LZ early and this part I remember all the time because it was just like out of the movie *Platoon*, we crash landed in this village. It's burning. Artillery's coming in. The gunships are strafing. People are shooting all over the place. Little figures are running around. They're shooting back at you.

"And jets are screaming overhead. We all come in and hit the deck. And we landed our 4 Eagle Flight in one area. And next, a B Company came in. And they hit a mine field. So the first guy jumped off the helicopter, got blew right back in. The next guy jumped off, blew right back in.

"They literally had to lift off again and get out of there. So we came in and we were going to go secure the village and blow up the bunker and our colonel gets out. And there was this moment of quiet. And we call him the 'Gray Ghost.' And he came out and literally he had .45 strapped across his waist. Pearl handles. And it was just like out of the movie. He started like, 'Goddamnit. This is war. This is what it's about. You guys are really going to enjoy this.' And we were just like, 'Oh, my God.' Because he was kind of a gung ho guy. And so we went and swept the villages.

"We got firefighter contacts. Booby-traps. You know, combat's kind of funny. It's not like John Wayne. You don't see somebody shoot back and forth. A lot of times, you're just ducking and fire is going over your head. We hit a lot of booby traps. There were a lot of times, I walked point and took the booby trap that didn't go off.

"And there was another time where we were in a pineapple plantation. Because this was all south and an old pineapple plantation had big rows about five or six feet apart and they'd have a canal. And I was carrying the radio at that time and there was about 30 of us strung out and all of a sudden there was like this boom. It was just like a sudden shock. And you're kind of, you're stunned. And all of a sudden the medic goes racing out and he said booby trap. And we're all kind of standing around and I got my 30-pound radio on with my gear and I'm kind of hunched over and we're looking and jumps into this canal and he pulls up Joe Donnelly, who's actually from Milwaukee and he said, 'Help me, guys. Help me.'

"And so basically I look around and the guy behind me was hit. Two guys in front of me were hit. And I was like totally unscathed so I dropped off my radio and a couple guys went in and we pulled him out of it. And he's kind of moaning and talking, he had a radio on. We unstrap him. We're all like 'Where does it hurt? Where does it hurt?'

"And the medic's going over him and all of a sudden somebody said, 'Well, there's blood coming out of his pant leg there.'

"So the medic says, 'Ok, let's see what he's got.' So he cut the pant leg open and all this blood gushed out and his artery was just flopping. 'Cuz he had all the meat on the inside of his leg blown off. And so then it was like they never really teach you in training to go through all this stuff.

"And so the medic was like, 'Grab his artery.'

"So me and another guy just put our hand and held his artery down while they tied it off. Got some medic bags on it. And he got him patched up and it was a booby trap. We didn't get any fire. It was broad daylight. And so we just kind of put him off in a helicopter. And that was it. But we had a lot of engagements like that. You'd be walking around and you'd hit a booby trap. You'd find a bunker complex. You'd blow up.

"You get into these little firefights. And the only difference is that Cambodia was like war because there were tanks. The artillery was gone. One night when the CIA would be working with Cambodia mercenaries, we were out probably about 200 meters from where the artillery pieces were. Because they'd have platoons just strung out as trip wires we were called. And then these Cambodian mercenaries came in with some special forces guy. They set up a little further away.

"And about half way through the night, they had a big ambush. Everything's blowing off. But for us, the hard part was we're all sleeping and all of a sudden, guys behind us starting firing heavy machine guns and so they're going through right on top of us. Three or four feet so we had to kind of crawl around. We couldn't do anything. We just kind of had to hug the ground there because all the stuff was going around. The dirt's flying and all that kind of stuff. The next day, you go out, you help pick up bodies. Clean up the body field. The battlefield and that.

"I was very lucky. I don't know why I was never hit. I always tell my wife God must have paid me back to marry her. I don't know. But I never was wounded, but there's plenty of times where I was with guys who were wounded.

"And after Cambodia, Nixon started pulling the troops out. So in August, my unit left. But I didn't have enough time to 'leave country,' as they called it. So from there I went to the 199th Infantry Light Brigade, which was around Saigon. And so I had a couple of days as they process you, took a bus and went up to the rubber plantations. So I had been in the swamps, had been in some of the mangroves and all that and then we had gone to the swamps.

"And then I went up to the rubber plantations. So I got there. And they had 4.2 mortars. But they had enough people. So when I got done, when I got there, they had attached me to as recon platoon. And I'm like, 'Ok. I've been in combat. This is OK.'

"They came over, checked me out, asked me questions. 'How do you handle this? How do you do your weapon?' Cleaned a weapon.

"I cleaned a weapon and showed it to them. Put my gear together and they're like, 'Ok, you can come with us.' So we go out, we got a mission. We're going to scoop and poop—basically go out and kind of recon. Get somewhere and wait.

"So we got up the first day. The next morning, we wake up and the guy picks up the radio and says we got to go back. And we're kind of going like 'What?' And so we ended up going back to the firebase.

"That unit went home. They were getting pulled out. So then I went back to Tan Son Nhat. Couple days later I went to the 25th Infantry Division. And so when I got to the 25th Infantry Division, which was the Bobcats, it was a mechanized unit. So I was a little delighted. Because at the time, it meant I wouldn't have to hump. But once I got to that unit, we got into a mortar platoon. And so there was six tracks and we were working with the Australians and the New Zealanders. They were building roads, and we would go out and do road security and we would fire the mortar which was a big, heavy mortar, 4.2. It's like a 55-caliber, 155, 105 round. And we would fire their support when we got into contact and we'd do the roads.

"Well, I got there and they said, 'Ok. You're the track driver.' And I said, 'It's not my MOS' *(Military Occupational Specialty).*

"They said, 'Don't worry about it. We'll show you what you have to do.'

"So I was still 19. I thought this is kind of exciting. And then I got into the track. And after a couple of weeks, I said, 'How did you make me the driver?'

"He said, 'When you roll over a mine, the driver gets killed. You're the new guy.'

"And at that point, I was like, 'Holy cow. I'm the new guy.'

"We had some contacts but we fired mainly support for the Australians and New Zealanders. And then after that, that unit went home. So, at this point, I'm in December. I'd been there almost...I'd been there 11 months. But I still didn't have enough time. Because Nixon had declared no more combat troops so every time a unit ended up getting casualties, they were taking guys from other units. Combat vets to go fill the slots.

"And so then I ended up going to what they called the First of the 21st, the Wolfhounds. And I went back to a straight-leg unit. So the next thing I know, I was out humping, assistant machine gunner. Walking point and do that. And that point was almost as dangerous as Cambodia because we ended up going in to an area that was supposing to be Vietnamization. And the ARVNs hadn't been patrolling. So we ran into numerous firefights. We ran into booby traps, a large bunker complex. Hospital complexes.

"At that point, there was one day that...it's ironic. It's how you feel when you get close to your date to be sent home. You feel confident. But then you start getting nervous. And I was lucky. I got in with a bunch of squadded guys. Nobody smoked. We were tight. We had been out in the field. But we weren't regulation and the captain always kind of punished us by putting us out on flank and stuff. But we were really good. 'Cuz out of the company, they had about 40 percent casualties. We had very few casualties and nobody killed.

"And so that was really good. But we had a couple of things where we ran into a bunker complex. One of the sergeants was looking for souvenirs and we had this big firefight because it was a training complex. He got shot by the cook. We ended up kind of having this firefight. There were two other casualties. We killed a couple of them.

"But on the other side of the ridge, the captain had come along and there was a big trail, a well-marked trail. And they had a marking post. And the marking post was a stump, and it has three rocks on it. That was their field of fire. And so he was radioing to us, you know we're going to go do this. What should we do?

"'Well, get ready to do this, guys. So you guys support us. And some of the old guys were calling the other old operators, saying don't do that. It's a marking place. And at the time, with the ARVDs doing Vietnamization, the ARVNs refused to move on. We walked in, huge ambush. We lost about 10 or 12 guys.

"After that, we were on the other... probably 1000 meters the other way. We had to put our gear on, and we actually had to go through the field of fire. And as the bullets are going over his head, we had to get in there and basically bail him out. And when I mean bail him out, is by set up the perimeter and that we had night choppers come in and evacuate.

"And that was like another scene form the movie *Apocalypse*, or no, *Platoon*, where the tracks had come through with tanks that night with the lights on and crashing thorough. And they crashed through. So we set up the perimeter and then basically, the next day we collected bodies and one of the things that we found was we had set up and they had taken their wounded NVA and they had put Claymore mines in tying the clippers through bandages to their hands. Most of them had wounds, and if they were woke up, they would just set off these Claymore mines and just cleaned out the middle of us. We didn't even find...They were like 10 feet away."

You saw a lot of intense action but there was one incident that had a major impact on your outlook on life.

"We were at the main base of the 25th, and we pulled berm duty. And what happens there is kids would sneak in the wire and steal the Claymore mines. And they would sell them to the VC. And they were doing it to earn money. At the time, we kind of knew it but we didn't know. And so on guard duty, you would fire warning shots over their head. That was the whole thing. You'd fire tear gas, you'd try this, you'd fire warning shots.

"I remember one time these kids just wouldn't quit. And so one time, I raised my weapon and I fired a shot. And I know I was damn close because the kids stopped. Well, all of them stopped. They all left that fence. At that moment, I felt like, 'What kind of person have I become to shoot kids?'

"And so I carry that. And that was in December. And I always feel that was one of the reasons I don't have children. Because I felt there was a well of anger that could be tapped at any time and I just didn't want to get into that. People always say, 'You're great with kids. You do well. You're a great teacher.' But I always carry that in the back of my...yeah, maybe I would have been, but I didn't want to take that chance after I came back home.

"When I came back home, I was very different. Probably was an angry young man for a while. And when I came back, one of the things I always talks about is I was met at the airport. I was 20 years old. So I had 401 days in Vietnam, so a little over 13 months. I came home. I flew in. Part of the thing that always stays with me is ...you got off the plane. You've been up maybe a couple of days. And then they give you all this money. And so when I went to San Francisco, one of the things, first off, they give you is 'Do you want to re-up?'

"And I'm like 'Oh, God. Just get us out of here.'

"And then the next thing that they have to tell you is you got to go at least four to five in a cab because the cab drivers will take you in town and there's people that are going to rob you of your money. They have prostitutes, pimps, all the bars. They tell you they're going to knock you out and take your money. And I had like $1,200. I had nowhere to spend money. So I got on a plane to...and I went to the United Airlines and they take all of your identification and when people talk about being treated badly, this was probably my episode."

"I got up into San Francisco, I went United Airlines. I said, 'I got to go to Milwaukee.' And so they're like looking at me and I'm a little guy, tanned, got my little uniform on, got my little kit bag along. And so I paid for the ticket and all I had was 50s and 100s. So the woman's going, 'Wait a minute.' And they get the manager over and the next thing you know, he's like, 'Well, where did you get this money?'

"Well, I'm like 'I just got out of the service and got paid. And he's like, 'Where's your orders?'"

"I'm like, 'I don't have any orders. I'm going home. I've been discharged.'

"And he says, 'Where's your ID card?'

"I said, 'I don't have one.'

"He said, 'Well, wait a minute here. Stand over here, young man,' because there's all these people standing here.'

"And I'm really starting to feel humiliated. Getting mad. He finally hems and haws and calls somebody and says, 'You know, you got a lot of big bills and you shouldn't have that. But I'll let you go this time.'

"So I got on the plane and I was just like, 'Jesus Christ.' And some other choice words. We're flying home and the stewardess asked me if I wanted a drink. And I said, 'Yeah, I'd love to have a beer.'

"She says, 'Do you have an ID?'

"I said, 'No'.

"And she says, 'You guys from Vietnam are all same. You all think you come home and you're supposed to get a beer and I can't give you one.'

And I remember tears welling up in my eyes and I just like of like cried. The couple next to me was going to buy me a beer and it was like, 'No that's alright.' So I got in a cab, went home.

"It was March 29th. It was colder than heck. Knocked on the door and there I was. I was so happy to be home. And the thing I remember was my poor mother, she hugged me and she said, 'Thank God, you're home. You haven't changed.

"I thought, 'You have no idea what I've been through. Bodies ...putting people in body bags, they used to make us dig graves. We'd go out and find a bunker complex, dig up the graves, find out how they died. Look for a weapon caches. You know, there are some things that you never tell that go to the grave, but you're going through dead bodies, putting your friends on. And for me, I kept going from unit to unit to unit. So I had some strong ties but really never had strong ties other than the PAT unit you came from in Wisconsin. You hung out with the guys from Wisconsin.

"And then when I came home, I went to UWM because there was a program, it's was called the Experimentation Program in Higher Education. And it was the original program that got me in and it was for low-income kids. And when I went into the program, before I went into the service, there was probably about 200 kids and there was like 10 white people...And that was me. Otherwise, they were all minorities. So I came back and they were all happy to see me.

"And I said, 'Ok. I'd like to reapply.'

"So went down to where the Chancellor's office is, where the offices for the program was, and got in there. And you sit around, and they can tell by the short hair. And I'm sitting there and there's all the college kids. And they weren't trying to be mean. But then I get in, I give them my records.

"They pull me up, 'We're really happy to see you.' And how's everything going?'

"And somebody always asks that question, 'Well, where were you?'

"You'd be like, 'Vietnam.'

"And it was like, 'What did you do there?'

"And by that time, it was like, 'We went there and we killed people. That was our job. That was how you stayed alive. They shoot you. You shoot them. That's what we're there for is to kill people.'

"And the whole room gets quiet. And then I said, 'Ok, I'll give you a call. And I'll come back.'

"They gave me a call.

"I went to UWM and I didn't last very long. There was an English class where they have a professor from New York. He did his story about the baby killers from Vietnam and I got into a big argument in the class with him. And then he threw me out of the class. And at that point I thought, 'OK, enough.'

"So I went back to who I was—a blue-collar worker. I went to A.O. Smith. I went and worked at A.O. Smith running punch presses, being a welder. And I did that. And I didn't get married 'til I was 45. One of the things I always think is, because of Vietnam. Because there was a time, and not that I'm proud of to admit it.

"And so I worked blue collar for a long time. And then I got into the bar business. By this time I was hanging around, drinking a lot, playing softball, doing everything you can. Because I was trying to live like 90 years old. Recently, we had a softball game with some guys I graduated with and I was taking to a guy named Mike.

"He said, 'Man, I remember when you came home. You know, you would call me up. You didn't have money. You'd say let's go out.' And it was like every night. Going to little joints around Milwaukee. I was working, living at home. I had a lot of money. Didn't save anything. I was living like the world never ended."

John got a Business Management degree from Cardinal Stritch University and has worked at Rockwell Automation as a customer service leadership team lead since 1997.

JOHN MALAN

JOHN MALAN WOULD BECOME a famous TV personality in Milwaukee. But while watching him update blizzard forecasts and regale them with outlooks of sunny summer weekends, many of his viewers didn't know Malan fought with an armored unit in Vietnam, where he had several close calls in battle.

John's young adult life started on a baseball diamond and wound up in the jungles of Southeast Asia.

"I was a big baseball player all my life," Malan said. "You know, I was short and fast. And I really could hit well. And went to, you know, a lot of championships, Little League, Connie Mack League. And in high school, I

went to Proviso East High School in Chicago. And I transferred
from a city school where I was on the varsity at the city school as a
freshman and went to Proviso East, which is a huge, huge school.

"And played...my first year I played on the sophomore team.
But then made varsity the next year. But I was really just pretty
good baseball player. I was fast, stole a lot of bases. I actually hit
more home runs than anybody else on the team. And they would
put me at short. They'd put me in center field if they'd need me.
They'd put me at third, second, you know. I was a pretty versatile
player. So I did play ball. Or I tried to play ball.

"I got a letter from Pittsburgh, the Pittsburgh Pirates, saying
they were having try-out camp in Muskegon, Michigan. And I was
in the Chicago area. And so I'm thinking colleges. You know,
should I put in for college? Because they were getting into the draft
for Vietnam so...but I said, nope, Pittsburgh wants me. I'm going to
try out. I tried out.

"Made the last cut. Started playing with the team and after two
weeks, slid into third base in a game and cracked a bone in my
ankle. So I got sent home, where I got this report in October to the
induction center, whatever they called it, and so I was in the wrong
draft. I should have been in the baseball draft. Which wasn't there
at the time.

"So I went to the doctor right way. Military doctor. Said, well,
I'm hurt. I can't even go back and play ball. Because they said after
you heal. And he said, 'Yeah, it's looks like seven to eight weeks of
healing.' This was like end of June, so that takes you through
August-September. Aw, you'll be good for October. And that was
it. So I went into the service."

What was it like at the Induction Center?

"Oh, it was unbelievable. I'm like, 'What is this?' And you grow up fast because, you know, back in those days, we didn't go with our parents for spring break to Florida. Nobody had any money. I lived on the South Side of Chicago. My parents, God bless them, they've passed, but my dad was a printer, a blue-collar worker. My mom, after the kids grew up, worked at the post office part-time. So, you know, it's...we never went anywhere.

"My first airplane ride was when I went in and they said you're going to Ft. Campbell, Kentucky. Get on that plane and go. So you start learning about the world when you get into the service.

"I originally got a draft notice. Then I went in as regular Army because I said, 'No, I don't want to. I'll do three years so I can pick my job. Because if you go for three instead of two, you can pick your job. So I picked my job and was in for three. But then when I eventually got sent to Vietnam, I went back and got an early out. Exactly how many months I don't know, but it was more than two years and a little less than three years."

Why sign for an extra year?

"Well, the reasoning was...I think it's a scam. No, it was...they tell you, they say, look, two years, you're probably a grunt infantry and you're probably going to go to Vietnam because infantry was going to Vietnam. And I said, 'I really don't want to do that.'

"The recruiter said, 'You can pick any job you want if you extend for another year.'

"And I said, 'It's a year.' Then I said, 'I could do something.' So I looked over things and said, 'Wow, I could go into armor and they're sending all of the armor people to Germany. And then you get to see Germany and Europe and wow, how cool is that?' So I said OK, signed up, but I wanted to go to armor school. So out of Ft. Campbell, Kentucky, after basic training, I'm in for three years. And they sent me to Ft. Knox, Kentucky for armor training.

"And I go through Armor training and then I go through non-commissioned officers' training and all that stuff. And I'm feeling good because everyone's going to Germany, right? And then I'm in the middle of non-commissioned officer training school and the president at the time says we need armor in Vietnam. So they sent the 11th Armored Cavalry, which I was training with. So I got my Vietnam orders as soon as I was done with school. Thinking I'm going to Germany, but I actually went the other way and wound up in Vietnam with the movement of all the armor there."

What was it like when you got to Vietnam?

"First of all, I never, prior to this, thought of being a weatherman. Thought of learning meteorology, OK? I get to Vietnam, I thought I had just entered hell. I'm talking weather now. Not the war. Not the fighting. It was like 93 with a dew point of 80. And it was hot. And when you first get there, they give you two weeks just working around the bases, filling sandbags, building bunkers, stuff like that, just to get you acclimated to the weather. They don't put you out in the war right away. Or assign you to a troop. They just want to get you acclimated...that's how bad it is. I mean, it's like—have you ever been to Florida in the summer in like August when it was just so hot, you could hardly breathe? That's what Vietnam was when I got there. Because I got there in the summer.

"I was sent to the 11th Armored Cav regiment. And I got assigned to drive an armored personnel unit for the headquarters unit. The headquarters unit goes out...they got out in battle with all the other tank artillery battalions which are like the 155-meter Howitzers. They look like a tank with a monster barrel, and these are really Howitzers shooting big rounds out there. And so I was... we sat...I sat...would always sit in the middle with our APCs, our Armored Personnel Carriers, and we would collect all the information and we would have all the radio conversation back to the base camps, if there were any fighters coming in to give us air support, which had special radios and things like that. So I drove the APC for that unit.

"But during the day they'd say, 'OK, we're going to have... we'd have to send out a patrol. We'll pick Malan, Joe, him, that, you know. Get on that tank or get on that APC and go out and do a patrol.' So we did that from inside our mobile base camp. But I... my job was to drive the headquarters APC.

"Day to day is bad enough. Day to day, you pull guard duty at night. You're sitting out there. I'm sure the Vietnam vets have told the story before...my first day out in the field...so you can think of a wagon train, the old Western movies. Essentially, that's what all our APCs and tanks were lined up as perimeter with your barrels pointing down so if you had a ground attack during the night, you could easily repel it.

"But you had to sit on your APC or your tank at night and pull guard duty. And so you'd take three hours and then you'd wake up the next guy and take your place, you go to bed. First day, very first day out there, no one tells me anything, we're in the middle of a jungle somewhere and you hear the little noises at night, you know, stuff like that. I get the Claymore mines set up out there and I start hearing this...this like choral arrangement of a word that begins with F and end with You. I know I can't say it, but I'm saying it sounds like F-You, F-You, F-You. And I'm like...so I get on the radio and I think we have...I think the enemy's out there and they're taunting me.

"And the guy in the headquarters said, 'What did they say? And I said, 'F-You' and he said, 'Aw, that's a lizard. He makes that kind of sound.' And there's an actual lizard in the jungle that makes that sound that you become, after the first day you get used to those sounds. But it is the most incredible sound at night because it's just all by itself out there. And usually it's eight or 10 of them in a group. So scared to death. First day out and then the guy calmly tells me on the radio, 'Meh, that's just a lizard.' True story. True story. Ask any of the Vietnam vets about the F-You lizard.

"Let me go a little further. Because I brought a little comedic relief into the...but every day, you know, in the daytime, you're always...your ears are perked when you're out in the field because they rocket you. So you'd be going from one tank to another, or pulling some duty, or maybe going in for some chow, you're making something for food or whatever, cleaning rifles, blah, blah, blah, and all of a sudden, you hear this pop in the distance and you know that it's a mortar. Or you hear a *whoosh* and you know it's a rocket and they're probably shooting them at your base camp. And then you haul into your tanks, or bunkers, or wherever you're at, and it takes about five or 10 seconds and then all of sudden, things are exploding around you everywhere. And so that our daytime problem or fear.

"At night, same thing, you're listening for sounds of movement in the jungle and you'll hear movement. You'll hear people out there. You'll actually hear sometimes whispers and people out there. And it's just nerve-wracking. And then all of a sudden you'll get some tracer rounds shot into the perimeters. And then all of a sudden, a big battle ensues. It just might be a couple of guys sniping at you out there. Stuff like that. But that's your nighttime regimen. And this doesn't go on every day but it goes on most days."

How did you adjust to that?

"I don't know. I don't know.

"There were a couple of bad battles. But my worst. I think it was November of 1969, it's a blur. We went...we were getting ready to go close to Cambodia and we went past the farthest, northern-most base. After you get past that basecamp, it's tough. There's a lot of NVA, North Vietnamese Army, Viet Cong, and you're right by the Cambodian border where the Ho Chi Minh trail was. And it's active. Active, active, active.

"So we pull up and we're about maybe 10 miles from the Ho Chi Minh Trail. At the border of Cambodia. And we pull up and we were to establish a base camp here. And we did, just like we normally do. Put out the Claymores and everything. The first night, we didn't know it but we set up kind of right over an underground Viet Cong base camp. So they were underground below us, where we set up.

"And all of a sudden, about 2 in the morning, they start coming at us. And they came out as a wave of troops, you know?

And a couple of guys came out of the ground; they were throwing the satchels, which are the bombs. They're what they call satchel charges, which is a homemade kind of a bomb. And so we had people inside the perimeter and a bunch of people outside the perimeter. And so we're shooting like crazy. I mean that jungle was lit up.

"But sometimes you'd be like this and you'd have a firearm, and you go boom, like that. So that was a crazy battle. That was the worst battle of...I've had a few...but that I think, that November I think it was 1969, I think it was the worst. We had many tanks blown up, people killed, many injured, including myself. But my injury was, you know, not that bad. Just a shrapnel, just a piece of shrapnel, through the knee."

You also lost a special piece of equipment in that battle,
a bayonet your dad gave you that he used in combat during
World War II.

"Yes. They sent it to me—I couldn't take it through because we could take only Army-issued stuff when you're in the Army. But they sent it to me. It wasn't like it is today. You could send stuff actually. So I had it there pretty much my whole tour and that battle that we had just talked about, our trailer—the APCs would carry a small trailer, you'd put all your personnel belongings in there and your extra stuff and maybe some ammo, an extra...all your personal stuff like clothes—took a direct rocket hit and it was burnt down to the ground. And so I lost everything. I lost all my clothes. I lost my dad's bayonet. What else did I lose? Everything I owned at the time.

"But that was my worst battle. But I had some bad ones going into...we went into Cambodia, then the second year. The end of my first year. That was tough, too. Cambodia, they owned Cambodia. And that's why we were going in there. I think it was President Nixon, at the time. Said let's go to Cambodia and get them out of there. And so we had some...I remember, we were about to go in... it was pre-dawn and our whole line of tanks, armored personnel carriers, were ready to go into Cambodia and they said they were going to do a bombing first.

"So these B-52s come over and we know, we're being told they're about to strike and they strike like five miles in front of us with these 500-pound bombs. And I mean, you're sitting in your tank like this, and you know the bomb, where we're at five miles away, makes the tank jump up and down. And the APC jump up and down. We're like, 'Whoa!'

"When we went in, we had to make sure we were careful because of the craters. The craters left by a 500-point bomb about the size of this room. And almost this deep. So like 10 feet deep and the size of this room."

Reception when you got home?

"If it wasn't family and close, close friends, no one liked you. It was like 'Hey, I'm a war hero.' 'No, you're not. You're a baby killer.' And I'm like...and I was there like two years, so I came home for a 30-day break in between and went back and went into aviation, so I was a crew chief on a helicopter, sat behind the gun and that kind of thing. I never saw an atrocity in Vietnam. Never. Ever.

"Matter of fact, we were always good to the indigenous folks. We were always giving them our C-rations and doing things like that and candy to the kids, which they loved from our C-ration packs and stuff like that. And we would get freaked...when we were out in the field, I think they called them SP packs and they were just boxes filled with candy and cigarettes and whatever, you know for recreational use because we're out in the field and you couldn't go down to the 7-11 every night, right? So we'd give 50 percent of that away to the young kids that would come around our tanks and stuff. But home? Not a good feeling.

"You know, now...now, after 9/11, I can say I'm a Vietnam vet with pride, you know. But back then, you really didn't speak about it. You really didn't wear your flag. You know, the only people who would wear the field jackets, the Army field jackets, were the protesters back then. If I wore a field jacket to proudly display that I was an actual soldier, people would give me bad looks, dirty looks, say, 'What happened over there? Why were you killing babies?' Seems like it was killing babies all the time. I don't know what you're talking about. It was that one picture. With napalm. Very famous and we all know it, you know. That and My Lai are the two things that, I think, turned everybody against...but it wasn't the soldiers. We were asked to serve and we served. Period. End of sentence. If there were some problems, it certainly wasn't because of us.

"I grew up a lot. And I mean...I don't know, I say it's part war and part just military. I mean I went into basic training, get there first day, we're all lined up with our duffel bags, you know, at Ft. Campbell, Kentucky. And no one told me this, you know again, any advice. I was from Chicago and this big drill sergeant comes out and he goes, 'I want everybody from Chicago in the front.' So I'm thinking, 'I'm special.' So me and about eight other guys pick up our duffel bags, we cut through and he's, 'OK, drop and give me 50 and I'll tell you when I'm not going to torture you because I'm going to torture you gangsters from Chicago to make sure you're...you're going to do the right thing.'

"So we got tortured for a couple of weeks until we got to know everybody. And they backed off of us. But we were treated like gangster kids, you know? You learned certain things but you grew up fast. And you learned authority and you learned responsibility and you learned camaraderie. And I'll tell you the greatest thing— and I played on sports teams—and still play on sports teams, you...there's always one hero at the end that hits the game-winning homer. In war, unless you're a Medal of Honor winner, you have your buddy's back. Everyone's a teammate. It's team, team, team. And you hear that thing about you have my back, I'll have yours, like I'll always have my buddy's back. I won't ever leave one of us behind, that's all true. And that's the greatest camaraderie—the greatest camaraderie—you can ever find on this planet.

"I've done a couple talks at the VA, the Veterans Hospital, about PTSD, Post Traumatic Stress Disorder. And they ask me, 'Well, you were kind of successful in your life and got out of two years in Vietnam. And you obviously don't have PTSD.' I don't think I do anyway. They ask me, 'What was different with you than say somebody else,' because I've seen people blown up and I've seen burnt bodies, and I've had to put them into a body bag and I've had tracers flying past my head and stuff. I don't know. You know, it's really...a psychologist once came up to me after one of my talks, and I talked about how I'm just like all you guys who have PTSD.

"I have good family. Or I've had a groups of friends in the neighborhood and I had a pretty decent upbringing. Nothing special. But, you know, war can be so horrid and horrific. I think there's just a part of you that can't deal with it. I don't know what it's called. It's in your body somewhere, in your brain somewhere, in your make-up somewhere. And me...whatever is in me, filtered it and I didn't...and to me it was like when I left on my last plane, let me tell you, three or two weeks before going to leave, right? To go home forever and you don't have to have war with you any-more, are the most nerve-wracking days of your life. I mean you're hiding behind...you don't even go out of your tank to go to the bathroom, like you just go around the corner and just like, 'Hey, I'm not going out there to, you know. And it's just ... it's just a horrendous feeling.

"So why, when I left, did I treat it like Fantasy Island? Like the little guy, you know 'da plane, da plane?' I just left it back there. I just left it there. Why? I didn't, there was no cognizant feeling that I left it behind. I just did. I was just happy to get out of there. I don't know and I'm glad, you know, God bless that I didn't have that kind of situation.

"I'm proud to have served. Still have a group of buddies that I contact here and there, you know? All over the United States, from New Jersey, Cleveland, best friend through the war was Cleveland. My closest friend, Johnny Jones, was from Houston and he died in that same battle we were talking about. His tank took a direct hit and it exploded; it burned down and his body was burned pretty bad. And I've been to the Vietnam Memorial in Washington and I looked him up. We left some flowers there."

John went onto a successful TV career and became a Milwaukee icon as chief meteorologist at WISN TV and WTMJ TV.

LUPE RENTERIA

Lupe Renteria's biggest initial challenge in Vietnam was finding shoes that fit him.

"But the thing that I remember most is that I took a size 5 extra-wide boot," Renteria recalled. "So I couldn't get boots. So I wore tennis shoes all through boot camp. And even in Vietnam my first six months, I wore leather boots and everybody else had jungle boots. So I had the jungle rot."

Renteria survived his battles in the jungle but like many Vietnam vets, faced more battles when he got home.

"When I first got to Vietnam, I guess you go back and think about what you saw in sixth-grade geography.

"And you say 'Wow, people do live like this?' So beside the smells and the humidity and all that, it's an eye-opener for sure. And then you don't know what's going to happen from there.

"The first few days, you're still in your regular military stuff before you get your jungle clothes and stuff. But I always make sure that I tell people that it was important within those first couple days to, because as important as it was in sighting your rifle, you had to see a man of the cloth. Except those Jewish kids, they got to wait for the rabbi. I'm Catholic and we ended up with a Protestant minister. And basically they begin to tell you, 'Boys, you're going to be called upon to do some stuff over here and not morals you came from and all that if you will. So I tell people in short, basically the Fifth Commandment doesn't count any more.' And you say, 'Oh, wait a minute, man. That's not what they taught me.' But you know, that's war.

"Initially, I was a basic grunt infantryman and from November to May, I became a squad leader. And it was in the high corps most of the time, north of the DMZ where we had spent 79 days with seeing civilians, saw civilians three times, took two showers. But everybody stunk. People don't realize it was a big camping trip. I spent my first 10 months living on the ground or below the ground.

"I got wounded. Coming out of Khe Sanh on patrol. June 9th. In the face. These dark marks here, a hole here and another hole here *(points to different spots on his face)*. Grace of God and a lot of good luck. Very fortunate.

"We lost a bunch of guys. And I killed and captured some people in September and got a Bronze Star for that. Purple Heart for being wounded. And I have a Navy Achievement Medal because basically none of my guys got killed and we did things the right way, if you will. Yeah, so that's three personal decorations. But what I'm proudest of is I had been 20 years old. And I was a sergeant in the Marine Corps, at 20, only 22 months in the Marine Corps.

"Our battalion, I was with Foxtrots 2nd Battalion, First Marines, and we had 18 major battles that we were in but it was nothing. Sometimes...I recall getting ambushed five times in the same day. And it's not a major battle. Ambushes was...could be a daily occurrence. We were in the DMZ and it was not a safe place to be so we didn't run patrol outside the wire. You know, you're living with the rats, in the holes and stuff. And that was it.

"You know, we'd set up at nighttime, we were south, it was very white sand. You could go out at night and think you were in the Northwoods because of the pine trees right along the gulf there. And then all that white sand. And you'd think you were in northern Wisconsin walking in the winter wonderland, if you will. There was a leper colony right there and that stunk pretty much. Yeah, yeah, down there was VC and booby traps and up north was the NVA, the hardcore regulars up there with uniforms."

How were things for you after you came home?

"It changes you in the fact that you're old quick. You know, you come home at 20, you're a lot older than everybody else. Worrying about going to a dance or what to do. I would focus that it was a higher degree of maturity, if you will. You learn some strong leadership qualities, following orders type of thing. It definitely has it positives. I don't look at it....You know, the negative was nobody liked us.

"Well, when you think about the 60s and the war. But a great coming-home story is you know, they had warned us. We had flown Da Nang to Japan, to Okinawa, Okinawa in Japan, and you had to get everything re-done in Okinawa because you know you lost like 20-some pounds. We made a quick stop in Kyoto, then Travis Air Force base, and you go through a quick customs there. And it was $50 to get to the San Francisco Airport so five guys get in and see our bags put in the back of the trunk and they warned us, 'Get in and get out,' when I was going through camp. They don't like vets. So I go into United, and my seabag, and my little gym bag and I see this guy on the telephone, who said, 'Can I help you?' and I said "Sure, I want the first plane going to or going near Milwaukee, Wisconsin.'

"He says, 'Are you a Marine coming back from Vietnam?'

"Yes, sir.'

"And he says, 'Your baggage won't get there, but you will.'

"What?"

"He gets back on the phone, grabs my seabags, grabs my ditty bag, and puts me in a golf cart. Drives me around San Francisco Airport. I go on a plane. First seat. First row. I thought, 'Wow. This is very cool.'

"So we're flying and flying and they get on and say we'll be landing at O'Hare International Airport next. And I'm thinking 'What? Man, that's 90 miles, you know.' And you have a lot of money. Well, at that time, it was $1,300 you got because we had no place to spend money over there. You know you got $20 for a month because you didn't see anybody, you know, or near anything. So I thought I could take a cab home. I got relations in Chicago, I could call them, take the bus or I could sleep at the airport.

"So the plane stops and all this stuff is running through your mind and because you're used to thinking like that all the time. And the door comes flying open and a guy comes in and says, 'Are you the Marine coming back from Vietnam?'

"I said, 'Yes, sir.'

"He said, 'Come with me.' He takes me down the steps right there by the door, puts me in a station wagon and drives me around O'Hare to a waiting flight. That was really cool. I get to the taxi stand and I said to the guy, 'Hey, 1224 N. 32nd St.,' where I live and he says, 'Aw man, I don't want to drive all the way to the north side for one person.'

"'Wait a minute. I got airlines waiting on me hand and foot and I get pimped by a cab driver?'

"So we waited. Anyway, I made it home.

"And you want to talk to somebody. You haven't talked to anybody but military people for a whole 13 months. And him and the other person are carrying on a conversation and I thought, 'Hey, talk to me. You know where I was?' It was interesting.

"I think I got home on a Thursday. Friday the boys stopped by. And Saturday, 'Hey, let's go party.' 'Nah, I don't think so.' 'Yeah, yeah, yeah, you gotta go. A lot of women. A lot of drink.' So I went. I was in this kitchen. These north-side flats and I'm in the kitchen. And these two young guys come in and—young guys are probably 18 and I'm 20—and they say, 'Hey, where do you work?' And I said, 'I don't.' And they said, 'Where do you go to school?' I said, 'I don't.' And they take off. And I said, 'Talk to me!'

"So another guy comes in and he's in a coat and tie so I'm saying he's a little bit older, 20, maybe 22 or something. He's in a coat and tie. And he said, 'Where do you work?' or 'Where do you go to school?'" And I said, "I don't." And he said, 'Oh, how do you like the Army?' And I said, "I'm in the Marine Corps." And he said, "OHHHH, Marine Corps." and he starts doing this.

To this day, I have no idea what look I gave this guy but he just went, 'Sorry.' He's like, 'Sorry, man.'

"I said, 'Nah, that's OK., I just back from Vietnam on Thursday.'

"He says, 'Two days ago?'

"And I said, 'Yeah.'

"And then he—and then a pretty lady comes walking through and I looked at her.

"And he said, 'Oh, you know her?'

"And I said, 'No.'

"And he said, 'C'mon, I'll introduce you.'

"And I said, Nah, that's okay.'

"You don't know how to act anymore. So anyways he introduces me and she's very pretty and very nice...'Oh, nice to meet you.'

"And he says, 'Lupe just back from Vietnam.'

"And she says, 'Oh, really?'

"I says, 'Yeah.'

"She says, 'Ever kill anybody?'

"I says, 'Yeah.'

"And she says, 'You sadistic bastard.'

"As big as I could make my ring finger, as loud as I could scream, Sly and the Family Stone was playing in the background and all my buddies were in there, and I just screamed. I screamed, 'The first person I killed was a bitch about your age.'

"The place goes silent. My buddies come up and said, 'Let's get out of here.' And I was home for 20-some days and that was day three. And I spent the rest of the time denying being over there.

"I was...I was less fortunate. I still had 30 months to do. So on December 1, '69, when I had to report to Camp Pendleton. It took 82 of us—all fresh back from Vietnam—and made us one guard detachment. Camp Pendleton. Main side, they call it. That was probably the best we could do for Post-Traumatic Stress, you know, because you're with your peers.

"And I've seen a thousand times more action than some of these guys but there are guys that saw 10,000 times much more action than me. So you would tell these stories—at times horrific— we could tell each other things. But then you see these guys that you know have gotten out, still had time to do, go sent back after being wounded and everything. You see these guys in the showers "Man, put some clothes on." Because you know, that shrapnel just rips your body apart, scars and stuff. But you tell these stories and then you laugh until you cry."

Lupe fought in Vietnam for the U.S. Marines from November 1967 until December 1968.

273

FERNANDO RODRIGUEZ

Fernando Rodriguez joined the Marines to prove a point, to his teachers at a Milwaukee area high school.

"In 11th grade, I decided that I needed to go to summer school because I needed to prepare for some courses I would need for college," Rodriguez said. "I would have been the first one in my family to go to college. And I went to summer school at Bay View and when I got there, they put me in a Home Ec class and another class that I don't remember.

"I went to the counselors and finally ended up with the principal and said, 'I didn't come to summer school to take these classes. I came so I could prepare for some college courses.'

"And the principal said, 'Well, this is what we got for you. This is where we can fit you in. And this is what you have to take.'

"And I was like, 'I don't have to take those.'

"'What do you mean you don't have to take them?'

A little bit of back and forth there.

"And I said, 'Well, I'll show you.'

"And I went and joined the Marine Corps. So boy, I really showed him, eh?"

How tough was it?

"Well, a bunch of other people did it. So I figured I'm no different than them. I can do it just like they can. To me, it wasn't that much of a transition from being in a home where you have a lot of children. I have two brothers and five sisters. You had the duties and when your father tells you to do something, you do it. You're supposed to do what your mother tells you, but you don't do what your mother tells you. If your father tells you, then you do it. Plus you're growing up in the '50s. I learned that I had to take...I had to do what I had to do with what they were telling me to do."

Tell us about basic training.

"I'm what they call a Hollywood Marine. Do I look like a movie star? And Hollywood is the...they call the Marines that go to boot camp in San Diego. Call us Hollywood Marines. Looking back on it, I thought it was...I think it's something that a lot of young men should be doing. Especially Marine Corps boot camp.

"Yeah, it was tough. It was in during the time when they still disciplined you, I guess that's what they call it. But they were actually hitting and doing a whole lot of stuff to you that probably be illegal now. It was tough but the drill instructors, they expected a lot from you. They made you work at it but it's not like they wanted you to do 10 pull-ups the first day you were there. So they work you up. First, they build you all the way down and then they start building you all the way up. And I don't know if you've heard it from Marines before, but you're not a Marine until you actually graduate from boot camp, so we were called everything but Marines until after graduation.

"After boot camp, when you graduate, you get your Eagle Golden Anchor, which is what you work to get in boot camp. Because once you earn that, it can never be taken away. After that of course, I got a 30-day pass to go home. We came back, went through some advanced what they called Battalion Infantry Training, or BITS. And that was 30 days. And then I was shipped over to Vietnam. Flew over on Japanese Air Lines.

"My first recollection is the blast of heat coming at you. And then I remember that one of the guys got off the plane and he got down to the bottom of the stairs, he collapsed. And found out later that it was heat stroke. It was that bad. I mean, that's how hot it was. And I think they sent him back on the same plane. Won't say they did, you know, but that was the story we told that they sent him back on the same plane.

"So from there, we were marched up to a tent and to me, being in boot camp and being a Marine and always having your rifle with you, even when you went to sleep. You took your rifle to bed. And this is in boot camp. It was strange getting off of the airplane into a war zone and not having a weapon.

"When we got to that tent, we were told we were secure. But later on that evening, we started getting mortar rounds. And what I did, I ripped out one of the legs from the cots that they had there, the fold-out cots. So that was my weapon. Of course, none of the mortars came close to us, but that's how the training kicked in. A few others did the same thing. Some just waited around like nothing was happening and nothing did happen.

"The next morning, we were taken out to...to the... well, actually it was a big rock with a big field in front of it. And we were dropped out. There were five of us. And we were told to wait there. And someone would come and pick us up. And again this was a thing to me right away that, what are we doing out here? We're in the middle of a war zone. And we don't have any weapons with us. So we started looking around for rocks, every-thing, anything, just to have in our hands.

"And a little bit later a helicopter dropped down in the field and took us away. One of the recollections of that field also was... was seeing some of the people working in the field. And it took me back to the days of growing up in the migrant stream here in Wisconsin. And it looked like our families and our friends. What we used to do. Stoop labor.

"My job was to provide company artillery with the mortar, so we carried the M-60 mortar out in the field with company-sized strength. And when we settled in for the night, when we formed the perimeter, our crew captain would...he wasn't a captain but that's what we called him. The crew captain would select the place where we would dig the mortar pit and we would set the mortar in. And then the job of...we had the tripod carrier, he carried the tripod and the two.

"And we had the base plane. So when they sat in, they sat in together. And my job was to disperse the other men—the ammo carriers they called us, and you worked your way up—to different locations in the perimeter and pick up all the mortar rounds because every Marine had to carry a mortar round or two in his pack.

"Because we could only carry so many. And I believe I was carrying eight high explosives and two illumination rounds, or Willie Peters, or white phosphorous rounds. So we would have them if we did need them that night. And we did need them. But most of the time, when we saw them, we got fired upon at least once or twice throughout the night. Nothing real damaging and everything but the first thing for the mortar crew to do is determine where the fire is coming from and throw out an illumination round that way.

"I was wounded a little later on in my tour. We had travelled all night. To me, I mean I know now that it was but at that time, they told us it was Ho Chi Minh's birthday. It was May 3rd when I got hit. 1969. And so we travelled all night and set up in a village. And of course, the village was supposed to be friendly because our mission was to secure the food supply for the village and keep it away from the hands of the enemy at that time.

"So we got into the village, and the captain sent out a search-and-destroy force and the rest of us surrounded the village or put up a perimeter up around the village. And because some of the people were out doing the search and destroy, the mortar team had to send the demo carriers to the perimeter and me and a...my partners were there maybe about five or 10 minutes when we saw two people coming in on our location and we had to wave them in and they had their hands up so they were...they were surrendering. So of course we had to talk them in and walk them in and when we got down, we were...you know, we secured them and we started to search them. Little things can give them away to you as the one doing the searches that they may or may not be friendly.

"In this case, I...one of the guys had a Zippo lighter and it had the name of a Marine on there. So we knew most likely he didn't ...the Marine didn't give it to him. So we kind of treated him as not friendly. And when I was searching the other one, my partners, of course, was watching me in the back here and I had my rifle in my left hand. And I kind of bent over with my right hand to do searching and at the hand up here, all of a sudden I just felt my rifle drop from my hand.

"They say that your life spins in front of your eyes, goes by in seconds. It seemed like everything was like slow motion until I hit the ground. And it came back real fast and the first thing I said was 'my rifle.' A Marine without his rifle is not a Marine. So I was trying to get my rifle back and couldn't move my arm. And then I heard some shots and my partner shot one of the prisoners. And then the other one laid back down because he was going for my rifle. That's what he told me afterwards.

"It's like something that happens in...in 30 seconds that just stays with you forever. At the same time that I got hit, the villagers were friendly. The villagers were supposed to be friendly. So we had...we allowed them to move around and there was a couple of them watching us doing the searching the prisoners.

"And I always think that the bullet that went through me is the one that hit the lady sitting there watching this going on. And it hit her in the head. When I fell, she fell on top of me. And I have my arm that won't move with her on top of it which makes it even harder. And I have her brains falling on me. And all I could do with my right hand was try to take them out and try to get them away but I guess as I was doing that, I was putting like more blood all over me. And I was finally able to push her off to the side.

"And I remember some guy getting up and saying 'I'll get them.' You know, John Wayne-style. And I just kept saying, 'No, stay back,' because by this time we are getting fired on. There were more rounds coming into the...into our perimeter. And I tied my own tourniquet. We were taught this at boot camp. If it was just coming out, don't worry about the tourniquet. Put pressure on it. If it's squirting out, tourniquet. So I remember I took my white belt out–I still carry it–and tied it around me. And until the corpsman got to me and was able to do what he could do there and I was medevac'd out in a helicopter.

"I was hit in the upper arm, here. I was out of action. That was what Forest Gump called the million-dollar wound. And like Forest Gump, I never saw the million dollars, but I did spend some time in Japan. Well, the night first, the medevac unit there and they patched me up but they didn't sew me up. They stopped the bleeding and had a lot of bandages on me. And after about three or four days in there, I was sent to Japan.

"And it was in Japan where there treated me a little bit more and I was not able to move my hand at the time. And after a couple of weeks, they decided to ship me stateside. So they shipped me to the Great Lakes, via Alaska. So from the jungles to Alaska to the Great Lakes Naval Hospital."

When you came back to the States, how were you received?

"I was medevaced out, which makes me a little bit different from the guys that were coming back, one by one. Like I said, I was in the medevac transport plane and that stopped in Alaska. And from there we went to...it was in Chicago, there was an airfield in Chicago and then we were put on busses and shipped right to Great Lakes. All in the middle of the night. So I didn't really see civilians until I got to Great Lakes Hospital. So I don't have those bad experiences that other vets talk about, coming back and being treated bad by the public.

"After the war, In my whole 20s I really didn't know where I was going. Tried a lot of different things. And again, not until I was 30 did I stop to think about getting a family and, you know, being a normal, a normal workingman, I guess. The VA at the time has rated me with Post Traumatic Stress Disorder through all this my physical wounds and the wounds that you can't see because of Agent Orange.

"I started working with other veterans. I started out as a volunteer in '80, '81. I was 30 years old. I had started seeing...I had started seeing some of the old guys in the neighborhood that we grew up with and found out that a lot of them had the same shared experience. They finished high school and they went into the military. Or they got drafted. I went in a year ahead of them. So when I was coming out, my graduating class was just graduating. And I was already back. I was back here, I was still 18. I was a disabled veteran. And didn't know...I didn't know that I had PTSD. Because they hadn't determined or diagnosed what it was at that time. Didn't have a name for it.

"My work started out with working with homeless veterans. Well, working with some of the veteran's service organizations and from there it led me to homeless veterans. And working with homeless veterans, you start getting into the underserved population of veterans and you start getting into the Veterans Incarcerated. And when we say Veterans Incarcerated, it's a Vietnam veterans thing. We say 'Veterans Incarcerated' because we figure that you were a veteran first and then you were incarcerated. And people with less than honorable discharges.

"At first it was a little depressing because you hear the stories and you're saying, 'Damn, that's what I went through.' Or, 'I remember that. That happened to me.' And then after a while, it became more of a therapeutic thing for me. It was good to hear that sometimes. Because I know I wasn't alone. Sometimes the stories were a little rough but my story's just as rough, you know?

"And I did that almost through the end. I think I helped a lot of veterans get their benefits. I think I helped veterans that thought that they were never receive benefits because of an other-than-honorable discharge, get their discharges. I helped a lot of people with other-than-honorable discharges get them upgraded to a more favorable discharge. Helped a lot of people retrieve their records and their medals which is always rewarding. For them and for me."

When he returned to Milwaukee, Fernando began a long and distinguished career at the Wisconsin Department of Veterans Affairs, assisting homeless vets and helping many vets get their benefits.

RUBY SCHEUING

RUBY SCHEUING WAS PART of a M.A.S.H. unit as a U.S. Army nurse. She cared for countless wounded soldiers. The Army had a major impact on Ruby's life. She met a major, Gary, from the Corps of Engineers, the man who would become her husband. It all happened pretty quickly.

"I graduated from nursing school and then I knew that I wanted to do something," Scheuing said. "I just didn't know what I wanted to do. I wanted to go somewhere and I didn't know where I wanted to go. And so I walked into the Army recruiter and said, 'I want to go to Vietnam' and he said 'You have a guaranteed assignment.' So I signed on the dotted line and my mom was so angry at me. She said, 'Well, you can't do that.' I can and I did.

"Then I went to Ft. Sam Houston for basic and then my first actual duty station was at William Beaumont in El Paso. And then I met my husband in El Paso before we went and he was taking a company over, of engineers and he was...took a company over about two weeks ahead of me and then I came after that."

"We got married during the Tet Offensive. I was a convert to Catholicism and I stay in touch with the chaplain that married us. So it's...we've always stayed in touch with him and we also had Father Sheehan. He came from the battlefields to our wedding in his fatigues and said a few words. Blessed us and then he left. But the priest that married us was an Air Force Chaplain."

Were you and the other doctors and nurses swamped during the Tet?

"Well, we weren't busy...I mean, weren't busy 24/7. But then when the push came and you started hearing choppers coming in and then everybody was just on their game. And so the corpsmen would go out to the choppers, bring the casualties in; they'd be triaged. And then I was a post-op nurse. So I didn't take care of the patients until they actually came out of surgery.

"And I think one of the things that I always...you could see them visibly when they came out of anesthesia, was count extremities. And then their first question was always 'Where's Joe?' 'Where's my buddy?' And we did not keep them long in our hospital because it was a Mobile Army Surgical Hospital, a M.A.S.H. unit. They just treated them and as soon as they were stabilized, they were moved to Saigon, and then out of country. And those that could just be treated medically and then just sent back to duty, there were those also. So we didn't keep any of them very long in the hospital because it was a M.A.S.H. And so they were moved on."

Did you do a lot of post-op handholding?

"Yes, yes. And I think just being there helped a lot. And seeing a woman helped them a lot. Just to hold their hand. You know, and then they would...they were so strong. These guys were just...you know, they would come out of this and they'd just enjoy talking, you know, as they came out of the anesthesia. And you never got a chance to get to know them because they were just moved...moved back. Sent on to another Evac hospital.

"Our helipad was maybe a football length away from the hospital. So every time that came in, all that dirt. So infection was a big thing. A lot of our major wounds were left to heal on the outside, from the inside out and so they were left open. And so there were...there were things we did that we didn't do stateside. You started IVs and you did those kind of things.

"And it was...it was an experience that you...I came home with a good feeling because it was happening whether I was there or not. And I felt that I was able to help many of these young soldiers in spite of their injuries. So I think it was reassurance, was a big thing and just...obviously just taking care of them post-operatively. But we didn't have them there that long.

"We had one experience where our hospital moved out in November—the M.A.S.H. unit moved—and then we went to an Evac hospital, the 71st Evac, and we had one time where there were mortars and we were under fire and it was just getting all of the patients out of the floor and there was one particular soldier I remember because he had just had a new trach and you have to suction new trachs. And we didn't have power. And so he was on his own, just expectorating this mucus from his trach, and he...he did it.

"Sometimes the options were few and far between and that's what he had to do. And he did it. They were just tough. On the other hand, I had a colonel who pulled rank on me, that he had chest tubes, that he had three and you have to cough and deep breathe with these chest tubes, because otherwise you just get pneumonia and die. And so, you know, we support them and hold them so the coughing is easier. And he told me that he was NOT going to be coughing and deep breathing and I was not going to be telling him what to do. And so I said, 'Well, here's your choices. If you don't do what I say, you're going to die from pneumonia. Or you can do what I say and we can get these chest tubes out and everything will be much better because you won't have all that drainage in your chest.' So he listened to me.

"And I worked with a staff that was pretty well set. There were a couple of nurses there that were going into their second year. And that's waaaay too long. But they had chosen to do that.

"I don't remember any individuals, but they were all characters. They just...they were happy that people were there just to be with them and as they suffered from their injuries. But they were just...they were just tough guys. I mean, they didn't...so many times, it just seems like your patients, they're whining about something. These guys don't whine. They were just tough. They were just tough. And they were just happy for you to just hold their hand and be there with them.

"I was 2nd lieutenant. My husband was a major and wouldn't marry me until I was promoted to 1st lieutenant. So I was by the time we got married.

"I got my dress in Singapore. The girls, the bridesmaids got their dresses form the Sears catalog. So we were young. We had everything. And they carried our reception on for a month after we left. People didn't even know who we were anymore and they were still having a drink on us. So that's a happy ending in that it worked out that well.

"We actually, we got married and from the reception, we got on a plane with a Vietnamese general that was flying to Saigon. And we flew right after the wedding, right to Saigon. We had to wait a couple of days because they were fighting in the streets in Tan Son Nhat. And so...and then we got out and yes, we were able to take a 41-day honeymoon, getting off and on planes and finally ended up at my parents' place in Illinois, who had never met him. And then we went on to Brooklyn, NY, for his parents, who had never met me. And then on to our duty station in Ft. Lee, Virginia. And then we had two of our children born there. And then our third was born in Korea.

"My husband planned all of this. I did nothing. He planned it all as well as being the...a combat engineer with the 299th Engineer Battalion. He was the operations officer. And so he was a very busy man."

On their honeymoon, Gary and Ruby travelled through Asia, Hawaii and San Francisco. Ruby became a stay-at-home mom for the couple's three children. Gary passed away in 2008.

WILLIAM SIMS

WILLIAM SIMS WAS wounded in action during one of many firefights he experienced in Vietnam. But his closest brush with death happened before he fired a shot when he first reported to the front lines after being shipped out from Hawaii.

"I was standing in a line and the sergeant came up to me and asked, 'What's wrong with you?' and I said, 'I don't know.'

"He says, 'Step out of the line.'

"So I stepped out of the line and they sent a medic over to take my temperature and I had 104-degree temperature. So they sent me to the hospital and I'm recouping in the hospital where all the wounded guys are coming through that same hospital. I stayed there for a whole week and a half before they sent me up front to my unit. I was thinking because I was sickly like this and coming from Hawaii, they would send me back, but they didn't.

"Every day was survival, my personal experience being up front and they sent me down and watched our whole unit bomb a hill. So that was my first experience being in Vietnam, bombing a hill.

"We didn't go back to base, base camp, Camp Eagle for about three months. We were out in the field. We didn't have the correct type of boots; we had leather boots. One of the guys in our unit, he was a specialist and one of his uncles knew someone in Congress or whatever was happening, anyway he wrote them and told them about our condition in terms of our boots and some stuff we didn't have. Well, in the next week, we ran into an ambush and he got killed but about three days after he died, a whole truckload of boots and stuff come in. So we granted that to him and the knowledge somebody he wrote to that he got us those boots.

"There were close calls all the time, man, I've had, I was in a number of firefights. If you look up the unit's exposure, we were exposed a lot to the enemy. The one thing I recall is when I got my bronze star for saving my lieutenant's life.

"I had come upon the unit that morning and they had had some action. I was in the rear. And they came back and got me from the rear to go up to the action. When I get up there, the lieutenant tells me to take the left flank. I was point man and I told him okay. But before I could get up, I had a young rookie behind me the guy who had just came here about two weeks ago. He jumps up and hits the bushes to the left flank which I was going through, as soon as he gets through the bushes, I hear a yip. Yip. And I look, and he's laying on the ground, so I think we got action here. That's what I yelled back and by that time, and when I said I think we got action, all hell breaks loose.

"Okay. We had walked into over some months, a brigade hospital, a three-tier hospital and it was secured by a brigade. All right? They had 50-caliber machine guns on each flank. A three-tiered hospital with over 1,200 people in it and they was fighting for their lives. And it turns out we had to call in the First Cav. We had some Marines working with us and they were bombing this hill from the bay, with the ships."

Tell us how you were wounded in that battle.

"The guy throws a grenade and I see it bounce and see it coming and I turned my head to the side 'cause I knew it would bounce and certain like that it's gonna bounce past me. It bounced and it bounced close to my leg and it blows up and when it blows up, I feel my leg lift up, right? And I said, 'Oh no, I don't even want to look at this,' but I looked and my leg was still there.

"Then I see a little trickle of blood coming out of there. If I didn't have my boot on real tight, it could have did some serious damage."

But you kept fighting?

"Oh, yeah, you got to. One of the VC had seen me, this is before anything happened. My weapon had jammed and the guy next to me's weapon had jammed and I said, 'Hey we got to get out of here.'

"I'm looking around, I'm crouched down and I see him laying on the ground—the lieutenant—so I know that I ain't got no weapon and the nearest weapon is him, okay? So I go and grab him, pulls him about 15 or 20 yards to a foxhole.

"When I saved the lieutenant's life, one of the machine gun's had gotten hit, so when I was putting the LT into a foxhole and loading his weapon to protect himself, I saw this happening. The guy had gotten raked on the side and killed him instantly and he fell over the machine gun, so I runs to the machine gun after I put the LT in there and I push his body off and he done bled into the chamber so I gotta clean that chamber out before it's gonna fire, so I'm wiping it with my elbow and everything I got. Pick up the machine gun and clear it and go over to the left flank. As I said, I hold that position until I'm relieved. That was terrible because I lost most of those people, most of our platoon.

"I carried that for a long time, all that material, you know. And we were, we had been in that area a number of times but we just happened to be too close to 'em that time, we was right up on 'em. And that's why they did what they had to do."

William was awarded the Bronze Star for saving his lieutenant. He has worked at Milwaukee's VETS Place Central since 1970, helping veterans of all wars with various support services.

SYLVESTER WATSON

SYLVESTER WATSON IS STILL fighting a war 50 years after his active duty ended. He's not dodging bullets in a literal sense, but there are psychological firefights that can present themselves unexpectedly.

"Watching movies with all of those Hollywood movie stars, I was under the impression that joining the Marines Corps, you get to see the world you get to see different parts of the country," Watson said. "And going through basic training and seeing San Diego, that formed a different picture altogether. It's not all lights and bells and whistles. Especially when you start dealing with your drill instructor and learning what the Corps has for you.

"I had a pretty stern mother who taught us discipline. So with that good foundation, basic training was basically a piece of cake."

VIETNAM

What was it like when you got to Vietnam?

"Here you are in a place you've never been before and people are trying to kill you. Heavy equipment, heavy rounds, heavy mortar rounds, rockets and you had bunkers, places you had to get away from the rockets. It was kinda scary. Here you are you don't have weapons, you just landed.

"I was in motor transport. We would unload the heavy equipment that was needed plus a lot of supplies. We spent a lot of time at the airstrip. At night, we'd got out beyond the line at listening posts and basically just out there, hoping and praying there was no offensive during that time. Once Tet broke loose, they tightened up the lines a little more. *(The Tet offensive was a coordinated series of North Vietnamese attacks on more than 100 cities and outposts in South Vietnam.)*

"We were on our way to Hue City and we came under a mortar attack. I was riding shotgun. That's one thing I never wanted to do was get caught inside a moving vehicle if it were to get hit with a mortar. I was heading for the door of the truck and had my hand on the latch getting ready to jump out and my driver caught me by the hand and told me to stick it out. So that was one.

"Just before the Tet offensive, we went out for a truck ride, not knowing the perils or the dangers that were imminent. We went off into an area where we didn't understand that it was dangerous because the next day everything was completely blocked off, the road was blocked off. The heavy bombardment, the infiltrations of the NVA, was all over the area.

"When you do silly things like that, the impact of the danger doesn't really fall upon you until you sit still for a minute and come to realize what danger you were in.

"For a great period of time when we would pull into the motor pool, there would be bodies of the NVA outside the gates that were killed the night prior. And when you see stuff like that it brings reality right in front of you.

"When you're out in no-man's land, they can rain down on you at anytime. I've seen guys flying through the air once a rocket hit them."

Were you ever hit?

"No. I was one of the lucky ones. No, I was never hit, but just seeing your friends dying. I've heard that being over there you don't make friends and after a while, you find out why. And even now, going through groups and PTSD, your wife, your kids, you can't really exhibit your feelings, you know that they're going to die one day. The grief that comes from post traumatic stress, it just causes you to just get off by yourself.

"Oh, I could tell you some stories about folks asking questions about why is he always by himself. Why is he always sitting in the dark? So often I sit in the dark and I ask myself, 'Why do I do this?' And then it dawned on me one day that we were mortared sitting in our hootch *(sandbagged bunker or foxhole)* you don't want to be caught in your rack, all turmoil, guys running from each other. And I finally realized the reason that I prefer the dark was because it was safety in the dark, you can't be seen. During the daylight hours, you're exposed, but at night you have a chance.

"And I've often asked myself, 'Why, why, why, did I survive? Why couldn't I die over there to come back to die a slow death of memories not being able to socialize like regular people?'

"War has a tendency to shatter and remain in the mind. You can...you can get healed but those memories have a tendency to come back. Your friends from days gone by, you can never rekindle from where you left. You can never regain what you've lost.

"As the days and the years go by, you come to realize the point behind people and why the mind shows these horrific moments and not being accepted. You know you're always standing in the shadows because you're not really, you don't feel like you belong. You know the average war veterans, they have seen death, they have experienced life altogether different for civilian life.

"When you sit in a restaurant and you look around and you never want to have your back towards the door. You know, you see people laughing having camaraderie. In just these last few years I started going to church, I've been able to recapture some of these moments of love. And there's just times where I want to die because I see what so many guys that took their lives and what they were facing.

"I would love to be natural again. Be able to laugh and joke without having any kind of guilt behind it. It took me a long time even to start with memorabilia from the war. I wanted to separate myself from that part. I don't. I have problems with people saying welcome home. I have and even when I go into my groups at the VA, I can see some of the guys having a joy about them. I get angry because they've been able to release themselves from their memories.

"Never let anyone say war is not hell. Because they'd be lying to you. War is hell. It's not what you leave over there; it's what you bring back."

"But I'm just so happy my God has given me a reason to live. I got my kids, I got my grandkids. They come over every summer, we go fishing, we cut wood but they give me a reason to live. If it wasn't for my children, for my wife, I'd be dead. If it wasn't for the group meetings where I could take the rough edges off my memories, and I just thank God for Jesus, because he gave me a reason to live."

Sylvester returned home to Milwaukee after Vietnam and drove a Milwaukee County bus for 20 years. His two sons, two nephews, and two grand-nephews served in the Air Force and Marines.

AFGHANISTAN / IRAQ

Number of Wisconsinites who served: 34,792

Number of Wisconsinites killed in action: 127

(Source: Wisconsin Historical Society)

DAN BUTTERY

WHILE MANY PEOPLE struggle to figure out a chosen profession, that was never a problem for Dan Buttery. But for an injury he suffered in Iraq, he's still be on active duty today.

"I enlisted in the United States Army in 1995," Buttery said. "I went in after college. I wanted to serve right out of high school, in fact. I have a letter, when I was ten years old, that I was trying to enlist apparently. And I received a letter back form the Marine Corps saying, 'Talk to us in eight years.'

"I had two uncles who were active duty. An aunt who was the first female command master chief in the United States Navy and so my family serves. I had a grandfather who served in World War II. And just that sense of honor and duty and I wanted to enlist right away, out of high school, but I had the option of going to the university, so I went. And also my mom was dying of cancer and she had loved her brothers dearly and they both had been on active duty their entire life, multiple tours of Vietnam. She had asked me not to serve because she...you know, moms doing what moms do. And I honored her wishes until she passed. So I graduated from college and enlisted that next summer.

"I deployed more as a reservist because I was in the Guard, Army National Guard after 9/11. So the world changed, of course, on 9/11. I was currently serving as a company commander for a combat engineer unit in Wisconsin. And we had a mission where we went to Nicaragua in 2002. And it ended up becoming a precursor for the mission in Iraq the next year. Mostly because we went in and we were working with villages and we were working on ...I mean, there's a combat side of engineering and there's the forest protection and helping the community and societies rebuild in their villages so that was something we had been doing in Nicaragua.

"But it was a good training experience for our unit, I would say, because we almost ended up doing very similar from a rebuild kind of, win the hearts and minds as a lot of people were hearing in Iraq under General Petraeus and his guidance in 2003, once the major conflict, or the major war, land warfare effort has subsided.

What do you remember most about your experience in Iraq?

"The combat unit engineer unit we were tied to, 724 Charlie Company Engineers. I was the company commander, which was the captain's rank, we were doing quite a bit of the villages through all of Iraq. We covered pretty much every corner of the country and in fact, when the Italian compound was hit by a car bomb in

November of 2003, we were just blocks away. It killed upwards of 35 of the Italian forces that were there. We had been working closely with the local Iraq populace, setting up schools and clinics, setting up forest protection. The Italian, the Korean forces, the Republic of Korea Special Forces were in country. And we were just blocks away when that compound was hit. And a number of IEDs had hit our vehicles. Fortunately, none of them were close enough or—if you want to call an IED a dud when it goes off—but it ultimately was more of a dud than an IED and didn't have the mass blast than it should have had. Fortunately for us.

"I was never wounded but we had some close calls. Yeah, we're very fortunate. We brought everybody home after our first deployment. 124 soldiers. And there's some injuries that were non-combat-related that sent a few soldiers home early. But there's no question that we were close many times. And call it luck, call it skill, call it 'It just wasn't your day.' And you just keep going. And you drive on and continue to do the mission.

"I was injured in Iraq. And that ended up ending my military service. I should still be in. It's called the Military Medical Review Board. And spinal cord injury. Nothing to write home about. It's an injury that the spinal cord...you have to take very seriously. So my ability to deploy any more was nonexistent. If you're not deployable, you really are not a soldier.

"Yeah, the vehicle hit a structure. It was surrounding a situation where the driver lost control of the vehicle. I mean I got out and I dropped instantaneously. I didn't realize what happened. Some of the guys who I was with thought I got shot because I dropped so quickly. And I said, 'I'm fine.' But you realize, if you've never been shot before, what that feels like. So I ended up realizing now after the MRIs and everything, it's just a blown-out spinal cord back injury.

"I like to argue that serving in the military in the armed forces didn't change me that much because I've always felt like it was something that was a part of me. However, going into combat is always going to change you. You may not recognize it or acknowledge it but it changes you. Just being fearful. And if anybody says they were never afraid in various situations, they're lying to you because you can be the toughest individual in the room, it's still scary.

"What's most scary—the most frightful events—are those that you don't know. You don't know what's around the next curve. You don't know what's going to happen next. And it can either paralyze you and not let you make decisions or keep moving on a daily basis or you just live with it. And I think when you come home from that, and you live in fear that long, this is something that has impacted all generations. It was called different things over time.

"You come back and you realize you're a different person in alertness—driving through the Marquette interchange. I didn't drive for three months. We were advised not to. And fortunately, I didn't. And I still remember driving through the Marquette interchange which is a very complex intersection and I could tell you what every driver, what every assistant, you know, person in the passenger side, what was in the back seat, what was in the window of every car that was around us going both directions. Because you become incredibly alert. And you have to because if you get lazy or you lose that ability to be extremely alert, it could kill you. And you carry that with you for, if not months, years.

"To serve is a very selfless act. You have to have that sense of purpose. And it's not just about going to war and wearing a uniform, it's what's behind the uniform. It's what's beneath the fabric. And I saw that with so many of the soldiers I served with. I served with some of the most amazing individuals I'll ever meet in my life were in that unit and they were 19- and 20-year-olds. They were 25-year-olds. I saw them making decisions in a split second that would have—they could have easily lost their life. But they made the decision to protect the innocent.

"They made the decision to maybe not fire their weapon when an Iraqi was driving erratically, and under the rules of engagement, they have the right to fire but didn't and it ended up being someone who was just driving like they're driving on Interstate 94 in Milwaukee. Just driving poorly. So you just see this character of these individuals and they don't put themselves forward, which is very rare today in today's society. Having served with these incredible individuals, that's the greatest accomplishment and experience for me.

"And having been one of their leaders and working with them, we accomplished some great, some great work in country. In fact, with the current ISIS scenario, there's a lot of areas I'm familiar with that we were at and you wonder if, of all those people we worked with, the good people, the Iraqis we're working with, are they still here? And I have no way of knowing that.

"They're no different than us. They want freedom. They want safety. They want to be able to have their children go to school, learn, and be safe. It's horrific what's happening today because of knowing the accomplishments that we had made with a lot of these local Iraqis. That's the hardest part today for me is seeing that country being torn apart again."

Dan started the Milwaukee chapter of Fisher House, a place where soldiers' families can stay while visiting loved ones receiving treatment at a hospital. He also helps with the marketing efforts for the Wisconsin Department of Veterans Affairs.

MICHAEL HOFSTEDT

IN HIS LATE TEENS, Michael Hofstedt never thought much about joining the military. That all changed when he visited his girlfriend, a camping instructor at an area campground.

"This was about six months after 9/11," Hofstedt said. "And I went up and visited her and stayed at a campground, next to where I could stay with her in a cabin so I stayed. And the guy who was running the campground asked me to help him chop some wood. Was an elderly guy, probably about 65 or 70. And he was listening to a radio at the time—we were chopping some wood— and he didn't charge me for the campground, which was perfect because I was an 18- or 19-year-old kid.

"And he asked me—you know, the news came on—talked about the war and he asked me why I wasn't there and I didn't have a good answer for him. And so that kind of stuck with me and I talked about it with my girlfriend that night. And about two months later, I was in the recruiter's office.

"I went to Iraq first and that was about four or six months after I got to my unit. So I was fairly new. Still trying to get my feet wet and gain the trust of everybody. I spent six months in Iraq and probably five days after Thanksgiving and we went originally for the inaugural Democratic elections.

"And so we were assigned tasks to post security around some of the more heavily populated areas in Bagdad. So we took over four to five of Saddam's palaces. He had many. I don't know, this one, what kind of value it held. But it was nice because it was within walking distance from every aspect that we had to control and oversee. It was a pretty hectic time. They obviously didn't like us in his palace. They didn't like us pulling security to a lot of people who vote. And so...we all just kind of slept with one eye open. And we were attached to—being paratroopers in a ground unit, we weren't used to tanks but that was the unit they attached us to so we had some tanks along with us.

"So being crammed in those were of all experiences in Iraq. They crammed 12 of us in the back and it was horrible. And we weren't used to it. We like to stretch our legs out and...But yeah, we spent six months there and for the most part, people there were allowed to vote. People were happy. So it felt like we did the job that we were asked to do.

"Roadside bombs weren't prevalent but indirect fire was a pretty common thing from the palace. The palace was on the Tigris River and so we had a nice fortified position but there was tall buildings on either side. And tall buildings being seven-, eight-, nine-story buildings. A lot of windows. So it was sometimes hard to guard. And sometimes we'd keep units out, small units outside those apartment complexes, just a little added security.

"But indirect fire happened every day. It wasn't uncommon. Grenades were...But when we were there, it was common for the enemy to convince families to use their children as the enemy of the U.S. in exchange for food, money, and sort of life support. So kids with grenades was a common thing. Three or four times a week. And then the Iraqi police unit was fairly new at the time and we kind of took and try to train them every now and then. But it didn't seem to work. It didn't seem like they were any sort of passion behind them. You couldn't really trust them.

"You know, I never knew what was going to happen. And there would be a couple of times where they thought we were the enemy and shot at us and we started shooting back at them and there was firefights between essentially two friendly units. So there was a bit of a mess there too with that. I guess on a daily basis there'd be something, something would happen.

"The issue of the 82nd, the all-American squad, was something I attached myself to right away. Being from Wisconsin and growing up the way I did, I never really had any reason to judge or dislike anybody before I knew who they were. And the all-American terminology comes from the fact that when the 82nd was started, it had people from all over the United States that would come together and fight. And I really respected that history and knowledge of the 82nd. And I attached myself right away. I don't know if I got lucky or not but the unit I was a part of was really close. We had 30 people that were brothers within six months. So obviously the camaraderie was crucial. And jumping out of airplanes was fun.

"I had a lot of good friends. And we were very much our own person and we would put that, or bring that to group on a daily basis. So the friend from Texas was a stereotypical Texan teenage kid. And the guy from Georgia was a stereotypical Georgia kid. And they didn't necessarily, I guess, inspire me to become like them, but who they were and who I was inspirational. Like I guess sort of bring your individuality into the group find a way to make it work."

What was the least favorite part of your Iraq experience?

"Well, I've learned to not like lines. The hurry up and wait. It's very common. Every day, you're sitting in some sort of line. And you sort of have to deal with it. And you know eventually you just become immune to the idea, but I certainly don't like sitting in lines now. So I guess off the top of my head I could say that.

"The first couple of days in the Army before you get to boot camp, you're sort of in this holding tank, you know, having your head shaved, your blood taken, and your medical and your physical essentially starting your personal packet with information that you'll carry with you throughout your entire career. And it was miserable, to say the least.

"Some people had it a lot worse than I did. I wasn't in tears...I wasn't crying trying to make a call home or trying to escape or anything. But there was people around me trying to do those things so. It was sort of a miserable 72 hours of tests taken.

"I wasn't wounded. I've been near...I've heard bullets fly near my head presumably. I've had friends wounded. So, yeah I feel fortunate.

"I'm not a gung-ho...gung-ho about it. I'm very proud of my military experience. Everything that I wanted to do, I did in my first term. I was very happy to get out without any sort of physical ailments."

Do you feel like your service made a difference?

"I don't know. Certainly not in the Iraq war. I never really had any real inspiration to go to Iraq. You know, I never really approved or saw a reason why we were there in the first place. And in Afghanistan, we spent a lot of times...During my term in Afghanistan...we were sort of attached to this idea of winning the hearts and minds and I think there's been a couple of movies made that have made mention of hearts and minds.

"And it was very true. It's essentially a lot of times what we did is we'd go around to these villages and set up little mobile health spots and mobile clinics, pull security, and check everybody in the town. Give them free healthcare, somebody who practices medicine to heal them in some sort of way. It wasn't necessarily trying to find the enemy. And we spent 15 months there. And I'd say half of that was spent wining hearts and minds and then training the Afghan army.

"But it just didn't seem like it was anything really groundbreaking. A lot of times, we'd go into these villages that have really no communication to the outside world and they didn't even know that we were in their country, let alone why we're in their village. It's just a landscape that's hard to traverse. It's hard to conquer. So I like to think that there was something good that came out of it, you know, 18 months I spent overseas, but who's to really know?"

Are you glad you served?

"Yeah, absolutely. I think it goes back to the question of being changed from the Army. I think that I'm definitely a different person, more resilient, more stubborn, more knowledgeable. I'm calmer in situations that are chaotic. I don't expect any place to... here in the United States...at least in the near future to be as chaotic as it was over there. And there were certain trainings we did that were also very stressful and there were times where I saw some of my friends fall out or I convince my mind that I couldn't go any further and we did it. We went as far as we needed to go and accomplish what we needed to accomplish.

"And I've never met anybody who's never been in the military that's had that training, that real life, real mind training. So that's never going to go away. I'll never forget that. That in and of itself was worth it."

Michael became food and beverage manager at Milwaukee Hilton City Center in September of 2014.

ALISON KITZEROW

ALISON KITZEROW HAD AN Air Force ROTC scholarship at Marquette University. She planned on attending law school. But for Alison and legions of others in the military and civilian worlds, everything changed after 9/11.

"September 11th happened my sophomore year of college, and a couple months later, I decided to straight out enlist in the Army Reserve. So I ended up giving back my Air Force ROTC scholarship and then during my sophomore and junior year of college, I went to basic training and military police school. And then I was in.

"So I went to, it was basic training and military police school and it was all at Ft. Leonard Wood in Missouri. It was 17 straight weeks. So I honestly finished my last final exam as a sophomore at Marquette, went to training all summer, and I came back and started the semester again as a junior."

When were you deployed to Iraq?

"That happened four months after I got done with my training. So I came back to Marquette. I was a junior and then I got activated December 27th, 2002. And I served the entire 2003 in both Kuwait and Iraq. And the start of the war was in March 2003. And then I got home, I think it was February 10th, 2004."

Was it tough transitioning from college kid to full-time soldier?

"Well, I was 20 years old. And I guess scared. My parents were really scared. I just remember right before I left, my mom was like crying and I was just like, 'You have to be strong for me.' So she always remembered that, too. So my mom's hair definitely got a lot grayer after I was deployed for the year. But there was lot of unknown. The war hadn't started yet. I just remember when I was sitting in my dorm room, this was right before my unit got activated, watching *CNN* and *Fox News* and that was all when George Bush wanted Saddam Hussein to give up the weapon of mass destruction. And I just remember sitting there thinking 'Give up the weapons of mass destruction! I don't want to leave college.'

"And then I ended up getting deployed and we spent six weeks in Kuwait. Well, actually, let me back up a little bit. We spent a month training in Ft. Dix, New Jersey, and there was a ton of snow on the ground. So it really wasn't preparing us well for getting sent over to the desert. So then we got sent to Kuwait. We were there for I think another six weeks.

"The war started in the middle of March 2003. And it was scary. We were building camps out of nothing, just right there in the middle of the dessert. We actually built a prison camp. I was military police. Built it from ground up. I had 7,000 prisoners. It was just a scary experience at some points. But luckily I never saw combat. So I think the scariest things were just the unknown. Unknown if chemical or biological weapons were going to be used against us. Twenty years old. Just like the first major time I'd been away from home. Sandstorms were miserable. Snakes, rats, all that type of stuff."

Was there one moment that stood out where things got particularly scary?

"I would say it was March 25th, 2003. I enlisted March 23rd, 2002, by the way. So I'm one year into the military. I think it was like a couple days prior. My unit had moved north out of Kuwait into Iraq and we crossed the border and it was really scary because, like I said, there's a lot of unknown. What are we to expect? Plus, I was in the Reserves so a lot of our equipment, our Humvees, just the things that we wore, they were very outdated. Things hadn't really been updated yet, so some of our Humvees had no doors on them. So we're taking this huge convoy into Iraq. And we crossed the border. It's really scary. And we go into this village and there's lots of Iraqis lining the streets. And it was just really scary as we're through there and I just remember sitting in the back of this truck and we're all like a whole bunch of us packed in and we're in this big convoy.

"And I was like 'Oh, my gosh. I wonder if somebody's going to shoot at us?' And actually, it was like the complete opposite. All the Iraqis that were lining the street were thanking us. They're like, 'Thank you. Thank you for coming in and thank you for doing what you're doing.' So that was a defining moment.

"And then shortly after that, I think this all happened in the same day, Iraq had one of the worst sandstorms it had in a hundred years. It is insane. Like the Humvee. You can't even see ...You can barely see the outline of the Humvee. And I just remember we had to stop. Our entire convoy had to pull over because we couldn't even see where we were going. And I just remember like not even being able to breathe. Like I had to put a shirt over my mouth. It's like you felt you were being suffocated with sand.

"We ended up having to sleep either outside or in vehicles. And our vehicles didn't have enough room for people to sleep in them. So some people honestly slept outside with big ponchos over them. And luckily I got space in a vehicle to sleep. And I just remember sleeping horribly, by the way. And I woke up and I had like inches of sand all over me. And then we moved forward and kept going up farther into Iraq. But that was one year to the date after I had enlisted. And I was like, 'What the hell did I sign up for?'"

How difficult was it not knowing who the enemy was?

"Right and you know the military, the Army had prepared us for that somewhat, because a lot of military training now is called MOUT—Military Operations in Urban Terrain—where you do a lot of simulated exercises in villages and what look like little cities and stuff so we were kind of prepared for that. But you're right. It's not like just like the Civil War, where you got two different lines coming towards each other. Or medieval times with like swords and stuff. You have no idea who the enemy is and that's why I think of that initial convoy going through that village and you were just scared. Who is the enemy and who wasn't. So yeah, that was scary. I guess the enemy to me was always Saddam. But where was he? They found him while I was there. I think they found him December of 2003 when I was still over in Iraq."

What was the best part of your service in Iraq?

"Well, sometimes you have to go back to basics and...there's two different things. One of my favorite parts is just kind of going back to nature. Honestly, I felt that we were in the crappiest country ever, but that country out of all the places that I've been in the world and the United States, had the most amazing sunrises and sunsets. And I just remember one time we had to sleep under the starts literally and like the entire like sky was just full of stars. And that was amazing."

Are you glad you served?

"Uh, yes...I actually was just thinking about this yesterday. That, you know, I feel like when you're in college, you have a very defined path for your life where...I just feel like when you're in college; when you start college, you feel like you have a plan for your life. So my plan, when I started out at Marquette; was that I was going to join the Air Force or ROTC. I was going to get my degree. I was actually going to go to law school. I got into this special pre-law scholars program at Marquette. I was going to serve four years in the Air Force as a JAG officer, and that was my plan for my life.

"And then stuff happens like September 11 and then you make a decision that changes your life. And you can't say that making a decision at 19 years old, that you're as well informed. You just kind of like make decisions that are like a little bit more impulsive without thinking it a lot through and that was a decision that affected nine years of my life. But, and this is what I was thinking about yesterday, is that I don't think I would be where I am right now if it wasn't."

How did your experiences help you get where you are now?

"Actually, when I got home from Iraq, I ended up finishing up three semesters of my degree and then I graduated Marquette with a degree in psychology and English. And I ended up not doing as well on the law school admissions test as I had wanted to. So my plan didn't work out. I didn't end up going to law school.

"But I ended up working at a VA for four years. And that was very interesting because I was a veteran helping veterans. I worked in their pension program, which is like for low-income disabled vets. So there's compensation, which is for injured vets and there's this program for low-income disabled vets. And I met some of my best friends working at the VA. People I'm still friends with now. So even though it really wasn't the job for me, I did meet a lot of great people there. I ended up quitting there because I realized you shouldn't be in a job that isn't the job for you.

"And I ended up going to grad school. Used some of the safe education benefits that they have for service members. They paid for my entire master's degree and I got a masters in professional and technical writing. And then I was looking for a job. I was doing some freelance writing for a little bit and I ended up finding a job as a writer at this company called Zywave in Wauwatosa.

"I knew one of my friends had worked there before. I'm like 'Did you work for that weird 'Z' company?' *(Zywave, a Milwaukee software company)* And she was like, 'Yeah.' So then she put me in touch with a recruiter. So I started as a content writer. And then, it was so funny, my boss still remembers my cover letter for the position because I was going to have to write about a whole bunch of weird topics and I said that if I can assemble and disassemble a grenade launcher, I'm sure I can learn anything about a topic and write about it. So he still remembered that and he really liked that cover letter.

"So anyway, I think it was a little over a year into my job as a content writer that my boss wanted to promote me to a manager. So I definitely think that the military prepared me well for management. When I got out, I was a staff sergeant and I really didn't have any direct reports. Now I have nine employees that report to me but I just think that the military had taught me a lot of things about just leadership, resiliency, learning to adapt to things that aren't necessarily the best situations. Not being afraid of things. Being confident."

Alison is manager of internal communications and content development at Zywave.

JOHN WITMER

IT COULD BE ARGUED THAT parents of soldiers serving on the front lines undergo more emotional stress than their young adult children who are in the line of fire. Those close to combat often have detailed knowledge of their situation, a certain sense of control. For their parents, the fear of unknown dangers their loved ones might be facing can be overwhelming. Take that considerable amount of fear and triple it for Waukesha's John Witmer, who had three daughters deployed in Iraq at the same time. Only two would survive.

"I was surprised by my daughters' decision to go into the military," Witmer said. "My oldest daughter, Rachel, went in first. And Charity, her twin sister, and Michelle followed. And Michelle followed largely because she saw the difference it made in her sisters, as far as the way they were, their confidence level, etc., what being a soldier did for them.

"But I also think she caught kind of the...you know, we talk about the service, you know. We often don't really connect the word 'service' and the definition service with 'hey, they're serving.' And she wanted to serve. You know, and she saw how her sisters were serving and she wanted to serve, too. They were all in the Army National Guard and they all three served together in Baghdad.

"So, at the time, I started to have real problems with pain, different parts of my abdomen and I went to the doctor and I said, 'You know I this...I got this...I don't feel quite right.

"And he says, 'Are you under any stress?'

"And I laughed. And then I explained, you know. And you know he talked about how obviously the stress was not helping my digestive tract and things like that.

"But it was a full year of just being on high alert. And every time the phone rang, we were like, because they could only get to the phone at certain times. And a lot of the times when they got to the phone, it was a satellite connection and it was very choppy. And so you needed to get there and you needed to listen hard. We got used to getting up at 2:00 in the morning when the phone rang because we knew this might be the only time we heard from them for another week or two. So it was very stressful. Yeah, very stressful."

Were your daughters all in same unit?

"Two different units. So Michelle and Rachel went first with the 32nd, MPs. And then Charity followed later with the 118th Company B, medical battalion, out of Waukesha. So they...she went about, oh boy, five or six months after they did. But they were actually overlapped at one point in time. Charity and Michelle and Rachel were able to get together. I have pictures of all three of them in uniform in Iraq. So...and the week before we lost Michelle, Charity had actually gotten leave to go be with her and just hang out for a day. And it was in retrospect such a gift that she was able to be there with her for that day."

What happened to Michelle?

"Well, let me give a little bit of a prelude. Because when all three of them went to Iraq, the...the local media was kind of following the story because it was very much human interest, right? Three kids all serving together. And they followed it literally for months. And so it was not unusual for a guest to get a call saying, 'Hey, how are the kids doing? And you know, let's do an update on the story and whatever.' When they came home for leave at Christmastime and all three were together, the local TV stations all wanted to come talk to us and they all did.

"So then in April, on a Friday night, Good Friday, the doorbell rang. And I was on the phone and Lori answered. And I will just never forget her voice coming from the living room and it just didn't compute and she was saying, 'No, no, no,' like she was ordering someone away from the door.' So I ran into the room and saw the notification team at the door.

"And now, it's like, what's the next question? Is who? Whose name are they going to tell me? Right? And they wanted...they wanted to do their notification thing and they've got this preamble that they want to give you, and all I want to know is what name are you going to say? And so they told us that Michelle had been killed in an ambush. She had been part of a convoy going to reinforce police stations in Baghdad. It was night shift. It was midnight. That had just left for what they called midnight chow. There were six Humvees together. And then they split off and went different directions and as soon as they split off, what one of her teammates described as the most intense ambush they had experienced in the year that they had been there. Just unloaded on them.

"There was a sniper in the third floor windows. IEDs went off. One of the vehicles was crippled. And in that...all that turmoil, Michelle was in the gunner seat. And, you know, she was going to return fire and was killed. So the rest of the convoy was struggling to get out of harm's way. One of the vehicles has been crippled. They were actually forcing it, pushing it with the second vehicle, to try to clear this ambush zone. And when they got out of this area, that's when they realized that she had been hit. And they called for attention, medical attention, but it was too late. So, yeah.

"Even though it was a very difficult time for us, we felt that people needed to understand most about how this was impacting families. I think that's one of the reasons that we chose to stay in front of the cameras. I don't think it...most people didn't understand that this was the war that was largely fought with reservists and the makeup of the military had changed dramatically in the years preceding the Iraq conflict, where the new strategy was to rely on reservists.

"So you had people who in the past were weekend warriors. And who, you know, were joining the National Guard, you know, to serve locally. Or maybe they thought they would slide into stateside roles while other people were deployed. The whole world had kind of changed and, in the 90s I guess. And now National Guard was being needed on a regular basis in conflicts.

"And I think that was one of the things that we hoped people would understand, that war had kind of changed, that we were fighting with, you know, weekend warriors, people that...I'm not... that's not a term that's minimizing at all. It's just that this is someone who may have a business, who now is being called away for seven or eight months. Nine months. Twelve months to serve. And it's...it's...it's probably...you know it could have happened.

"But it was a...you've got mom at home with the kids and now she's trying to run the family business while dad is overseas. Or vice versa. Mom was the primary breadwinner as maybe a doctor, or nurse and now dad's at home trying to take care of the kids while she's deployed for 12 months. Some of them longer than that. So we hoped that people would begin to understand more about what military families in general went through. The hardships that they endured.

"One of the things that happened shortly after we lost Michelle was the unit that she was attached to, which had been there a year and had been scheduled to come home within a week of when she was killed, got extended. So now they had lost one of their, you know, one of their own, and they were told that they needed to be there at least three more months. And so now they were going into month 15 or 16. I think they came home in

September. But I think they came home in September. So they had been there, I think, 15 months by the time they got home."

You decided the write a book about Michelle.

"It started out as therapy and I was kind of writing it for a very small audience and my wife saw it she just kind of ordered me to... to put it out to a wider audience. Because it was, you know, thoughts that were...that she thought were very helpful to help me process grief. And in some ways, I was putting thoughts, words to thoughts that she had had, too. And she thought it was very helpful.

"So I started writing a series of really what were blog entries. And then after our granddaughter, Madison, was born, I kind of felt this mission to put it all down in a book. You know, pull it all together. Take these kind of disparate blog entries and unify them around the history of Michelle. The other things...you know, Michelle wanted to write a book. Michelle wanted to write a book. And she wrote us letters saying that when she got back, she was going to write a book about Iraq. So part of what her mission in that book was to take all of that correspondence and some of the very meaningful and touching stuff she wrote and incorporate it into this book. So, you know, that was the challenge, to kind of to create this narrative that included our story, her story, and, you know, just how this all unfolded for us. And where it took the family. The journey that it took us on.

"The thing that is most remarkable is it's still going on. I wrote the book in 2010. We still have people reaching out to us. And the fact that they continue to reach out after all these years is, I think, one of the most meaningful things to me. That Michelle's story does live on. And it still does makes a difference to people when they read the book. You know, the feedback I get.

"Again, my wife is my biggest cheerleader. So she's my book promoter. She teaches fitness classes and she's in her warm-ups or whatever—she's always telling people to read the book and things like that. And so she's touched a lot of people at least through that exercise and the book has circulated locally. And you know, there has been some...some national coverage of the book. But, so I do get occasionally letters, emails from overseas and things like that.

"But it has helped me stay connected to people that care about our story and that really helps me. And just talking about the book to people has always been very meaningful because it's a way to keep Michelle's story alive. And to me, that's one of the most important things. The mission of the book...the smaller mission of the book was to make sure than when Madison, my first grand-daughter, turned 16 or 17, her parents could hand her the story that involved not only Michelle but her mother, Terry, and her aunt Rachel. And she could see how this all fit together and understand who they were. Who they are and the difference that they made. And how they, in many ways, were kind of on the leading edge of change in America, where women, you know, long before they had this debate about whether women should be in combat, they were in combat.

"You know, there was just no...there was no...real...okay, so there may have been this prohibition about women serving in combat roles. But when women in the National Guard began getting pulled in to conflicts, all that kind of became meaningless.

"Because if you're military police, by job description, and you go to Iraq, you are in combat. Because there is a hostile zone all around you. And, you know, my daughters were under fire multiple times. You know, they took RPGs *(Rocket-propelled grenades)*. They took...they were exposed to IEDs, you know, sniper fire. It happened all the time and, you know, it was almost to me silly that they were still having this discussion statewide whether women should be allowed in combat roles. Because they already were.

"So the story basically said that, you know, while we were over here debating in the US, women were just quietly filling the gap. And the other thing to understand is that the ranks, I don't know if it's 1 in 4, 1 in 3, I don't know. I used to know the number. Of the National Guard, as far as women to men, they are an integral part of it.

"And one...shortly after Michelle was killed, somebody in Congress got the idea that, you know, all women should be pulled out of hostile fire zones. And, you know, it was ridiculous that would have just shut down the operation. It's not like it was just one or two scattered here. I mean they were...they were involved. They were doing important jobs and I guess that was kind of going without a lot of notice. So the book kind of speaks to the changing role of women in the military. And not because I'm an expert. I'm observing as a father, what was happening."

Is Michelle's story an inspiration?

"Well, that would certainly be what I would hope from the book. And there are letters she wrote that I think could inspire more, that could inspire to that end. You know, she spent a lot of time...some of her teammates would talk about how she would spend so much time with the kids over there. That she was always looking for little things to give them. Candy. Little toys. She would pose for pictures.

"One of the favorite pictures we have of her is her, you know, with these ragtag Iraqi kids hanging outside the police station, you know. There she's with the big smile and what they told us is that that was kind of who she was over there. She was always kind of looking after the kids in the neighborhood when she had free time. And you know, just talking to them and things like that.

"She did spend one day at the orphanage over there and she wrote us a very moving letter about that so it was...Yeah, I think if you learn anything about my daughter, through her writings and what we put together in the book, you would be inspired to try to be a better person."

Michelle's sisters returned safely from Iraq. Rachel is an art teacher in Milwaukee. Charity works as a lab technician in San Francisco. They are both mothers of three children.

GENERAL SERVICE

DIRK DEBBINK

DIRK DEBBINK ATTENDED the Naval Academy starting in 1973. He graduated as an ensign in 1977 and became a main propulsion assistant on a ship he helped navigate across the Pacific Ocean to Japan. From those humble beginnings, Debbink would rise through the ranks and become one of the most significant influencers on Navy policy in the history of the branch.

"My first deployment did take us to Japan at one spot, at one point, but it's a Western Pacific deployment. You head west, with stops in Hawaii, Midway Island, and then you head over, spend quite a bit of time in Japan. Mostly southern Japan, Sasebo, that area. Down through Hong Kong. Went to Subic Bay and then went through the Straits over to the Gulf. And all that was just in time, if you will, for Ayatollah Khomeini to take over the Embassy in 1979.

"We were sitting in Subic Bay at the time. We thought we were going to enter a three-week overhaul period. And literally, you know, that morning we started off-loading and that afternoon we were all called to quarters, saying put everything back on the ship because they had just taken over the embassy and we were sailing with the Kitty Hawk battle group to go over there and represent U.S. interests. Of course, that played out. It took 444 days, as we all recall. So we were just there until probably until March of '80, something like that. And then we got relieved and another battle group came over. We were the first ones over there, though. That was a pretty interesting time.

"I don't want to overstate it because, of course, there was no combat in the end. But, of course, you don't know that when you're sailing over, so literally it was daily general quarters drills. You know, man your battle stations. Practice all of our drills and things like that. And you keep sailing west, though. Into the ocean, the Indian Ocean. Formed up with other members of the battle group.

"Waiting for orders, or waiting for something to happen. That gets a little monotonous after a while. But at the same time, I always said, it was better to stay at sea because at least you had the routines, something to do every day."

Was there a sense on the ship of 'Let's go get 'em'?

"Yeah...I guess, you know, there certainly...there might be among some people that sentiment. And certainly at times you might feel that way. At the same time, it was a lot bigger picture than that. And I also like to say those of us in the military, we're actually the last ones who want conflict. You know, the goal as I saw it over there, we had a pretty large contingent of American firepower in this battle group and the goal was that we provide deterrents from anybody doing anything else. And further goal was that we would convince the Ayatollah that he needed to accede to our demands or else we would have. Not that we wanted to, but we could have. Maybe that's my perspective too now, 35 years later. But American firepower...the last thing you actually want to do is use it. Truthfully. You'd rather be able to solve the problem diplomatically."

You eventually retired from active duty and transitioned to the Navy Reserve.

Transitioning to the Reserve back in the '80s, especially, was totally different than it is today. You decide you wanted to transition back then, you were a quitter. You were quitting the Navy. It's like, wait, isn't this is still the Navy? No, you're a quitter. And you literally had to resign and had to go see a recruiter and come back into the Navy Reserve. That's how distinct it was. And in fact, that distinction lasted until I became Chief of Navy Reserve.

"Even my good friend, Pat Walsh, who was the Navy Reserve Naval Operations at the time, and a classmate of mine, we said we're going to end this policy so that now you can transition from the active Navy, the Reserve Navy, back to the active Navy, go back and forth without having to resign your commission and be re-recruited. That can't be that same Navy you know and love. So that transition was tough back then. But if the Navy or the service is a passion and it's in your blood, which is was for me, I just kept trying to find ways to serve. And that meant Navy Reserve.

"We used to joke about it. We said if you could get through a Reserve weekend and not have it cost you out-of-pocket money. Your reserve pay would pay for your airline reservation and any others costs that you would have, that was a successful drill weekend. So that's the kind of sacrifice that even yet today many of our reserves and some of our Guard service members make to be able to continue serving. But as I said previously, as long as they gave me real meaningful work to do, I did it. I was able to travel all around the world and do some amazing things."

You were promoted to Vice Admiral and became chief of the U.S. Navy Reserve in 2008.

"The goal for our Reserve and Guard should be that every time we call a reserve or guard serviceman forward, that's exactly what they need because they'll do a good job of it, first of all, and when they come back, they'll tell their family and their employer and everybody else 'Wow, that was an awesome two-week,' or whatever it was, 'two-month or year-long period, of duty. I was used every day. And I was, you know, effective at what I did.'

"And then our families and our employers will keep supporting these Guard and Reserve rotations. If we haul them out and they sit for two weeks or they sit for a month, or whatever and play basketball or cribbage or whatever, you know the whole thing breaks down.

"I think the Navy and maybe society too has changed a lot... has changed a lot in my 35 years of service. I mean literally as a junior officer in the ship, when you were standing watch as the command duty officer, the senior officer on duty at night, I felt like I was on the marijuana patrol. I mean literally, you know. Drugs were rampant in the Navy back then. We'd just gone through the Zumwalt *(Admiral Elmo Zumwalt, Chief of Naval Operations from 1970 to 1974)* years, which published all the Z-grams and were remarkable social change in the Navy, allowing beards which was eventually taken back again, but trying to conquer this problem. And then it was when Tom Hayward *(Admiral Thomas Hayward, Chief of Naval Operations from 1978 to 1982)* came into the office, as saying that, that I loved, 'That's not my Navy, you know? It's my Navy and you're not going to do drugs in my Navy.'

"And we conquered drugs in the Navy pretty well, primarily I think probably through urinalysis testing, frankly and getting really rigorous about that. Look, you take the drugs, you're not going to get away with it for long. We're going to catch you. We're going to throw you out when we do. That threat might have been idle in a good economy, but in a poor economy, it's a pretty strong threat. We're going to throw you out.

"I think later on, additional social change that came about beside drugs, probably maybe in the early 2000, when we had a lot of sexual assaults. And you know, the military is held, and rightfully so, to a higher standard than society. All these things, drugs, sexual assaults, you know any of the social stuff, is much less in the military because of, you know, there's a military order here going on that it is society. But it should be much less so when we were dealing with that, we resurrected that saying actually, not in my Navy. We will not tolerate sexual assault."

Debbink championed efforts to address the problem of sexual assault as the on-camera presenter in a YouTube video produced by the US Navy in April 2012.

EXCERPTS FROM YOU-TUBE VIDEO
https://www.youtube.com/watch?v=AXMeo6F8gkE

- "We are all working together every day to make sure we have the capabilities to defend our nation and to foster goodwill around the world. But every day, in our Navy, two to three and perhaps even more of our shipmates are sexually assaulted."

- "Too often these hideous acts are committed by one sailor on another. And all too often, alcohol is involved. No one, sober or inebriated, has the right to inflict the lifelong scars and emotional and physical damage of sexual assault upon another person."

- "That is why every Navy operations support center, every Navy Reserve unit, and every Reserve sailor must step forward and create a climate where everyone is treated professionally with dignity and respect at all times."

- "Your personal responsibility is to intervene when you observe a shipmate heading for a situation that looks dangerous. When we fail to do so and a sexual assault occurs, a shipmate is hurt badly, scarred for life. Our morale as a Navy is undermined. And our readiness and combat effectiveness are compromised."

- "Our ultimate goal must be a Navy culture of mutual respect where sexual assault is never tolerated and is completely eliminated. And where every sailor can serve confident and proud of their Navy."

- "The tools, knowledge and resources to prevent sexual assault are on the sexual assault prevention response website and are available to all hands."

- "So we've seen a lot of change. But the one thing that is definitely consistent throughout, consistently good but even they've gotten better, is the technical ability. And it has to be because our ships and our aircraft, everything, the submarines."

- "It's an amazing time right now. You know, firing laser weapons. They're real. This isn't just Star Wars stuff. We actually have lasers operating in the Gulf right now. Shooting a electromagnetic rail gun, you know, that propels the actual projectile at some 200 miles, leaving the barrel, I think, at 1,100 feet per second with no explosive, you know, just electromagnetics, you know, accelerating throughout the gun barrel."

- "And this is just an amazing time right now. Again, hopefully to deter those who want to do us ill because then they'll know you're not going to beat us."

Dirk retired in 2012 completing 35 years of service.
He is president of MSI General, an architectural design/build firm located in Nashotah, Wisconsin. He has an MBA from the University of Chicago and is a registered professional engineer.

EVELYN RIVERA

VETERANS OFTEN TALK OF how military service improved their lives, teaching discipline, self-control, and respect for others. But for some vets, service had an even bigger impact, leading to opportunities for citizenship and a path to a better life.

Evelyn Rivera grew up in Colombia and surprised her family by signing up for duty in the Marine Corps.

"I'm the first one, actually, in the military," Rivera said. "It's not usual in Colombia for females to join in the military.

"A friend talked to me about it and I talked to a recruiter and two months later I was in the Marines."

What did you do in the Marines?

"Supply. Logistics. Inventories. Working in warehouses. My first station was in Okinawa, Japan. I was also stationed in California."

What did you like most about the military?

"The life. The friends that you make. More like family. The brotherhood. Is something safe, secure. You meet so many people from different countries. Different parts of the States. I mean, it's everything, everything to me."

What was the hardest part?

"Actually, being away from my home."

Was boot camp tough?

"For me, it was. I mean physically; you're running all the time. And mentally; it's also hard but in the end, you understand why. Those three months are so hard. So that you can become a stronger person physically and mentally to be prepared for combat or actual life. For both. Civilian life and military life."

What was your rank?

"When I got out, an E4. A corporal. But because I'm still on inactive duty, now I'm a sergeant, but after I got out."

Did you have children while you were in the service?

"Yes, my first son was born in Okinawa, Japan. It was hard at first because you have to go back to work after a month and a half. But they understand you're a mom, you're a wife. You can be everything at once. You are military. You're a wife. You're a mom and everything works out."

Are you proud to have served your country?

"Yes, obviously you come out a different person from boot camp. And everybody look at you, your family, your friends, now you are a different person, but in a good way. Is honor because you serving your country, you are prepared for anything. For to do any job, and to do it for your country. So a lot of people, thanks for that and respect you for that. It is. It's an honor, actually. Wherever you go is always everybody thanks you for your service."

Your husband is a Marine?

"Yes. We met in Okinawa. He loves it. He loves it. He's gonna stay in the Marines. He was a recruiter for enlisting and now he's a recruiter for officers. And he loves it. He's supposed to do 20 years in the military.

"I am thankful to the military. I came to this country to be better, you know, to better myself. And out of the military, I got a family, I got a husband. I got kids. I met great people. And like I say, for myself, it makes me a stronger person. It did. I am really thankful to the military. And I became a citizen also. That was one of my major goals, when I joined and it happened."

Evelyn Rivera served in the Marine Corps on active duty from 2008 to 2012.

ABOUT THE AUTHOR

Mark Concannon is a four-time-Emmy Award-winning journalist who worked as a reporter/anchor at WITI-TV in Milwaukee for 23 years. He is currently president and executive producer of his video company, Concannon Communications. Mark and his wife Janet live in suburban Milwaukee.

For more information, please visit
www.mettleandhonor.com